WHEEL$PIN

THE AGILE EXECUTIVE'S MANIFESTO

MEET · THE · AUTHOR

http://bit.ly/mWrrRq

What is this and how do I use it?

It's called a QR code. It allows you to *Get In the Loop with me!* Use a barcode scanner on your smartphone to unlock special content, videos and rewards from the author. As you read, scan the QR content (updated periodically) throughout this book for an even deeper, richer experience of *Wheel$pin: The Agile Executive's Manifesto.*

WHEEL$PIN

THE AGILE EXECUTIVE'S MANIFESTO

Accelerate Your Growth,
Leverage Your Value,
Beat Your Competition

Mike Richardson

PUBLISHING

No Limit Publishing Group
123 E Baseline Road, D-108
Tempe AZ 85283
info@nolimitpublishinggroup.com

This book was printed in the United States of America

No Limit Publishing
No Limit Enterprises, LLC
1601 E 69th Street, Suite 200
Sioux Falls, SD 57108

RAVE REVIEWS FOR *WHEEL$PIN*

"A driving force for the new economy."
~ **Doug Duncan, Chief Economist, Fannie Mae**

"Mike transforms the oxymoron "organizational agility" into a powerful and actionable concept. If you're "in the driving seat" of your company, reading this book will spark you to steer with both more control and more nimbleness."
~ **Rafael Pastor, Chairman of the Board & CEO of Vistage International (The World's Leading Chief Executive Organization)**

"At last, someone who really understands the nature of our challenge. Where was Mike Richardson all my business life? I wish I had his framework 37 years ago when we started our business! We would have avoided wheel-spin which cost us Millions in lost profits."
~ **Tom Campanaro, Founder & CEO, Total Gym**

"A must read for improving cash flow through better execution, operational control and agility."
~ **Tom Fricke, CEO, Cartridge World**

"Mike Richardson helps me see the business superhighway in a whole new way, with which I can avoid wheel-spin and create traction. It's GPS for today's executive."
~ **Ray Lucia Jr., President & CEO, RJL Wealth Management**

"This book really helped me connect all the dots. If you're looking for real-world solutions to the challenges of simultaneously running and building your business, look inside."
~ **Ash Robinson, Executive Director of Franchising, Kidville (previously CEO of JW Tumbles)**

"Brilliant! I doubt if you have ever read a book like this. It will be your business bible."
~ **Jim Bayne, Area President, BB&T - John Burnham Insurance Services**

"The most comprehensive, integrated model I have ever seen for the moving parts of driving a business, and I've seen a lot!"
~ **Larry Hart, Vistage Chair**

"Having trouble sleeping because you are worried that your business is out of control, you are lurching down the road without a map? Here's the book that will EASILY show you how to keep your wheels on the road as you create - and follow - your own map to success. Sleep easy after reading this book."
~ **Joanne Pastula, President & CEO, Junior Achievement of San Diego & Imperial Counties**

"Mike Richardson is my mentor and friend since 2004. Mike has an amazing ability to implement just the right structure to influence positive and successful behavior in his friends and the people he coaches. I learn more from Mike about being a better person, leader and executive than in all my years of schooling. Mike and his *"In the Driving Seat"* model helps me see things from a unique strategic perspective and as a result I make better decisions for the development of my company and our brands. I am very excited about Mike's book Wheel$pin! Millions of people will now have the opportunity to experience the exceptional value of organizational agility by implementing Mike's strategic platform which I am so lucky to incorporate into my life and my business."
~ **Jesse Campanaro, National Commercial Fitness Sales Manager, Total Gym**

"Mike Richardson is filling a void for CEOs stuck with former economy rules and wishing to drive their companies forward in the new economy."
~ **Alan Sorkin, CEO, Premier Asset Management**

"If you are an aspiring leader, or *In the Driving Seat* of a company, this is the one tool you need to have in your leadership tool box. Focusing on the future while executing current strategies without missing critical daily details is a skill set that takes successful leaders decades to learn. Mike's Wheel Spin will get you there now."
~ **Jason Karches, General Manager, Today's Racing Digest, LLC**

"This is a well thought out book with valuable insight on every page. Wheel$pin to traction translates into a much bigger bottom line. Don't delay."
~ **Philip Lurie, CEO, CPS Printing**

"My 24 year business career has spanned gigantic multinational companies to starting a business from scratch. I have read many books, attended many lectures and hired many top consultants. Mike Richardson stands out amongst the very best. His techniques are not just theory. My experience in business is much more subtle than that. Mike provides proven techniques that are easy to apply and work. His efficient and effective techniques have helped MyOffice Inc to earn Top 100 Fastest Growing Company award 4 years running and increase our bottom-line profitability by substantially. But more importantly, we have trained and aligned our leadership and (entire company) to execute using his tools. I would highly recommend Mike and this book!"
   ~ Shaun Alger, CEO, MyOffice

"A practical blend of strategy and how-to insightfully presented from a place of experience by the author make this business book an essential all-in-one guide to getting your business on track to success. Read it. Implement it. Your business will get better. Guaranteed."
   ~ Andreas Schenck, CEO & Entrepreneur

"Mike's insights changes our mental model of what leadership is all about – agility to adapt to the "road conditions" and make continuous corrections while keeping one's eye on the destination AND the journey at the same time – not choosing one over the other."
   ~ Mark Neilson, Founder, Accretive Services

"Mike has become the voice in my head when I stray off course."
   ~ Pauline Getz, Owner & Principal, Getz & Associates

"Clear and concise approach to effective management."
   ~ Dave Lambillotte, President, IVD Research

"If your company is stuck in neutral, you have to read this book."
   ~ Mitchell Simon, President & CEO, The Simon Leadership Alliance

DEDICATION

To my parents and brothers, and to my wife Rhona and sons, Craig and Chris, to all of whom I owe so much.

Thank you to all of you who's paths have intersected with mine, for your encouragement, guidance and support, from all of whom I have learned so much. Many too many to name but you all know who you are.

CONTENTS

Preface

Wheel$pin can cost us a fortune in avoidable costs and opportunity costs. In the face of an ever changing business world, which is accelerating all the time, it is easy to lose traction, suffer wheel$pin, and pay the price. Sometimes with life and death consequences. The life and death of our business depends upon our agility as an organization.

In this new age of increasing uncertainty, turbulence, and volatility, with the speed of business and the pace of change accelerating all the time, we aren't sure what is going to happen next. When there is less and less we can count on with any certainty, we must be able to count more and more on our agility as an organization, team, manager, executive and CEO to cope, no matter what. Whatever happens next, we must have the *agility* to deal with it.

In this new reality, organizational agility is *the* core differentiator among businesses, whether they are competitors or not. It determines the winners and losers, the victors and victims, the first and the worst. It determines which organizations survive and thrive, and which don't. It sorts the best from the rest, separating those businesses which are accelerating their growth, leveraging their value and beating their competition, from those which aren't. Organizational agility has always been a determining factor, among many others, but now it is becoming more critical than ever.

As managers, executives, and CEOs, of any kind of organization, our responsibility is to be *In the Driving Seat* of our organizational agility. Individually and collectively, like never before, we must be fully filling that seat. Any shortfalls are increasingly likely to become evident very quickly, very fully, and very finally, with few second chances. Just look at the carnage we have seen in business in recent years—banks, retailers, and automotive manufacturers—among many others you know of who don't make the news. Even Toyota, with its 2010 safety issues, recalls, and crisis of public confidence, was affected. Toyota had been a source of business wisdom and best practices for decades. And then the 2010 British Petroleum (BP) Gulf of Mexico oil spill, cleanup, and aftermath caused its share price and CEO to plummet.

While organizational agility is a timeless problem, today's reality is placing new and unfamiliar demands upon us and our skills. It is asking new questions of our executive strengths, which are being tested in new ways. To pass the test, we need new answers, a new manifesto.

Where do we get those new answers? That was a question I constantly asked myself as a manager, senior executive, and then CEO, running small to medium sized, fast moving businesses in a corporate environment. I ended up running an aerospace division of such businesses, as part of a British public company. I am originally British, having become an American citizen a few years ago.

Looking for those new answers, I experienced an increasingly frustrating sense of void, a vacuum. Something was missing. It was evident to me that most coaches, consultants, and trainers who came into my office offering to help me didn't really understand what it was like to sit in my seat. Also, although I was an avid reader of business books, most of them only partly illuminated my challenge, often from a high altitude without much pragmatic advice that I could apply for immediate effect. None of them seemed to put it all together, addressing the whole challenge, the whole problem, and the whole solution of being *In the Driving Seat*.

I have yet to find the book that I want to read, so I decided to write it myself! This book is about filling that vacuum. If you share my "sense of void," then this book is for you. A manifesto for you to be an agile executive. It addresses the whole challenge, the whole problem, and the whole solution of being *In the Driving Seat* of organizational agility. It provides a unifying architecture, framework, and system of concepts, models, and tools, uniquely integrated, aligned, and attuned with the changing nature of our challenge today. The concept suite, model set, and toolbox will help you be more ready, willing, and able to translate more strategy and execution into more traction, with greater agility as an organization to cope, no matter what.

As such, this book is designed to be a manifesto which:

• Provides an introduction to the *why, what, when, where, how,* and *who* of organizational agility.

• Unifies the necessary parts and the necessary whole to fill the void. You will find many new parts and perspectives. You will also find included many existing parts and perspectives, from the most influential books, authors, and thought leaders who have informed my thinking throughout the years, as an integrated system and solution. My focus is on helping you put it all together, not least of all integrated with your own thinking, perspectives, and parts. The unifying architecture, framework, and system you will discover act as a keystone, a central organizing concept with which you can integrate, align, and attune all your existing investments in strategic initiatives, and change programs, training, and development. In so doing, you will help the whole emerge and see more clearly any of the missing parts and any lack of integration, alignment, and attunement. In my experience, oftentimes many of the parts are there, but the whole hasn't emerged and/or isn't working well.

• Supplements your learning and application with online content, giving you pragmatic tips, techniques, and tools that will continue evolving over time. This lets you choose what you want to delve more deeply into, without getting in the way of the introductory flow of the book as a keystone summary. You will find reference hyperlinks throughout, which you can either click on directly (if you are reading an electronic version of the book) or indirectly (by visiting www.mydrivingseat.com/booklinks, where you will find the master list of numbered hyperlinks, which you can use as your entrée to the online content). If you have online access presently, consider going now to www.mydrivingseat.com/booklinks booklink #1 to read more. Not least of all, this first booklink will provide a link to a file containing all the graphics you will discover in this book and more. This includes full-size and animated graphics, for you to use any way you choose—perhaps to bring your team up to speed or put on your wall as reminders.

• Helps you diagnose sources of wheel$pin, understand what that wheel$pin is costing you, and have the agile treatments you need to regain traction.

My hope is that by reading this book and exploring the online content, you will begin recognizing and developing agility as the core differentiator in your business these days:

- **Executive Agility** as the core differentiator of you from your peers, as someone who possesses the executive strengths to be filling your role fully *In the Driving Seat* of organizational agility.

- **Team Agility** as the core differentiator of your function, department, or business unit from its peers, as one that seems to execute more proficiently, adaptively, and dependably in a team context.

- **Organizational Agility** as the core differentiator of your business from its peers, as the competitor in customer markets and/or financial markets, the one that stands out as the better bet.

Whether you are a manager, executive, or CEO, seasoned and experienced or a newly appointed novice, in a turnaround mode or growth mode, this book is a manifesto dedicated to you and your agility. It's about future-proofing your competitiveness as a business, your contribution as a department, and your strengths as an executive. No matter what the future brings, you have the agility you need to cope. You will be accelerating your growth, leveraging your value and beating your competition.

As outlined in the chapter by chapter overview that follows, after we have answered the *why, what, when, where,* and *how* of organizational agility in Chapters 2 through 6, Chapter 7 helps us understand who we need to be as Breakthrough Leaders and how we need to put it all together to be Architecting a **BREAKTHROUGH!** Journey. We conclude in Chapter 8 by asking about your readiness, willingness, and ability to pass the test of organizational agility.

Chapter by Chapter Overview

Let the journey begin.

A Sense Of Void And Filling It

"Everything should be made as simple
as possible, but no simpler."

—Albert Einstein

December 29, 1972, Eastern Airlines Flight 401 is at 2,000 feet on final approach into Miami International Airport. It's nighttime and the aircraft is an L-1011 TriStar, the latest generation technology jet of its time, with three crew members in the cockpit. They reach that phase of approach in which the captain pushes the lever to get all three landing gears down (the nose gear and the two lateral gears), expecting three green lights to confirm they are down and locked. Instead, the captain sees two greens and one bulb that fails to illuminate.

The captain recycles the landing gear to try again, in case it was just a transient fault. He does so, but no luck. Still two greens and one bulb that fails to illuminate. So the captain says, "Put this darn thing on autopilot and let's figure out why this light won't go on."

Let's pause at this point. I ask you to consider the sequential path of goals that the crew had in mind at this point in their journey:

- **Goal No. 1:** Fix the bulb

...and after that...

- **Goal No. 2:** Recycle the landing gear and get three greens

...and after that...

- **Goal No. 3:** Land safely, relatively on time, and ready for what's next, with passengers none the wiser and everyone continuing on with their journey. After that everyone continues having a nice life and the crew having a nice career.

Let's resume our tragic story.

With the autopilot engaged and holding altitude, all three members of the flight crew began to focus on the detail of fixing the bulb, as their sequential goal #1. It was a little bit tight in the cockpit, and, as they concentrated their focus on the bulb, one of them nudged the yoke. In those days, nudging the yoke disengaged the autopilot from its altitude-hold mode. Kind of like dabbing the brake when you are in cruise control in your car. The autopilot obliged.

The plane went into a very gradual, imperceptible descent. It was nighttime, and the plane had been diverted out into the darkness over the Florida Everglades. They couldn't see the horizon as a reference point but, sure enough, the altimeter showed that they were slowly losing altitude. The crew remained focused on the detail of fixing the bulb. The imperceptible descent continued.

At 150 feet, one of the crew spotted the altimeter (indeed, reading 150 feet) and disbelievingly said, "We did something to the altitude... we're still at two thousand (feet), right?" A few seconds later, the aircraft crashed, traveling at 227 miles per hour and 18.7 miles short of the runway. A total of 101 crew members and passengers died. Tragic. Thankfully, 69 of the 163 passengers and six of the 13 crew survived.

Recovering and listening to the cockpit voice recorder (CVR), the National Transportation Safety Board (NTSB) concluded in its final report that the cause of the crash was pilot error and specifically: *"the failure of the flight crew to monitor flight instruments during the final four minutes of flight and to detect an unexpected descent soon enough to prevent impact with the ground. Preoccupation with a malfunction of the nose landing gear position indicating system distracted the crew's attention from the instruments and allowed the descent to go unnoticed."*

My translation: In other words, the cockpit crew became so focused on the detail of fixing the bulb ("malfunction of the nose landing gear position indicating system") that they became distracted from flying the plane ("monitoring the flight instruments" and "allowing the descent to go unnoticed").

Their attention to their No. 1 goal on their sequential path of goals undermined the subsequent goals in their journey, with disastrous results, for which they were held responsible. In that cockpit that day, their organizational agility got tested, initially only mildly (it's just a bulb) but then brutally (at 150 feet). Tragically, they failed the test. I don't want that happening to you with your business.

How many Eastern Airlines scenarios have we seen in business lately? Big banks (Bear Stearns, Lehman Brothers, Washington Mutual), retailers (Circuit City), automotive companies (General Motors and Chrysler going into bankruptcy, and Toyota with its 2010 recalls and crisis of public confidence), and BP, with the 2010 Gulf of Mexico oil spill and its subsequent handling of the crisis, are all recent examples.

These are all terrible scenarios in which organizational agility failed the test, and, therefore, to some degree, they can also be attributed to pilot error! They all involved an imperceptible descent, followed by a nosedive, followed by a tailspin, followed by a smoking hole in the ground—a smoking gun of pilot error and a lack of organizational agility to cope, no matter what.

And who would have thought that we would see Toyota added to the list, with its 2010 safety issues, recalls, and crisis of public confidence? I personally held the Toyota Production System and innovation of new philosophies and approaches for quality control, assurance, and continual improvement in high esteem. I am on the board of a Toyota dealership, which is a family business, in my hometown of San Diego, and so I have been experiencing the whitewater rapids somewhat from the inside. Of course, some of the pivotal incidents in the whole saga also happened locally in San Diego (the runaway Lexus and the runaway Prius). Following the recalls, legal cases are still ensuing, and Toyota is seeking to limit its liability based upon its research findings. In the official government report, first released by the Department of Transportation in February 2011 (conducted by a combination of the National Highway Traffic Safety Administration (NHTSA) and NASA (National Aeronautics and Space Administration)), Toyota was largely exonerated from speculation that electronic flaws had caused unintended acceleration incidents. No such flaws were found.

No matter what the findings were from here, it is a fact that Toyota suffered a crisis of public confidence. By its own admission, Toyota corporate became so focused on fixing the bulb of growth and becoming the world's No. 1 automotive manufacturer that it became distracted from flying the plane of its famed quality system, which went into some kind of an imperceptible descent, followed by a nosedive, followed by a tailspin, followed by a smoking hole in the ground!

Indeed, a smoking gun, involving congressional hearings, in which Mr. Toyoda himself owned up to pilot error, saying:

Quite frankly, I fear the pace at which we have grown may have been too quick. I would like to point out here that Toyota's priority has traditionally been the following: first, safety; second, quality; and third, volume. These priorities became confused, and we were not able to stop, think and make improvements as much as we were able to before, and our basic stance to listen to customers' voices to make better products has weakened somewhat. We pursued growth over the speed at which we were able to develop our people and our organization, and we should sincerely be mindful of that. I regret that this has resulted in the safety issues described in the recalls we face today, and I am deeply sorry for any accidents that Toyota drivers have experienced.

My translation: We became so focused on "fixing the bulb" of volume, our third priority, that we weren't "flying the plane" of our first and second priorities of safety and quality, which had gone into an imperceptible descent. Which then became very perceptible. Which then became a crisis of public confidence.

Thankfully, the brand equity has been dinged, but not dented too severely, and our dealership is doing just fine, not least of all because of the organizational agility we have developed, which we will explore further.

Then there's the BP 2010 Gulf of Mexico oil spill. With the blowout from the Macondo well on the Transocean Deepwater Horizon drilling rig on April 20, 11 rig personnel lost their lives, 17 others were injured, and the disastrous oil spill and aftermath ensued. BP issued its internal Accident Investigation Report on September 8, 2010. In this 192 page report, plus appendices, BP identifies and analyzes a sequential chain of events that led up to the disaster. Without expecting the technical jargon to mean much to you, here they are:

1. The annulus cement barrier did not isolate the hydrocarbons.
2. The shoe track barriers did not isolate the hydrocarbons.
3. The negative-pressure test was accepted although well integrity had not been established.
4. Influx was not recognized until hydrocarbons were in the riser.
5. Well control response actions failed to regain control of the well.
6. Diversion to the mud gas separator resulted in gas venting onto the rig.
7. The fire and gas system did not prevent hydrocarbon ignition.
8. The BOP (Blow Out Preventer) emergency mode did not seal the well.

"The team did not identify any single action or inaction that caused this accident. Rather a complex and interlinked series of mechanical failures, human judgments, engineering design, operational implementation and team interfaces came together to allow the initiation and escalation of the accident. Multiple companies, work teams and circumstances were involved over time."

–British Petroleum Accident Investigation Report, September 8, 2010

The technical jargon means a lot to me, as I used to be a petroleum engineer working on drilling rigs for Shell International. As a 21-year-old college graduate, fresh faced from the six-month training program, I was based in Holland, working 24/7, one week on and one week off, onshore and offshore. As on the BP Deepwater Horizon rig owned by Transocean, we were overseeing contractor rigs staffed with "roughnecks" and "roustabouts" of various nationalities (Dutch, German, other European nationalities, American, British). I was one of two Shell personnel on site: the "toolpusher" is No. 1, and the petroleum engineer is No. 2. Working onshore and offshore, in the shallow water shelf of the Dutch sector of the North Sea, we were drilling to depths of maybe 3,000 meters and maybe a 1,000 meter lateral offset, to hit the bull's-eye of our target, safely, on time, on budget, gathering and analyzing all the data we needed along the way.

Notwithstanding the technical jargon, my point in sharing the chain of events from the BP accident investigation report is to help you understand the "complex and interlinked series" of events and participants which "came together to allow the initiation and escalation of the accident" as a journey "over time."

It's all about the journey. Tragedies, accidents, and disasters like the BP blowout, Toyota's recalls, and the Eastern Airlines crash, unfold as a journey, at first mildly and slowly, and then brutally and all of a sudden! Our organizational agility gets tested progressively, coming down to the final few moments in which we have the possibility to avert disaster. In the case of Eastern Airlines, at 150 feet, the tragedy could still possibly have been averted. A few seconds later, with impact, it wasn't. In the case of BP, at 8:00 p.m. on April 20, the tragedy could still possibly have been averted. One hour and 49 minutes later at 9:49 p.m., with the first explosion, it wasn't.

In the congressional hearing on June 17, 2010, the CEO of BP, Tony Hayward, owned up to pilot error, saying:

The explosion and fire aboard the Deepwater Horizon and the resulting oil spill in the Gulf of Mexico never should have happened. I understand people want a simple answer about why this happened and who is to blame. The truth, however, is that this is a complex accident, caused by an unprecedented combination of failures. There are events that occurred on April 20 that were not foreseen by me or BP, but which we need to address in the future as lessons learned from this terrible tragedy. Based on the events of April 20 and thereafter, we need to be better prepared for a subsea disaster. Based on what happened on April 20, we now know we need better safety technology. We and the entire industry will learn from this terrible event and emerge from it stronger, smarter and safer.

My translation: We became so focused on "fixing the bulb" of being perceived as the leading innovator of deep water drilling and keeping the well on time and on budget, that we weren't "flying the plane" of safety on board and decent contingency planning (remember the famed three page contingency plan, reported in the news and apparently copied and pasted between the major oil companies), which has gone into an imperceptible descent, which then became very perceptible. Less than two months later, Tony Hayward was saying they already had masses of 20/20 hindsight about how to be much stronger, smarter, and safer!

Indeed, the official government report, released by the National Commission on the BP Deepwater Horizon Oil Spill and Offshore Drilling on February 2011, centered its findings on complacency, saying:

"In the years before the Macondo blowout, neither industry nor government adequately addressed these risks. Investments in safety, containment, and response equipment and practices failed to keep pace with the rapid move into deepwater drilling. Absent major crises, and given the remarkable financial returns available from deepwater reserves, the business culture succumbed to a false sense of security. The *Deepwater Horizon* disaster exhibits the costs of a culture of complacency.

If we are to make future deepwater drilling safer and more environmentally responsible, we will need to address all these deficiencies together; a piecemeal approach will surely leave us vulnerable to future crises in the communities and natural environments most exposed to offshore energy exploration and production."

Yes, "a piecemeal approach will surely leave us vulnerable to future crises" - fixing bulbs and not flying the plane!

As we progress through this book, we will leverage many examples, case studies, and stories such as these, not least of all, from my experiences with the oil and gas, automotive, and aerospace industries, among others. I now facilitate CEOs, executives, and their teams, and I chair Vistage groups. Vistage International is a global membership organization for CEOs, executives, and managers, founded in 1957, and, at the last count, with 15,000 members in 15 countries, growing rapidly all the time. Those members come together in small peer groups that are facilitated by a chairman or chairwoman. There are more than 500 persons chairing groups around the world, many of whom are former CEOs, presidents, or general managers like me.

So I am now lucky enough to work with members and clients from a wide diversity of industries and businesses, from startups to public companies, young and old, large and small, for-profits and not-for-profits, of all types, shapes, and sizes. At the last count, I have facilitated more than 500 group sessions and 1,500 one-to-one coaching sessions with CEOs. At the core, I am always working with them to be *In the Driving Seat* of their journey as a business and their agility as an organization, to avoid the kinds of pilot error we have begun to explore.

Avoiding Pilot Error

This book is dedicated to exploring why we see Eastern Airlines scenarios in business, whether on a macroscopic scale (like those we have mentioned, not least of all BP and Toyota) or on a microscopic scale (like you experience every day in your business), and what you can do to avoid them. Exploring macroscopically and microscopically, my purpose is to help you translate this learning into your everyday reality to avoid pilot error.

While few of us can relate to sitting in a *flying seat* (although I am sure there are many of you out there who are pilots), practically all of us can relate to sitting in a *driving seat*. I want to help you fully fill your role *In the Driving Seat* of your business. I want to help you avoid Eastern Airlines scenarios of any kind, of any magnitude, on any scale, macroscopically and microscopically. I want to help you differentiate yourself as someone who has mastered organizational agility.

This requires us to piece together the whole challenge, the whole problem, and the whole solution of fully filling our role *In the Driving Seat*. As was the case with the Eastern Airlines story, which we will further diagnose later (if you are in a hurry to know more now, visit www.mydrivingseat.com/booklinks booklink #2), any shortfall becomes evident very quickly, very fully, and very finally, with few second chances.

Just like that day in the Eastern Airlines cockpit, our new business reality is asking questions of our executive strengths and testing our agility in new ways. To pass that test, we need new answers. Where do we get those new answers?

An Expanding Universe

While we live in an expanding universe of inspiration from the gurus of leadership and management, my experience is that it tends to be cluttered with faddish concepts, how-to principles, and celebrity formulas.

When I was running small to medium sized and fast moving businesses, I began to experience a frustrating sense of void—a void of support, a sense that there was something missing, a kind of vacuum. I realized I might have to wait a long time for others to fill the void, so I decided to fill it myself.

First, I realized I needed to understand the void, top to bottom, side to side, and front to back, bringing some skeletal structure to it. Half the solution is in fully understanding the problem in an organized manner. My sense was that there was a missing architecture, sufficiently integrated, aligned, and attuned to the changing nature of our challenge these days, which would bring organization to the clutter, in a decluttering manner. There was a missing meta-model and organizing concept. Peter Drucker said it so well:

"When we create a central organizing concept, everything else gets easier. Unless organized, information is still data. To be meaningful, it has to be organized. Only the individual, and especially the individual executive, can convert data into information, deciding how to organize their information so that it becomes their key to effective action, turning the chaos of data in the universe into organized and focused information for the executive."

–Peter Drucker

I set about crystallizing a central organizing concept and architecture, to declutter the expanding universe of inspiration, into focused information for effective action. For effective action, it must be highly integrated, aligned, and attuned with the changing nature of our challenge these days. After a lot of pondering, researching, and experimenting, the void began to take shape like this:

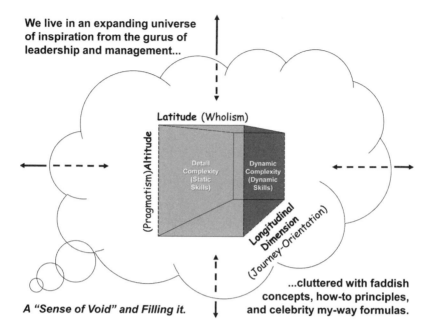

Let me explain. Being *In the Driving Seat* of our business is a whole-person challenge, just like being *In the Driving Seat* of our car (or the flying seat of a plane), at the intersection of three dimensions:

- **Latitude** (Wholism): This is about understanding the high-level concept and big picture *whole* of our business, and the breadth of issues, problems, and opportunities we face at every level; it's about looking at our business laterally and exploring the possibilities that present themselves when we do.

- **Altitude** (Pragmatism): This is about understanding the small picture parts of our business and the depth of *pragmatic* issues, problems, and opportunities we face at every level; it's about looking at our business vertically and translating high concepts into practical realities at ground level, between the rubber and the road.

- **The Longitudinal Dimension** (Journey Orientation): This is about understanding our issues, problems, and opportunities longitudinally, across multiple time horizons, from the present forward and the future backward, in a *journey-oriented* way; it's about looking at our business as an unfolding journey of the whole and the parts, in breadth and in depth, conceptually and pragmatically, all at the same time.

Just like *In the Driving Seat* of our car, it is a complex, three dimensional, whole-person challenge, and, to be fully filling the seat, we must master those complexities. In fact, there are two particular types of complexity involved, and we must master both and their interplay. In his 1990 book, *The Fifth Discipline: The Art and Practice of the Learning Organization*, Peter Senge explains it well:

> "The reason that sophisticated tools of forecasting and business analysis, as well as elegant strategic plans, usually fail to produce dramatic breakthroughs in managing a business—they are all designed to handle the sort of complexity in which there are many variables: *detail complexity*. But there are two types of complexity. The second type is *dynamic complexity*, situations where cause and effect are subtle and where the effects over time of interventions are not obvious.
>
> Conventional forecasting, planning and analysis methods are not equipped to deal with dynamic complexity. The real leverage in most management situations lies in understanding *dynamic complexity* not *detail complexity*."
>
> *–The Fifth Discipline: The Art and Practice of the*
> *Learning Organization, Peter Senge, 1990*

As depicted in the graphic above, *detail complexity* is at the intersection of the latitude and altitude dimensions. It's about the big picture whole, the small picture parts, and the detail of how they interrelate. For example, when we were developing software products in the aerospace business I used to run, we needed to get the architecture of the product right (the wholism of the latitude dimension) and dot all the i's, cross all the t's and get all the commas in the right place, in thousands and thousands of lines of software code (the pragmatism of the altitude dimension). If we didn't do either of those things very well, it wasn't a very good software product!

As also depicted in the graphic above, *dynamic complexity* is in the *longitudinal, journey-oriented plane of thinking*. In my software business, our bigger challenge was the dynamic complexity of developing multiple software products in parallel, managing the simultaneous evolution of versions of our standard product and customized, bespoke variants, dealing with setbacks, and constantly figuring out how best to deploy and deconflict our very limited resources. All at the same time, we facilitated the change leadership and change management challenge of our clients in undertaking these large-scale software deployments (something that they are notoriously bad at) and influencing their journey to be prone to success, not prone to failure. We kept trying to persuade them to understand that they weren't buying software but were buying into a business transformation. All in all, it was a very dynamically complex unfolding flow of a journey in the longitudinal dimension.

This is the challenge: to be mastering both of these types of complexity and their interplay. In trying to deal with the unfolding flow of dynamic complexity, we can overlook details, and in trying to deal with the unfolding flow of detail complexity, we can overlook dynamics. There can be a "gotcha" either way.

In more general terms, we can think of the two types of complexity as follows:

Detail Complexity	Dynamic Complexity
• Dotting the i's and crossing the t's • Many to one (many people applied to one project, client, opportunity, etc.) • Having a detailed plan, defining who does what and when, as a cascading milestone chart showing interrelationships and critical paths • Managing our attention span through traditional time and priority management • American football • Book/classroom learning *"The Devil Is in the Details"*	• The 24/7/365 blur/real time/ online all the time/flat world • One too many (one person wearing many hats, serving multiple projects, clients, opportunities, etc.) • Managing a portfolio of plans and their interrelationships/replanning on the fly/shifting goalposts • Managing our attention span through an ongoing, dynamic process of triage • British football (soccer) • Experiential/field learning *"The Devil Is in the Dynamics"*

The saying "the devil is in the details" is certainly still very much the case, more than ever before. However, with the increasing speed of business and the accelerating pace of change these days, we have had wave after wave of dynamic complexity washing over us. So I also suggest to you that "the devil is in the dynamics."

Think about it. We live in a 24/7/365 blur of a world. Everything has become real time, online all the time. It's a flat world of hyper competition and a level playing field, especially if we have had to lay off some employees and everyone is wearing multiple hats, serving multiple projects, clients, opportunities, change initiatives, sites, and roles. We are constantly managing a portfolio of plans and replanning on the fly in response to moving goalposts and reshuffling priorities. Traditional approaches to managing our attention span through time and priority management don't work very well anymore, with the challenge becoming much more like an ongoing, dynamic process of triage.

It's kind of like the difference between American football and British football (the real football!). In American football, we have a defensive team or an offensive team on the field at any one time, and each is paying attention to the detail of its role in that moment. In soccer, we have one team on the field at all times, ebbing and flowing between playing defense *and* offense, all at the same time—and defense can become offense with one long pass down the field. It's not that there isn't dynamic complexity to American football, which clearly there is; it's just that soccer (or something similar like basketball or ice hockey) involves a different and greater mix of dynamic complexity. (To read more about detail complexity and dynamic complexity, visit www.mydrivingseat.com/booklinks booklink #3.)

"Change Agents" to "Travel Agents"

You have probably been experiencing the wave after wave of dynamic complexity washing over us in recent times, with an ever-shortening wavelength in between. Have you noticed that? The time in between major upsets seems to be getting shorter all the time, with things coming at us thicker and faster. Each wave seems to bring with it a new level of turbulence, uncertainty, and volatility.

That's the new normal. In the old normal, we used to refer to ourselves as *"change agents,"* leading and managing change from one fixed state to another fixed state. It was mostly about getting the detail complexity right in the change between those two fixed states. Not anymore. These days, there is no fixed state, and it is much more about the dynamic complexity of being in a constant and accelerating state of change. As a result, our emphasis must pivot to the longitudinal, journey-oriented plane of thinking. In other words, we have morphed from being "change agents" to being *"travel agents,"* helping our organizations travel better in our unfolding journeys of dynamic complexity.

The longitudinal dimension of journey orientation has emerged not just as a third dimension, but also as the primary dimension around which we must reframe our approach as CEOs, executives, and managers. More than ever before, we must see our challenge *In the Driving Seat* of organizational agility as three dimensional. To fully fill that seat, we must develop new skills for the third dimension of dynamic complexity, fully becoming the three-dimensional CEOs, executives, and managers we need to be. Any shortfall in filling the seat is increasingly likely to become evident, very quickly, very fully, and very finally, with few second chances, just like in our tragic Eastern Airlines story.

Our education, training, and development systems have done a reasonable job in giving us the skills of detail-complexity that lend themselves to book and classroom learning. The problem is that developing the skills of dynamic-complexity is something you only really learn the hard way, experientially, in the field.

Developing Dynamic-Complexity Skills

In their 2002 book *The Communication Catalyst: The Fast (But not Stupid) Track to Value for Customers, Investors and Employees*, Mickey Connolly and Richard Rianoshek put it this way:

> "It is very possible that you already possess the leadership and communication skills that meet the challenge of static conditions. They have been honed since the dawn of the Industrial Revolution. The *dynamic skills* are unusual, and developing them fully requires considerable personal interest.
>
> *Static conditions* are based upon predictable challenges. The crucial variables are known. Although no business challenge is completely static and unchanging, some are definitely more static than dynamic. *Dynamic conditions* are substantially unpredictable. Many times you cannot safely predict the commitments, capabilities, and actions of customers, investors, employees, and competitors. In those times, leadership and communication must be more dynamic than static.
>
> The guiding principles for leaders are dramatically different. In dynamic situations, the static imperatives cause damage and create waste rather than value."
>
> *–The Communication Catalyst: The Fast (But not Stupid) Track*
> *to Value for Customers, Investors and Employees, 2002,*
> Mickey Connolly and Richard Rianoshek

That's our challenge as leaders *In the Driving Seat* of organizational agility these days, to bring our *dynamic skills* up to the same level of development as our *static skills*. As Mickey Connolly and Richard Rianoshek point out, we must also recognize that applying static skills to dynamic conditions can easily do more harm than good—that would be like applying an old static/detail-complexity solution to a new dynamic-complexity problem. We shouldn't be surprised if it doesn't work very well these days! That's what Peter Senge reminded us of in the extract from his book, *The Fifth Discipline*, earlier in this chapter, that, "Conventional forecasting, planning and analysis methods are not equipped to deal with dynamic complexity." Yet, how many times in business do we still see conventional, detail-complexity approaches (100 page strategic plans, with long action lists and detailed spreadsheets, sometimes leather bound and gold embossed!) applied to unconventional, dynamic complexity times? That's insanity! Doing what we always did and expecting a different result! No wonder it doesn't produce any breakthrough results.

The trouble is, as the saying goes, when all you have is a hammer, everything looks like a nail! Our school and college education, corporate training and development systems, and business schools do a good job in giving us the "hammer" of *detail complexity*. But when did anyone ever sit you down and give you a training class in *dynamic complexity* and the dynamic skills required? Probably never, not least of all as these are the kinds of skills you can only really learn the hard way, in the field, and experientially.

In other fields of work that are acutely journey oriented, these dynamic skills are already highly developed, experientially and in the field, from which we can learn. Consider these scenarios:

- A jet fighter pilot heading into a dogfight
- A fire crew arriving at a burning building
- A patient being wheeled into an ER

In each of these acutely journey-oriented situations, and many more like them (not least the Eastern Airlines story at the start of this chapter), a journey is unfolding in real time, with life and death consequences. Depending upon what happens in the next few moments, the next few seconds, the next few minutes, and the next few hours, people will live or die.

When in these circumstances, the professionals involved are acutely oriented to the longitudinal dimension of the journey and their journey-oriented agility to find a path that is prone to success, not prone to failure.

The dynamic skills of these professionals get tested in situations with the very high stakes of life and death consequences. They don't have the luxury of any void in fully filling their role, in all three dimensions of the challenge, and mastering the detail complexity and dynamic complexity involved. Any void becomes evident very quickly, very fully, and very finally, with few second chances. This takes us into the domains of such things as Situational Awareness, Intuition, Complex Adaptive Systems, and Naturalistic Decision Making (read more at www.mydrivingseat.com/booklinks booklink #4).

The reason that we invest so much time and money in the field training and experiential learning of these kinds of professionals is so that they can develop their *dynamic skills* in the most real world situations and simulations possible. That's the only way you can really hone these kinds of skills and develop the kind of intuition required.

In his book, *Intuition at Work: Why Developing Your Gut Instincts Will Make You Better at What You Do*, Gary Klein puts it this way:

> "Intuition is a natural and direct outgrowth of experience—the way we translate our experience into action. Our experience lets us recognize what is going on (making judgments) and how to react (making decisions). Because our experience enables us to recognize what to do, we can therefore make decisions rapidly and without conscious awareness or effort. We don't have to deliberately think through issues in order to arrive at good decisions.
>
> Analysis has its function, and intuition isn't perfect, but trying to replace intuition with analysis is a huge mistake. Intuition is an essential, powerful and practical tool. Flawed though it sometimes may be, we could not survive, much less excel, without it."

> *–Intuition at Work: Why Developing Your Gut Instincts Will Make You Better at What You Do*, Gary Klein, 2003

I first started to develop my intuitive gut instincts for dynamic complexity and the dynamic skills required, experientially and in the field, when I was working as a petroleum engineer on drilling rigs, as I mentioned when we were discussing the BP Gulf of Mexico oil spills and the Transocean Deepwater Horizon drilling rig. Based in Holland, I had to converse in Dutch to coordinate local subcontractors of supplies and specialist services. In the middle of the night, in driving wind and snow, during a heavy operation (maybe running casing into the hole and cementing it in place), one element of detail complexity missed or one element of dynamic complexity mismanaged and things can go bad, in a big way, in a hurry. As we saw with the BP oil spill! I realize now that this experience first started to inform my intuitive gut instincts for journey orientation and dynamic complexity.

I was lucky enough to have these kinds of experiential opportunities in the field, early on in my career, to develop my intuitive gut instincts for dynamic complexity and the dynamic skills required. Our problem in our organizations is that many CEOs, executives, managers, and employees have not had much experiential field learning of the kinds of dynamic complexity we are talking about and are increasingly experiencing in business. They have not had the benefit of developing their intuitive gut instincts for journey orientation and dynamic complexity in other fields of work.

However, most of us experience a very analogous situation every day, for which we have experientially honed our skills and developed intuitive gut instincts in the field. *In the Driving Seat* of our cars!

Learning to Drive Again

Do you remember when you first started learning to drive a car? We have all been there. This is all fresh in my mind as I am now teaching my 16-year-old son to drive, having taught my 19-year-old son a couple of years ago.

When we first start learning to drive, we are faced with an unfamiliar, overwhelming, and, let's be honest, downright scary amount of detail complexity and dynamic complexity to master, especially if we are learning with a stick shift (which is typical in the U.K.). When that is the case, we have the added detail complexity of which gear we are in, what speed we are going, and what gear we should be in for the circumstances: Are we going uphill, downhill, approaching a curve, and are the road conditions wet or dry? We also have the added dynamic complexity of mastering the clutch and making smooth gear changes with one hand off the wheel, sometimes while halfway around a corner, while checking our mirrors, and changing lanes.

Look at us now. We have mastered the detail complexity and dynamic complexity of driving to an advanced degree, fully filling the three dimensions of our role *In the Driving Seat*. We don't have much choice but to achieve this level of mastery. Because, when we are driving our cars, any void can become very evident, very quickly, very fully, and very finally, with few second chances.

Think about it. *In the Driving Seat* of our car, we are able to be strategic and operational, leaders and managers, long-term and short-term oriented, all at the same time, hardly giving it a second thought, at the same time changing the channel on the radio, making a cell phone call (hands-free, of course), talking to a passenger, and thinking about life, usually arriving at our desired destination, safely, on time, and ready for what's next. Amazing!

So, we know that we have the dynamic skills to be *In the Driving Seat* of our car. The only question is, when we park in the lot outside our office and walk inside, what happens to these natural abilities? Where do these dynamic skills go when we need them *In the Driving Seat* of our business?

With wave after wave of dynamic complexity washing over us these days, we must be in the same mode *In the Driving Seat* of our business as we are *In the Driving Seat* of our car. Facing this reality is like learning to drive again; fulfilling the three dimensions of our role *In the Driving Seat* of our business is unfamiliar, overwhelming, and, to some degree, downright scary!

http://bit.ly/oewX9x

This is what this book is about:

• In the new normal of uncertainty, turbulence, and volatility, tuning into the sense of void and filling it.

• Understanding the whole challenge, the whole problem, and the whole solution of our role *In the Driving Seat*, at the intersection of the three dimensions of latitude, altitude, and longitude;

• At an intersection of the static plane of thinking and a dynamic plane of thinking, recognizing the combination of detail complexity/static skills and dynamic complexity/dynamic skills required;

• In particular, understanding the need to develop our dynamic skills to master the longitudinal, journey-oriented dimension of dynamic complexity;

• Developing the higher-order executive strengths of journey orientation required;

• Becoming the three-dimensional CEO or executive we need to be these days, fulfilling the three dimensions of our role *In the Driving Seat* of our business.

In the dynamic plane of thinking of the longitudinal dimension, we must develop our higher-order executive strengths of journey orientation:

> \+ Execution Excellence
> \+ Executive Intelligence, Intuition and Resilience
> \+ Pathfinding
> \= Organizational Agility

As we progress through this book, we will review each of these executive strengths, how they relate to mastery of the journey oriented dynamic complexity/dynamic skills we need, and how they add up to a bottom line of organizational agility. It's like learning to drive again. By the time we are done, you will have learned advanced driving skills. First, let's review some underlying premises.

Three Underlying Guiding Premises

There are three guiding premises underlying this work:

Premise No. 1

Without Traction, There is No Journey!

*Strategy and execution are only as good as the traction they create
and sustain on the higher road of a breakthrough journey*

Just ask those drivers who end up in a ditch at the side of the road that first icy morning of the winter season: Without traction, there is no journey! When you lose traction, no amount of horsepower or all-wheel drive helps you. Without traction, there is no journey, except a short journey into the ditch, at best. We lived in Wichita, Kansas, for a while and this would sometimes be proven to me the first icy morning of the winter season when it caught people by surprise. In my short, 10 minute commute between home and work, I would pass half a dozen cars, trucks, and SUVs in the ditch, despite four-wheel drive.

Strategy and execution are only as good as the traction they create and sustain, on the higher road of a breakthrough journey. Why are we so often disappointed with our investments of time and money in these areas? In my experience, it's often because we are only addressing parts of the challenge, parts of the problem, and parts of the solution, and the whole hasn't emerged and/or isn't working well. In some way, shape, or form, there is a thinking knowing doing gap. We have heard of the "knowing-doing" gap before, and I am extending that by adding the thinking component. Traction comes from thinking *and* knowing *and* doing. *Thinking* without *doing* or *doing* without *thinking* means we are losing traction.

To fulfill our role *In the Driving Seat* of our business, we must fully address the whole challenge, the whole problem, and the whole solution with building blocks of thinking knowing doing.

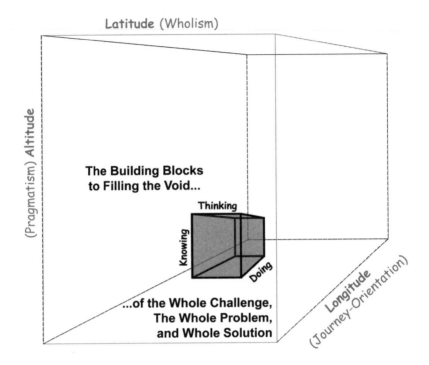

Latitude (Wholism)

(Pragmatism) Altitude

**The Building Blocks
to Filling the Void...**

Thinking

Knowing

Doing

**...of the Whole Challenge,
The Whole Problem,
and Whole Solution**

Longitude
(Journey-Orientation)

Each building block of thinking-knowing-doing is a microcosm of the whole, a fractal of the whole challenge, the whole problem, and whole solution of being *In the Driving Seat*. We can lose traction for two reasons:

- If each fractal is not a self-contained learning object of thinking-knowing-doing;

- If we are not accumulating all the fractals we need to progressively fill the void of the whole challenge, the whole problem, and whole solution.

This is at the heart of the sense of void I experienced: We get little help in fully filling the three-dimensional space of the whole challenge, the whole problem, and the whole solution, with all the fractals of thinking-knowing-doing that we need, not to lose traction in some way, shape, or form. For instance, in my experience, most business books typically only partially fill this space:

- Books like *Good to Great* (Jim Collins, 2001), *Execution* (Larry Bossidy and Ram Charran, 2002), and *Blue Ocean Strategy* (Kim & Mauborgne, 2005), provide new fractals at a high-altitude, conceptual level of about 30,000 feet but don't do well in translating things down to ground level and into the dynamic-complexity of our unfolding journey.

• The series of books by Kaplan & Norton on the *Balanced Scorecard* do a reasonable job of bringing high altitude concepts down to ground level, but my experience is that, in getting into all of that detail, they tend to be anchored in the static plane of thinking. When I saw their latest book, entitled *Execution Premium* (2008), I thought they had cracked it and would be building out their content in the third dimension of the dynamic plane of thinking. Alas, I was disappointed. It was still full of flow charts which, for me, are still stuck in the static plane of thinking.

• Books like *The Leadership Challenge* (2008, 4th edition) by Jim Kouzes and Barry Posner, *Now Discover Your Strengths* (2001) by Marcus Buckingham and Don Clifton, and the series by Malcolm Gladwell, *The Tipping Point* (2006), *Blink* (2007), and *Outliers* (2008), all provide us some other fractals in the mix and don't really attempt to fill the whole.

Don't get me wrong; these are mostly great books, and I am so grateful for their research and authorship. I am an avid reader of these and many others, and they have each hugely informed my thinking-knowing-doing through the years, providing valuable parts to help me piece together the whole. But typically, in my experience, we are left to figure out how to integrate these fractals of learning into the whole challenge, the whole problem, and the whole solution of being *In the Driving Seat* of our business.

Oftentimes, and counterproductively, the time, energy, and attention we consume in implementing partial solutions subtract from traction rather than adding to it because they fail to produce the breakthrough results we were hoping for. Remember what Peter Senge said: "The reason that sophisticated tools of forecasting and business analysis, as well as elegant strategic plans, usually fail to produce dramatic breakthroughs in managing a business" is because these conventional approaches were designed to address detail-complexity, not dynamic complexity.

In my experience, another reason for not producing "dramatic breakthroughs" is also because these books and the professionals that base their work on them tend to be primarily in one mode or another—consulting, training, or coaching.

Interpreting, Translating & Facilitating leading edge Thinking-Knowing-Doing...

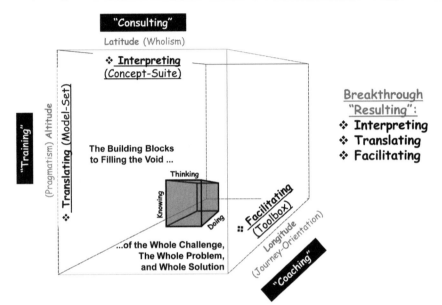

...with a Concept-Suite, Model-Set and Toolbox for Breakthrough "Resulting"

In my experience, consulting tends to be mostly about thinking, primarily about big picture stuff and high-altitude thinking. Training tends to be mostly about knowing and giving people the pragmatic know-how to bridge the thinking knowing gap. Coaching tends to be mostly about doing and creating accountability with people to bridge the knowing-doing gap.

In reality, to create traction and produce "dramatic breakthroughs," we need a blend of these modes, which I call "Resulting." This implicitly speaks to the whole challenge, the whole problem, and the whole solution of producing results. We must be "resultants," *In the Driving Seat* of our business, with an inescapable responsibility for results.

Now I realize why I had such a sense of void when many of those coaches, consultants, and trainers came into my office offering to help me when I was a CEO. Whether they were big or small firms, generalists or specialists, they were typically offering me one-dimensional or, if I was lucky, two-dimensional solutions to my three-dimensional problem. It's the same with many of those books, whether broad or narrow in focus, conceptual or practical. They typically only attend to some subset of the three dimensions, leaving a void in some way, shape, or form, on one dimension or another. As a result, they are guilty of oversimplification. As Einstein said in the quotation at the head of this chapter, *"Everything should be made as simple as possible, but no simpler."* Business is increasingly complicated these days, and to lapse into oversimplification by leaving thinking knowing doing gaps is a big mistake.

Relating to the three-dimensional challenge we have been developing in this chapter, I define "resulting" as the combination of interpreting, translating, and facilitating:

- **Interpreting**: providing a concept-suite helping us interpret leading-edge thinking, experience, and understanding of our challenge these days.

- **Translating**: providing a model-set helping us translate this conceptual understanding into relevance and applicability in our business, addressing the whole problem and the whole solution.

- **Facilitating**: providing a toolbox helping us apply and sustain these ideas, with commitment and accountability to facilitate driving things through to results.

This combination of interpreting, translating, and facilitating and the "resulting" which they add up to is why I love my work as a Vistage chairman so much. Being a chairman is about helping our members interpret leading-edge thinking and experience from speakers and each other. It's about helping them translate that into relevance and applicability in their particular business, in their particular situation, and with their particular needs and wants. It's about facilitating their commitment and accountability for applying these ideas, sustaining them, and driving them through to results. It's about "resulting." Tapping into the power of a peer group process, we help them tackle all three dimensions, to be architects of their journey, creating traction in business and in life. (To read more, visit www.mydrivingseat.com/booklinks booklink #5.)

So, that is the first underlying guiding premise of this work: Without Traction, There is No Journey! Strategy and execution are only as good as the traction they create and sustain on the higher road of a breakthrough journey.

Creating and sustaining traction is everything. Any shortfall of our strategy and execution in addressing the whole challenge, the whole problem, and the whole solution (interpreting leading-edge thinking, translating that into know-how at all levels, and facilitating the doing of what needs to be done) results in a loss of traction and a lack of "dramatic breakthroughs."

Let's also be clear, "the higher road of a breakthrough journey" may not be primarily about the profitability and growth of your business. It could be more about just sustaining your business with less stress, more time off, and improving profitability and cash flow; whatever definition of breakthrough is right for you. Talking about cash flow brings us to our second underlying guiding premise.

Premise No. 2

Cash is King!

Growing cash flow by reducing wheel$pin
and increasing tra¢tion, for cents on the dollar

Cash *is* still king! There is no denying it. Cash always has been king, it still is, in particular during recessionary times, and it always will be. Surviving and thriving in business is about not running out of cash. As we discussed above, while breakthrough journeys may be about many other things too, in some way, shape, or form they are also invariably about improving and/or growing cash flow.

That's the focus of our work and this book: helping you develop the organizational agility you need to turn around, improve, and grow cash flow by diagnosing and reducing wheel$pin. Note the substitution of the $ sign; wheel$pin is costing you a fortune in avoidable costs and, more important, in opportunity costs.

By wheel$pin, I mean you are putting a lot of energy into the equation, in the form of time, energy, attention, and money, but you aren't getting the results out in terms of traction and momentum. As we discussed above, your "resulting" isn't working well, with gaps in your thinking-knowing-doing, and you are spinning your wheels to some degree.

Wheel$pin is costing you a fortune in avoidable costs and opportunity costs:
• **Avoidable Costs**: If you are not getting the results out, why are you continuing to invest the time, energy, attention, and money in?

• **Opportunity Costs**: What market share are you not winning, what productivity gains are you not getting, and what profitable growth are you foregoing?

My work on organizational agility is about helping you diagnose where wheel$pin is coming from (in any way, shape, or form in your business and organization), what it is costing you, and then deriving a treatment plan to regain tra¢tion (noting our substitution of the ¢ sign), for cents on the dollar.

That's right, for cents on the dollar! This means helping you do simple, simple, simple things, which cost you next to nothing and can provide a huge payback. These approaches will reduce wheel$pin and increase tra¢tion for cents on the dollar, thereby providing a very high return on investment (ROI) of improving and growing cash flow.

In my experience, and as we will discuss more throughout this book, there are simple, simple, simple approaches we can and should take to launch the inception of a breakthrough journey, incubate it during its early stages, and improvise ways to build momentum. These should come before incurring more significant investments in larger infrastructural innovations and institutionalizing bigger initiatives. Indeed, this "starting small and finishing big" approach is often essential to architecting breakthrough journeys, as we shall explore and discuss further.

<u>Premise No. 3</u>

The Rules of the Road Have Changed
Mastering Simplicity and Complexity

Our third and final underlying guiding premise is that the rules of the road have changed. Permanently! There is no going back to the "old normal." The "new normal" is here to stay. And then there will be another "new, new normal" after that. And so on.

In particular, in my experience and as we have already begun exploring, the rules of the road have changed around an understanding of simplicity and complexity. We already started to explore this with our review of the two types of complexity: detail complexity and dynamic complexity. Now we will continue with a review of simplicity, using the quotation with which this chapter started:

"Everything should be made as simple as possible,
but no simpler."

–Albert Einstein

Let's face it, being *In the Driving Seat* of organizational agility is complicated. If it weren't, we would have mastered it a long time ago, and we wouldn't have any Eastern Airlines scenarios in business. Our desire to simplify is essential. It is also essential that we don't oversimplify, as the Albert Einstein quotation reminds us. This is further illuminated by another of my favorite quotations:

> *"I wouldn't give a fig for the simplicity this side of*
> *complexity but I'd give my life for simplicity*
> *on the far side of complexity."*
> **–Oliver Wendell Holmes**

This tells us that, just as there are two types of complexity (detail complexity and dynamic complexity), which we discussed earlier in this chapter, there are also two types of simplicity. We will call these:

- **Stupid Simplicity**: This is simplicity this side of complexity, which ignores that complexity.

- **Elegant Simplicity**: This is simplicity on the far side of complexity, which embeds that complexity.

How often do we hear someone using the KISS principle, saying something like, "Can't we just Keep It Simple, Stupid," sometimes just quietly in his or her head and sometimes verbally in the room! It is usually followed by something like, "Let's just focus on this year's budget goals," maybe continuing with something like, "and then future years will take care of themselves." Thinking back to our Eastern Airlines story at the start of this chapter, that is equivalent to saying, "let's fix the one-year bulb and not worry about flying the five-year plane." That makes us vulnerable to the imperceptible descent and tragedy of an Eastern Airlines scenario in the future of our business.

The KISS of Death

As our Eastern Airlines tragedy illustrates, *just* Keep It Simple, Stupid can be the KISS of death. A telltale sign is when we hear someone (or perhaps ourselves) using the word "just" in that kind of context. It is often a dead giveaway that we may be verging on stupid simple, which ignores complexity.

Instead, our challenge is to move through and master complexity, by reaching elegant simplicity on the far side, which embeds complexity. There is no way around it, or over it or under it, or any other way to shortcut it. We must move through complexity, mastering it. As we discussed earlier in this chapter, keep in mind that there are two types of complexity to move through (detail complexity and dynamic complexity) and master. That's much easier said than done! It involves the journey to mastery.

The Journey to Mastery

In his book, *Mastery*, George Leonard helps us understand the journey to mastery of anything:

> "We all aspire to mastery, but the path is always long and sometimes rocky, and it promises no quick and easy payoffs. So we look for other paths, each of which attracts a certain type of person. *Dabblers, Obsessives and Hackers* go through life each in their own way, choosing not to take the Master's journey.
>
> There is no way around it. Learning any new skill involves relatively brief spurts of progress, each of which is followed by a slight decline to a plateau somewhat higher in most cases than that which preceded it. The curve is necessarily idealized. In the actual learning experience, progress is less regular; the upward spurts vary; the plateaus have their own dips and rises along the way. But the general progression is almost always the same.
>
> To take the master's journey you have to practice diligently, striving to hone your skills, to attain new levels of competence. But while doing so—and this is the inexorable fact of the journey—you also have to be willing to spend most of your time on a plateau, to keep practicing even when you seem to be getting nowhere."

–George Leonard, *Mastery*, 1992

Read more at www.mydrivingseat.com/booklinks booklink #6

Being *In the Driving Seat* of organizational agility is complicated, and there is a lot to master. It is a long, rocky path, with no quick and easy payoffs and long stretches on the plateau. *Dabblers, Obsessives, and Hackers* hate the plateau (read more at www.mydrivingseat.com/booklinks booklink #6) whereas *Masters* learn to love the plateau, keep plodding along, and wage war against the barrage of the quick fix, fast temporary relief, bottom line, anti-mastery mentalities.

In trying to be *Masters*, on the long, rocky path, we are under constant assault from *Dabblers, Obsessives, and Hackers*, trying to convert us to their ways and threatening to lead us astray. As a result, many CEOs, executives, and managers dabble, obsess, and hack, unwittingly choosing the stupid simplicity side of complexity. Walking around a business like that you might overhear things like these:

- "We tried strategic planning and it didn't work."
- "Our business is too fast moving for strategic planning, and we just like to keep things organic around here."
- "We don't have time for strategic planning, and what's the point of doing long-range planning when the future is uncertain?"

Big mistake! That's an Eastern Airlines scenario looming in their future for sure!

As an example, imagine if we took the same approach to being *In the Driving Seat* of the financial accounting of our business. Think about it. The financial accounting of our business is an equally complicated and analogous three-dimensional challenge.

Our financial accounting systems, processes, and disciplines have to master the integrated three-dimensions of our balance sheet, our P&L, and our cash flow and the implicit interrelationships among these. We must master detail complexity (of bookkeeping and dotting the i's and crossing the t's on all the invoices, etc., among many other details) and dynamic complexity (inflows, outflows, and timing differences), based upon such underlying guiding premises as double-entry bookkeeping, accrual accounting, LIFO/FIFO inventory accounting, budgeting/ forecasting, and disbursement authorities, among many others. We could go on. It's very complicated!

No matter what the size of our business, imagine if we were a dabbler, obsessive, or hacker when it comes to the financial accounting of our business. It would be an Eastern Airlines disaster for sure and cost us a lot of money!

Clearly, the financial accounting of our business is not optional. At least, not if we want to stay in business. So, instead, we choose the master's journey of amassing the systems, processes, and disciplines, together with the resources required, to move through and master the detail complexity and dynamic complexity of the challenge. By and large, we achieve the elegant simplicity of mastery on the far side, and we sustain the discipline to operate our system well and continually improve its operation. We invest in new software and training, for instance, for even greater mastery, so that we can close our books faster, get easier access to data/information for management accounting purposes, and understand more transparently where we make money and where we don't.

In total, think about the amount of time, energy, attention, people, processes, paperwork, software, and systems you invest in mastering the financial accounting of your business. It's not optional. Why? Because if you don't do it, you can lose a lot of money, real fast.

What about the "strategic accounting" of your business? By comparison, how much time, energy, attention, people, processes, paperwork, software, and systems are you investing in accounting for the strategic future of your business? What account-ability are you creating and sustaining to master the similar complexities involved of being *In the Driving Seat* of organizational agility and translating strategy and execu-tion into traction? How does that stack up, compared to your investments in the finan-cial accounting of your business? I'm guessing it's probably miniscule by comparison! How come? Because, for some reason, it's seen as optional, at least to some degree.

I urge you to consider that the "strategic accounting" of your business is also not optional—as equally not optional as the financial accounting of your business. Why? Because, just like for the financial accounting of your business, if you don't do it, you can lose a lot of money, real fast. Just look at the number of Eastern Airlines scenarios we have seen in business lately and the financial consequences for all concerned.

Somehow, along the way, the adequate "strategic accounting" of our business has been perceived as optional. Yet, it is equally the integration of systems, processes, and disciplines, just like for the financial accounting of our business. However, when CEOs, executives, and managers are faced with the reality of the time, energy, attention, and discipline that mastery takes, they perceive it as optional and that a lower level of effort (i.e., dabbling, obsession, and hacking) is okay. Big mistake.

The rules of the road have changed. We must master the whole challenge, the whole problem, and the whole solution of simplicity and complexity to develop the organizational agility we need to survive and thrive. Only then will we be doing everything we can to avoid Eastern Airlines scenarios in our future.

These days, any shortfall in fully filling our role *In The Driving Seat* of our business is likely to become evident very quickly, very fully, and very finally, with few second chances (like what happened that day in the Eastern Airlines cockpit). Throughout this book, we will be discussing how their organizational agility got tested that day and what you can do to avoid Eastern Airlines scenarios in your future. It's a journey to mastery.

Our Journey to Mastery with This Book

This book will give you an introduction to the topic of organizational agility, intentionally being skeletal in nature so as not to overwhelm you at this stage in your journey to mastery.

Organizational agility is necessarily complex, as we will discuss, and many people tend to bounce off that complexity (as dabblers, obsessives, and hackers) rather than moving through that complexity to the elegant simplicity of mastery. I don't want you to bounce!

I do want to present you with a pathway, via which you can move through and master the complexities involved, by learning, applying, and achieving in parallel. Practice is the key to mastery, as George Leonard reminded us, saying, "To take the master's journey you have to practice diligently, striving to hone your skills, to attain new levels of competence." Hence, the supplementary content online of pragmatic tips, techniques, and tools (www.mydrivingseat.com/booklinks).

I want to help you to "get an A" as a great CEO/executive *In the Driving Seat* of organizational agility, translating strategy and execution into traction, with nothing getting lost in translation. Nothing getting lost in translation means no wheel$pin! In my experience, the majority of CEOs, executives, and managers are getting Bs and Cs at best. I want to help you join the minority who are getting an A.

My intention is to provide you with a unifying architecture, framework, and system of concepts, models, and tools, uniquely integrated, aligned, and attuned with the challenge of being *In the Driving Seat* of organizational agility. My objective is to get you thinking about how ready, willing, and able you *really* are to develop organizational agility as *the* differentiator in business these days, developing it as a competitive advantage.

My hope is that, as a result of reading this book, you will change your relationship with dynamic complexity and will achieve a personal breakthrough, being more composed, confident, and courageous with less stress, more balance, and better perspective.

As Mickey Connolly and Richard Rianoshek reminded us, developing the necessary dynamic skills "requires considerable personal interest." The first step in your journey of interest was picking up this book.

"The most powerful force in the universe is compound interest."

–Albert Einstein

As the quote from Albert Einstein tells us, when you compound your interest in this topic, through the upcoming chapters and the supplementary online content, you will be ready, willing, and able to undertake the journey to mastery. Let the compounding continue, and let the journey begin.

Chapter 1 Summary

Our journey as a business is an unfolding of how we link and accumulate individual thoughts, questions, decisions, and actions. Here are some things to think about, questions to ponder, decisions to make, and actions to take from this chapter, to weave into your journey.

Things to Think About

- *Think about* the Eastern Airlines scenarios you have experienced in some aspect or another of your business
  1. With products?
  2. With processes?
  3. With relationships?
  4. With innovation?
  5. With performance?
  6. With other aspects of your business?
- *Think about* the ways in which your business has become much more dynamically complex in recent times.
- *Think about* the current state of dynamic-complexity skills in your business, broadly and deeply throughout your organization, starting with yourself and your team.

Questions to Ponder

- *Ask yourself* how can you reduce the risk of Eastern Airlines scenarios in your business?
- *Ask yourself* how can you reinforce the need to develop dynamic-complexity skills?
- *Ask yourself* how can you avoid the stupid-simple excuses for a lack of a strategy process and discipline in your business?

Decisions to Make

- *Decide* that you will develop organizational agility and execution excellence as a competitive advantage.
- *Decide* that you will learn to drive again, developing the higher order executive strengths of journey orientation.

Actions to Take

- *Hold* yourself accountable to compound your interest on the journey to mastery, daily, weekly, monthly.

Why Is Organizational Agility
Increasingly Crucial?

"Fasten your seatbelts. The turbulence has scarcely begun. With accelerating speed, we've transcended boundary after boundary of diversity and complexity. The past is ever less predictive; the future is ever less predictable and the present scarcely exists at all."

–Dee Hock, 1999, Birth of the Cha-ordic Age

Change has changed! The nature of change itself has changed. These days, it has become much more like a dynamic journey on a shifting landscape of increasing uncertainty, turbulence, and volatility. That's not abnormal; it's the new normal.

As a result, organizational agility has become increasingly crucial. When there is less and less we can count on with any certainty, we must be able to count, more and more, on our organizational agility to cope, no matter what.

Dee Hock puts it well in his quotation at the head of this chapter. I first used that quotation in 1999 when I was giving a keynote speech at an annual convention. And yet, more than 10 years later, it seems timelier and more relevant than ever! Let's look at it in its parts:

"The turbulence has scarcely begun."

Think back through the turbulence we have experienced during the last 10 years, including:

- The dotcom/telecom/NASDAQ bubble bursting

- 9/11

- Two wars (Iraq and Afghanistan) and continuing terrorism

- Following his retirement in 2006, the former chairman of the U.S. Federal Reserve, Alan Greenspan, wrote his 2007 book, *The Age of Turbulence: Adventures in a New World*, only to have to republish it in 2008/9 "with a new chapter on the current crisis." Even he didn't see the degree of turbulence coming! We'll talk more about that later.

- The oil price shock of 2008, with prices reaching $140/barrel

- The subprime mortgage and real estate bubble, credit default swaps, and the credit crunch that followed

- The "Great Recession," which threatened to become a depression, and associated stimulus packages (TARP and "Cash for Clunkers")

- The Madoff Ponzi scheme

- At the time of writing in 2010, we are eagerly awaiting the publication of Jim Collins' next book, which he reports will be the result of six years of "turbulence research." On the way to that, his 2009 book was entitled *How the Mighty Fall: and Why Some Companies Never Give In*.

- Some of the mighty who have fallen include major banks, automotive manufacturers, and retailers, among many others.

- Healthcare reform in the United States

- Natural disasters thrown into the mix (the 2004 Indian Ocean tsunami, Hurricane Katrina in 2005, the Haiti and Chile earthquakes in 2010) and the ever present trends of global warming

- Toyota's 2010 safety issues, recalls, crisis of public confidence, and bad press

- Greece's meltdown and economic turmoil in Europe

- The 2010 BP Gulf of Mexico oil spill, cleanup, and aftermath, causing the plummeting of its share price and CEO

- Financial reform in the United States

- Austerity measures and budget cuts in the leading economies (UK) and debt ceiling crises (USA)

- Egypt's revolution, downfall of Mubarack, assumption of military rule and democratization and ripple effects throughout the middle east

- Japan earthquake, tsunami, nuclear crisis and domino effect of supply-chain issues in automotive, electronics and other markets

- For a more complete and current list, visit www.mydrivingseat.com/booklinks booklink #7

You get the idea! The turbulence has scarcely begun. The flow of major upsets seems to be coming at us thicker and faster all the time!

"With accelerating speed, we've transcended boundary after boundary
of diversity and complexity."

Have you noticed how the half-life or wavelength in between the major upsets listed above seems to be shrinking? We are only just picking ourselves up from the last upset when the next one is upon us. Hopeful for a lull, we find that each wave of upset seems to come sooner than the last, with accelerating speed. Not only that, but mixed in with these big waves of upset, we have also experienced wave after wave of new "diversity and complexity" (i.e., dynamic complexity, which we discussed in Chapter 1). Not least of all, as an example, just think about everyday computing technology today compared to how things were 1, 3, 5, 10, or 15 years ago:

- **Only fifteen years ago** in the mid 1990s, e-mail and the Web were still somewhat in their infancy, at least in terms of adoption by the masses. Fax machines were still prevalent, and laptops were in the minority.

- **Only ten years ago**, as we changed millennia, things were still rather "dial-up," broadband was still rare, and mobile e-mail communication was a relatively new thing, dominated by Blackberry.

- **Only five years ago**, most of us were still mastering Web 1.0 and had no clue of what Web 2.0 (Wikis, social networking, MySpace, LinkedIn, Face-Book, Twitter and the like) was all about. In his 2005 book, *The World Is Flat: A Brief History of the Twenty-First Century*, Thomas Friedman put it well:

> "It is now possible for more people than ever to collaborate and compete in real time with more other people on more different kinds of work from more different corners of the planet and on a more equal footing than at any previous time in the history of the world—using computers, e-mail, networks, tele-conferencing and dynamic new software. Any activity where we can digitize and decompose the value chain, and move the work around, will get moved around. Work gets done where it can be done most effectively and efficiently.
>
> When the world starts to move from a primarily vertical (command and control) value-creation model to an increasingly horizontal (connect and collaborate) creation model, it doesn't affect just how business gets done. It affects everything—how communities and companies define themselves, where companies and communities stop and start, how individuals balance their different identities as consumers, employees, shareholders and citizens, and what role government has to play. All of this is going to have to be sorted out anew."
>
> –Thomas Friedman, 2005, *The World Is Flat:*
> *A Brief History of the Twenty-First Century*

- **Only three years ago**, the concept of cloud computing was relatively unknown to most of us, and yet now we are probably making some use of it (using online back-up services or synchronizing our smart phone with an online calendar and contacts database).

- **Only a year or so ago**, Google joined Apple, Blackberry, and others in the mobile communications fray, with its Android operating system and associated hardware devices made by various manufacturers.

Indeed, at the time of writing this in 2010, Apple just released its iPad, shaking up the market for tablet computer devices and e book readers, which are also a relatively new phenomenon.

Each of these technological innovations creates a paradigm shift that introduces new diversity and complexity—new diversity of what's now possible, who can do what, how they can do it, and when they can do it. Each brings more and more dynamic complexity to the 24/7/365 blur of a world we live in, which is real time, online-all-the-time. The pace of change just seems to keep accelerating all the time, bringing wave after wave of dynamic complexity washing over us.

"The past is ever less predictive; the future is ever less predictable and the present scarcely exists at all."

When everything is being "sorted out anew" (as quoted above from Thomas Friedman), the rearview mirror is increasingly useless. The journey of how we got here has little predictive value for the journey of where we are going from here. Not only is the rearview mirror increasingly useless, but the windshield is increasingly fogged up, even if we have our defoggers on full blast! The future is ever foggier and ever less predictable. And with the accelerating pace of change, speed of business, and the shrinking wavelength in between wave after wave of uncertainty, turbulence, and volatility, the present scarcely exists at all!

As a result, the nature of change itself has changed! As we briefly touched upon in Chapter 1, we have morphed from being "change agents" to being "travel agents," helping our organizations travel better in our unfolding journeys of dynamic complexity:

When the present scarcely exists at all, looking at things through the static plane of thinking doesn't serve us well anymore. That would be like looking at a freeze frame in a movie with a rapidly unfolding and unpredictable story line. It's not going to be very useful in understanding the past or foretelling the future.

We can think of it like a movie for which the frame rate is increasing all the time. It all started with a "flick"—a series of cards we "flicked" through with incremental changes between each which would create a motion picture. A low frame rate (maybe two or three per second) between one frame and the next, one two dimensional picture and the next. Then we invented mechanical technologies that increased the frame rate, with such devices as the Zoetrope, Mutoscope, and

Praxinoscope. With the development of celluloid film technology, the frame rate increased still further, initially to about 5 to 10 frames per second. The problem is that the flicker fusion point of our human visual system, where we shift from seeing flickering to a seeing a fusion of a continuous flow, occurs at around 30 frames per second. So, with the invention of TV we moved up to 24 frames per second, then 30 frames per second with video. Now in the era of large screen, high definition TV, we are moving up to 72 frames per second, 120 with some video games and even 300 for some high speed and slow motion playback applications. And now, of course, we are also moving into the era of 3-D movies and 3-D TV, immersing us more in the flow of the fast-paced action.

That is also how change has changed. Change used to occur with a slow frame rate, moving from one fixed state to another fixed state, for which a 2-D picture sufficed as a snapshot of things. But the frame rate of change has increased exponentially. It is now well beyond the flicker fusion point of our leadership visual system. There is no fixed state. We can't discern one 2-D picture from the next. Things have fused into a third dimension of the longitudinal dimension of the storyline, as the continuous flow of our unfolding journey in real time. These days, we must look at things orthogonally, in the dynamic plane of thinking, to understand the longitudinal storyline of our business, in the continuous and accelerating flow of the past, the present, and the future.

From our discussion of detail complexity and dynamic complexity in Chapter 1, this dynamic plane of thinking and the longitudinal dimension of journey orientation has emerged not just as third-dimensional, but as the primary dimension around which we must reframe our approach as CEOs, executives, and managers. These days, we must look through this dynamic plane of thinking to master dynamic complexity and answer the new questions being asked of our executive strengths. Otherwise, we will be trying to solve new dynamic complexity and dynamic plane-of-thinking problems with old detail complexity and static-plane-of-thinking solutions. It's not going to work very well! We need new answers.

"Fasten your seatbelts."

So buckle up, as you ain't seen nothing yet! It's only going to get worse. Think about the nature of the challenge we increasingly face, as outlined above, and the increasingly wild ride it now represents! We have to buckle up for that wild ride, *In the Driving Seat* of organizational agility, by:

• Understanding the anatomy of dynamic complexity and developing dynamic complexity skills

• Accepting the three-dimensional nature of the whole challenge and learning to drive again, *In the Driving Seat* of our business, mastering the whole problem and the whole solution

• Fully filling our role in that seat, with the higher-order executive strengths of journey orientation required these days. In Chapter 1, I introduced you to the equation of those strengths:

+ Execution Excellence
+ Executive Intelligence, Intuition and Resilience
+ Pathfinding
= Organizational Agility

Later in this chapter, we will begin to explore the anatomy of dynamic complexity in more detail, and how it maps with these higher-order executive strengths, at each level of our equation for the dynamic skills required. First though, let's understand more about why we need to develop these particular higher-order executive strengths of journey orientation.

Why "Execution Excellence"?

Because, as outlined by Larry Bossidy and Ram Charran in their 2002 book, *Execution: The Discipline of Getting Things Done*, "for all the talk about execution, hardly anybody knows what it is. They don't have the foggiest idea of what it means to execute."

They don't have the foggiest idea! That's been my experience of many CEOs, executives, and managers. They think they know what execution is, but in reality they don't, as we shall make clear progressively throughout this book. Larry Bossidy and Ram Charran go on to say:

"Most often today, the difference between a company and its competitor is its ability to execute. Execution is the great unaddressed issue in the business world today. Its absence is the single biggest obstacle to success and the cause of most disappointments that are mistakenly attributed to other causes.

Execution is not just tactics—it is a discipline and a system. Execution hasn't yet been recognized or taught as a discipline, whereas other disciplines have no shortage of accumulated knowledge, tools and techniques.

The leader who executes assembles an architecture of execution."

> –Larry Bossidy and Ram Charran, 2002,
> *Execution: The Discipline of Getting Things Done*

As we progress, you will better develop the journey-oriented, higher-order executive strength of Execution Excellence. You will be introduced to a unifying architecture of execution, as a system and a discipline of accumulating knowledge, tools, and techniques. The supplementary online content at www.mydrivingseat/booklinks will give you some resources to begin recognizing it and teaching it with your team.

Why "Executive Intelligence, Intuition, and Resilience"?

Because, as outlined by Justin Menkes in his 2005 book, *Executive Intelligence: What All Great Leaders Have*, "many people tend to get lost or defocused when addressing a complex issue… or navigating a complex situation."

That has also been my experience of many CEOs, executives, and managers. The topography of issues and the shifting landscape of business these days mean we always have to navigate complex situations, with increasing detail complexity and dynamic complexity, to have any chance of sustaining a trajectory of profitable growth. It becomes overwhelming for many CEOs, executives, and managers, as it exceeds their capability and capacity to cope. Justin Menkes goes on to say:

> *"What we are talking about is an internalized set of skills, those that finally make explicit the elusive concept of 'business acumen'*—critical thinking applied to business is a form of intelligence—an organic, adaptive, ever-evolving set of cognitive skills applied in the business arena.
>
> *It is what we call Executive Intelligence—a distinct set of aptitudes that determine one's success.* These people have what some would call an uncanny sense of direction… a highly developed intuition for the analytic path that will get them to their destination."

–Justin Menkes, 2005, *Executive Intelligence: What All Great Leaders Have*

An uncanny sense of direction! As we progress, we will help you develop the journey-oriented, higher order strength of Executive Intelligence, helping you develop your capabilities and capacities to cope, so as not to be overwhelmed. We will help you develop that uncanny sense of direction and highly developed intuition for what we will call "pathfinding," of finding a path through, no matter what.

Intuition will be an equally important component. In his 2003 book, *Intuition at Work: Why Developing Your Gut Instincts Will Make You Better at What You Do*, Gary Klein helps us understand the role of *"intuitive decision making."* He calls it "an essential, powerful and practical tool… a natural outgrowth of experience… the way we translate our experience into action… our ability to size up situations and recognize what actions to take." He goes on to say:

> "Where decisions are more challenging, situations are more confusing and complex, information is scarce or inconclusive, time is short and the stakes are high… the classical, analytical model of decision making falls flat… intuitive decision making improves as we acquire more patterns, larger repertoires of action scripts and richer mental models.
>
> Analysis has its function, and intuition isn't perfect, but trying to replace intuition with analysis is a huge mistake. Intuition is an essential, powerful and practical tool. Flawed though it sometimes may be, we could not survive, much less excel, without it."
>
> –Gary Klein, 2003, *Intuition at Work: Why Developing Your Gut Instincts Will Make You Better at What You Do*

Trying to replace intuition with analysis is a huge mistake! As we progress, we will help you develop your journey-oriented, higher-order executive strength of intuition and intuitive decision making, by helping you develop a richer mental model and a larger repertoire of action scripts and patterns to excel. Indeed, as we will keep revisiting throughout, this is at the core of this book—helping you develop a richer mental model of the whole challenge of being *In the Driving Seat* of organizational agility and the behavioral patterns of thinking and acting that we need in our repertoire for excellence and success.

Not least of all, our repertoire has to have deep and solid foundations of resilience. In their 2002 book, *The Resilience Factor: 7 Keys to Finding Your Inner Strength and Overcoming Life's Hurdles*, Karen Reivich and Andrew Shatte say: "Everyone needs resilience, because one thing is certain, life includes adversities. If you increase your resilience, you can overcome most of what life puts your way. Can you boost your resilience? Absolutely. It's all about changing the way you think about adversity." They go on to say:

> "We all know resilient people. They inspire us. They seem to soar in spite of the hardship and trauma they face. In fact, the most resilient people seek out new and challenging experiences because they've learned that it's only through struggle, through pushing themselves to their limits, that they expand their horizons. They are not danger seekers, yet they don't wither when confronted with risky or dangerous situations. Resilient people understand that failures are not an end point. They do not feel shame when they don't succeed. Instead resilient people are able to derive meaning from failure, and they use this knowledge to climb higher than they otherwise would.

> Resilient people have found a system—and it is a system—for galvanizing themselves and tackling problems thoughtfully, thoroughly and energetically. Resilient people, like all of us, feel anxious and have doubt, but they have learned how to stop their anxiety and doubts from overwhelming them. We watch them handle threat with integrity and grace and we wonder: could I do that? The answer is yes. Resilience is under your control. You can teach yourself to be resilient."

> –Karen Reivich and Andrew Shatte, 2002, *The Resilience Factor:*
> *7 Keys to Finding Your Inner Strength and Overcoming Life's Hurdles*

It is a system! As we progress, we will help you develop and teach yourself a system to galvanize yourself and your team, a system addressing the whole challenge, the whole problem, and the whole solution of being *In the Driving Seat*, with the resilience we need. We will help you think about adversity differently, so that the whole challenge of organizational agility becomes less of an ordeal. We will help you soar higher with expanding horizons and climb higher to new mountain peaks, inspiring others and yourself to push new limits.

We will help you bring together the threads of your journey oriented, higher order strength of Executive Intelligence, Intuition, and Resilience, by understanding and leveraging the interplay and integration of these elements and factors outlined above.

Why "Pathfinding"?

Because, as outlined by Rosamund Stone Zander and Benjamin Zander in their 2000 book, *The Art of Possibility: Transforming Professional and Personal Life*, "Draw a different frame around the same set of circumstances and new pathways come into view. Find the right framework and extraordinary accomplishment becomes an everyday experience... bringing possibility to life."

Extraordinary accomplishment becomes an everyday experience! As we progress, we will help you develop your journey-oriented, higher-order executive strength of Pathfinding, by helping you develop your ability to reframe circumstances, bring new pathways of possibility into view, and find a path through, no matter what.

Reframing is a crucial skill. In his 2001 book, *Reframing Business: When the Map Changes the Landscape*, Richard Normann goes further and says, "Today's market game is much more about who can creatively design frame breaking systemic solutions—reconfiguration of value creating systems—we must reconfigure or be reconfigured."

We must reconfigure or be reconfigured! We will help you reconfigure your executive strengths and value creating system for the whole challenge of being *In the Driving Seat* of organizational agility. What is at stake is clear. How many CEOs, executives, and managers get reconfigured out of the equation because they fall behind the reconfiguration curve? We don't want that to be you. Reconfigure or be reconfigured! Richard Normann goes on to say:

> "But change, even radical, in organizations does not mean throwing the baby out with the bath water. Whatever is retained—whatever is the continuity face of change—this something must be reframed into another systemic context, put into another business idea and management model. No change starts from nothing—the 'old' practically always has elements which have potentially higher positional value if put into a new context. This 'continuity hub' of reframing may be: physical assets; capabilities; customers. Such undervalued (because located in an inappropriate systemic context) assets can be identified and serve as the 'hubs' of reframing."
>
> –Richard Normann, 2001, *Reframing Business:*
> *When the Map Changes the Landscape*

We will help you develop your pathfinding skills to be reconfiguring value creating systems and leveraging continuity hubs of change. These path finding skills exist as the interplay between two realms of thought, which Richard Normann explores:

- **The Business Realm:** "Looking at the changing logic of today's business context and logic of value creation, expressed in opportunities for dramatic reconfiguration of business systems."

- **The Mental Realm:** "Investigating the mental, symbolizing processes of the collective mind, which allow institutions to change themselves and function in this new context."

–Richard Normann, 2001, *Reframing Business:*
When the Map Changes the Landscape

We will help you develop your journey-oriented, higher-order executive strength of Pathfinding, by exploring the reframing opportunities in the interplay and overlap between these two realms. Not least of all, the "mental realm," as Richard Normann explains, requires a certain mental agility, to be able to explore reframing and re-configuration options and possibilities. We will help you develop the mental agility required to bring new possibilities to life and make extraordinary accomplishment an everyday experience.

So, we have now reviewed the reasons for the top three levels of our equation of or-ganizational agility and the journey-oriented, higher-order executive strengths required:

> \+ Execution Excellence
> \+ Executive Intelligence, Intuition, and Resilience
> \+ Pathfinding
> = Organizational Agility

As we progress, we will help you develop each of these journey oriented, higher-order executive strengths, both individually and collectively, with your peers and your team, combining them to add up to the bottom line strength of organizational agility. We will review each strength in depth, understanding how it addresses the anatomy of dynamic complexity and the dynamic skills required in a journey oriented way. We will review the underlying intelligences we must develop and leverage as foundations for these strengths. We will explore a journey oriented model for each strength, and, via the booklinks (www.mydrivingseat.com/booklinks), we will reference associated online resources, tools, and templates that you can leverage.

First though, let's understand more about the bottom line of organizational agility.

Why "Organizational Agility"?

Because, as outlined in their 2007 book, *Leadership Agility*, Bill Joiner and Stephen Josephs say that "Less than 10% of managers have mastered the level of agility needed for sustained success in today's turbulent business environment. Leadership agility is directly analogous to organizational agility: it's the ability to take wise and effective action amid complex, rapidly changing conditions. Leadership agility isn't just another tool for your toolkit. It's the master competency needed for sustained success in today's turbulent economy."

It's the "master competency," and less than 10% of managers have mastered it! That is my experience with many CEOs, executives, and managers. It never ceases to amaze me how many are still trying to apply old, detail complexity solutions to new, dynamic complexity problems and wondering why they aren't working! These days, the devil is in the dynamics, not just in the details, and so many organizations are bedeviled with a constant state of being overwhelmed, dysfunctional, and stressed. Life has become a constant whitewater ride. The answer is to break out of that mode by mastering dynamic complexity, but so many organizations have given up, resigning themselves to their fate of constant whitewater. They believe that is situation normal, and there is nothing they can do about it. It's just the way it is. As we have discussed, that is what we call stupid simple.

Don't be in that majority! Join the minority by developing the higher-order executive strengths of journey orientation as the "master competency" for success these days. It is about a journey to mastery, and the majority doesn't have the staying power to stay the course, go the distance, and see it through. Instead, those people in the majority dabble, obsess, and hack! We will help you stay the course, go the distance, and see it through, joining the minority who are mastering the competency required these days.

It is increasingly clear from leading research and authors that the demands upon our agility as leaders and organizations are only increasing. Bill Joiner and Stephen Josephs go on to identify two drivers of increasing turbulence:

> "Underlying this turbulence are two deep global trends that have radically altered what it takes to achieve sustained success: accelerating change and growing complexity and interdependence:

- **Accelerating Change**: every year new technologies, markets, and competitors emerge at an ever-increasing pace. As change accelerates, so does uncertainty and novelty: future threats and opportunities are harder to predict, and emerging challenges increasingly include novel elements.

- **Growing Complexity and Interdependence**: with the globalization of the economy and the spread of connective technologies, it's increasingly clear that we live in a diverse planetary village where everything is connected with everything else. In this interdependent world, the most successful companies will be those that create strong, timely alliances and partner effectively with customers, suppliers, and other stakeholders.

While specific future developments are increasingly difficult to predict, we can make two predictions with great certainty: the pace of change will continue to increase, and the level of complexity and interdependence will continue to grow."

–Bill Joiner and Stephen Josephs, 2007, *Leadership Agility:*
Five Levels of Mastery for Anticipating and Initiating Change

So, buckle up! You ain't seen nothing yet! The pace of change will continue to increase, and the level of complexity and interdependence will continue to grow. In other words, dynamic complexity! As a result, what it takes to achieve sustained success is radically altered. Other authors reinforce similar challenges of increasing uncertainty, volatility, and turbulence. In his 2009 book, *Business Agility: Sustainable Prosperity in a Relentlessly Competitive World*, Michael Hugos says:

"Real time data flows cause the whole world to behave like a giant stock market, with all the volatility and uncertainty that goes along with such markets. And because real time data is available, we all doing business in real time now whether we know it or not. Because information is available in real time, people are learning to react more quickly.

Change ripples through markets much faster than ever was possible in the industrial economy. Supply and demand data for products and services are communicated quickly so the prices of those products change quickly (just like stock prices). Companies that succeed are learning to make continuous small adjustments in their operations to respond as conditions change, and they are learning to continuously enhance their products and services with new features as their customers' desires evolve. They learn to make money from many small adjustments and from some occasional big wins—just as stock traders do.

Companies must attain and maintain a level of 'good-enough' efficiency, but unless a company is a low-cost leader in its market, it cannot use efficiency alone to generate profits. Responsiveness trumps efficiency."

–Michael Hugos, 2009, *Business Agility:Sustainable Prosperity in a Relentlessly Competitive World*

So, buckle up! You ain't seen nothing yet! Change ripples through markets much faster than ever before because the whole world behaves more and more like a giant stock market with the volatility that goes with it. As a result, responsiveness trumps efficiency! We need new responses coming from a new mindset for the new normal of our increasingly chaotic environment these days. In their 2009 book, *Chaotics: The Business of Managing and Marketing in the Age of Turbulence*, Philip Kotler and John Caslione say:

"Today's economy, with its heightened turbulence is markedly different. Today, and for the foreseeable future, the new normality economy is more than just normal times of up and down the business cycle. We can expect more big shocks and painful disruptions, causing heightened levels of overall risk and uncertainty for businesses at both the macroeconomic and microeconomic levels.

Turbulence in the business world leads to all the wrong responses from management. Many businesses and their executives subscribe to one or two conventional approaches to turbulence and the resulting chaos: they take few (if any) precautions, acting as if the storm will blow over, or else they run for cover, either slashing costs or, desperately, caught in 'magical thinking,' investing in new and often unrelated businesses to hedge their bets.

Chaotic situations will occur time and again, creating opportunities and/or crises. Business leaders are forced to deal with their companies' previously unexposed vulnerabilities or their newly revealed opportunities—and do so with deliberate and sometimes bold action that oftentimes requires developing a new mindset, which is needed to push past now-obsolete strategies and business models.

The goal is for business leaders to create organizations that are responsive, robust and resilient—in short, organizations that have the ability to live and thrive. These are organizations that aspire to and attain Business Enterprise Sustainability (BES). BES is essentially focused on all issues integral to extending the life of the business enterprise for as long as possible."

–Philip Kotler and John Caslione, 2009, *Chaotics: The Business of Managing and Marketing in the Age of Turbulence*

So, buckle up! You ain't seen nothing yet! Business enterprise sustainability is under assault from increasing turbulence and, to make matters worse, old, conventional, and downright wrong responses from management. In other words, conventional, detail complexity approaches applied to unconventional, dynamic complexity times. When all you have is a hammer, everything looks like a nail! We need to develop new tools in our toolbox for a new mindset and new responses. It's about evolving so as not to be an unwieldy dinosaur in danger of extinction. In their 2007 book, *Corporate Agility: A Revolutionary New Model for Competing in a Flat World*, Charles Grantham and Cory Williamson say:

"How does a business evolve from a slow and unwieldy dinosaur to a nimble jaguar? The process is a collaborative, strategic approach to management that acknowledges and leverages the growing interdependence of human resources (HR), information technology (IT) and corporate real estate (CRE), a process called collaborative strategic management (CSM).

It is about management over time, because continuous environmental change demands continuous organizational and managerial change. CSM is the dynamic and ongoing process of internal decision making that is the essence of corporate agility.

Achieving agility requires executives and managers to adopt fundamentally new ways of thinking. They have to shift away from the old linear, industrial model toward a more collaborative, systemic and holistic view of the world and their role in it. There must be a significant shift in how decisions are made in agile corporations, as opposed to a more traditional organizing and governance style."

–Charles Grantham and Cory Williamson, 2007, *Corporate Agility: A Revolutionary New Model for Competing in a Flat World*

So, buckle up! You ain't seen nothing yet! Achieving agility requires CEOs, executives, and managers to think differently, shifting away from the old linear, industrial model toward a more collaborative, systemic, and holistic view and their role in it—*In the Driving Seat* and the three dimensions of the challenge, as we reviewed in Chapter One—wholism, pragmatism and journey orientation. Not least of all, aligned with the longitudinal dimension of the journey, it's about the continuity of a dynamic and ongoing decision making and management process over time, for which we need a clear strategic framework, system, tools, and techniques. In his October 2009 *Business Week* article, "In Volatile Times, Agility Rules," C.K. Prahalad said:

"Over the years, managers have developed tools and techniques to overcome challenges ranging from inconsistent quality to stagnant productivity. Now they need a system for addressing volatility.

Volatility is here to stay. Organizations can handle extreme change only when they can address it within a clear strategic framework. Otherwise companies can only wait and react. Some aspects of managing in a volatile environment, such as focusing on operational efficiency and staying liquid, are givens. But more important are the abilities to scale up and down and reconfigure resources rapidly. In this volatile world, more and more companies will strive to become 'Velcro organizations' in which people and capacity are rearranged and recombined quickly without major structural change.

The winners won't stop focusing on quality, cost, and efficiency, but they'll be paying a lot more attention to agility, too."

–C.K. Prahalad, October 2009, "In Volatile Times, Agility Rules"

Volatility is here to stay, and the winners will be paying a lot more attention to agility, within a clear strategic framework and system for addressing volatility. It's beyond the mode of leadership and current expertise of most CEOs, executives, and managers. In their July-August 2009 *Harvard Business Review* article, "Leadership in a (Permanent) Crisis," Ronald Heifetz, Alexander Grashow, and Marty Linsky said:

> "When the economy recovers, things won't return to normal—and a different mode of leadership will be required. Twists and turns are the only certainty.
>
> The organizational adaptability required to meet the relentless succession of challenges is beyond anyone's expertise. No one in a position of authority—none of us, in fact—has been here before. (The expertise we relied on in the past got us to this point after all). In this context, leadership is an improvisational and experimental art.
>
> The skills that enabled most executives to reach their positions of command—analytical problem solving, crisp decision making, the articulation of clear direction—can get in the way of success. Although these skills will at times still be appropriate, the adaptive phase of a crisis requires some new leadership practices: Foster Adaptation; Embrace Disequilibrium; Generate Leadership."
>
> –Ronald Heifetz, Alexander Grashow, and Marty Linsky,
> July-August 2009, "Leadership in a (Permanent) Crisis"

So, buckle up! You ain't seen nothing yet! Twists and turns are the only certainty, and the organizational adaptability required to meet the relentless succession of challenges is beyond anyone's expertise. No one has been here before, and the old conventional approaches don't work in unconventional times, in which new questions are being asked of our strengths as CEOs, executives, and managers.

So, that's why we need organizational agility! As we progress, we will develop a new mindset, new ways of thinking, and new responses for the new challenge of organizational agility.

We will develop new expertise *In the Driving Seat*, mastering detail complexity and dynamic complexity with the static skills and dynamic skills required. We will shift away from the old linear, industrial model toward a more collaborative, systemic, and holistic view of the world, mastering the three dimensional challenge.

We will address all of this within a clear strategic framework and system for addressing volatility:

So, buckle up!
You ain't seen nothing yet!

- What it takes to achieve sustained success is radically altered.

- Responsiveness trumps efficiency.

- We need a new mindset and new responses.

- Achieving agility requires executives and managers to adopt fundamentally new ways of thinking. They have to shift away from the old linear, industrial model toward a more collaborative, systemic, and holistic view of the world and their role in it.

- Organizations can handle extreme change only when they can address it within a clear strategic framework. They need a system for addressing volatility.

- The organizational adaptability required to meet the relentless succession of challenges is beyond anyone's expertise.

+ Execution Excellence
+ Executive Intelligence, Intuition, and Resilience
+ Pathfinding
= Organizational Agility

This is the equation for the higher order executive strengths of journey orientation we need for success these days. This equation will be evolved into providing you a clear strategic framework, system, and toolbox, for you to fill your role fully *In the Driving Seat* of organizational agility.

http://bit.ly/n1pFMg

http://bit.ly/rkpyea

While all of the quotations we have reviewed so far in this chapter are from great books and articles, my experience is that these books typically don't fully fill our sense of void in all three of its dimensions. As we began discussing in Chapter 1, they don't address the whole challenge or provide a whole solution to the whole problem, leaving thinking-knowing-doing gaps. In particular, they typically fall short in translating high altitude concepts down to ground level, in the form of pragmatic, practical, and tactical tips, tricks, and techniques.

Not with this book! We will help you evolve in addressing the whole challenge, the whole problem, and the whole solution, fully filling the void. We will help you evolve yourself into the small minority of managers, executives, and CEOs who have developed the master competency of organizational agility for success, in the new normal of uncertainty, turbulence, and volatility. We will help you evolve from a slow and unwieldy dinosaur (with an old, linear, industrial mindset) to a nimble jaguar (with a more collaborative, systemic, and holistic mindset), being robust and resilient, surviving and thriving with sustainability, and with responsiveness, trumping efficiency in your business.

It is all about evolution. In their 2009 book, *The Practice of Adaptive Leadership: Tools and Tactics for Changing Your Organization and the World*, Ronald Heifetz, Alexander Grashow, and Marty Linsky define adaptive leadership as "the practice of mobilizing people to tackle tough challenges and thrive." They go on to say:

"The concept of thriving is drawn from evolutionary biology, in which successful adaptation has three characteristics:

1. It preserves the DNA essential for the species' continued survival

2. Its discards (reregulates or rearranges) the DNA that no longer serves the species' current needs

3. It creates DNA arrangements that gives the species the ability to flourish in new ways and in more challenging environments

Successful adaptations enable a living system to take the best from its history into the future."

–Ronald Heifetz, Alexander Grashow, and Marty Linsky, 2009,

The Practice of Adaptive Leadership

These days, business has much to learn from the field of evolutionary biology, which celebrated a significant anniversary in 2009. It was the 150th anniversary of Charles Darwin's *Theory of Evolution by Natural Selection*. As outlined by the authors above, having the organizational agility to survive and thrive in business these days has become more akin to the theory of evolution than ever before. (We will return to this in future chapters, but if you want to read more now you can do so at www. mydrivingseat.com/booklinks booklink #8.)

We will help you evolve the organizational agility DNA of your business, preserving, discarding, and creating DNA, as an adaptive, living system, taking the best from its history into the future.

But, if Cash is Still King...?

But, hang on a minute! If "cash is king," which we began discussing in Chapter 1 with Premise No. 2, then why do we need to spend much time thinking about the more abstract concepts such as organizational agility and execution excellence? Frankly, it all seems a bit academic, doesn't it? Not if we want to keep cash as king in our businesses! For that to happen, recent surveys, reports, and articles say that we must master these concepts:

• "Organizational Agility is a core differentiator in today's rapidly changing business environment." That's the number one conclusion from the March 2009 report from the Economist Intelligence Unit, "Organizational Agility:

how business can survive and thrive in turbulent times." Nearly 90% of the executives surveyed (349 business executives from eight countries including the United States, representing 19 industries with revenues ranging from under $500 million to more than $5 billion) believe that organizational agility is critical for business success. Rapid decision making and execution were also identified as not only important but essential to a company's competitive standing. The report also cites evidence from MIT that agile firms grow revenue 37% faster and generate 30% higher profits than non-agile companies.

Well, that's not terribly surprising. March 2009 was the middle of the 2008/2009 economic meltdown, so it's not difficult to conclude that organizational agility is key. Duh! So let's look at something before the meltdown:

- "Execution is taking precedence over profit and top-line growth as a focus for CEOs around the world." That's the number one conclusion from the October 2007 report from The Conference Board "CEO Challenge 2007: Top 10 Challenges." Prior to the turbulence of the 2008/2009 credit crunch/ recession, when asked to rate their greatest concerns from among 121 different challenges, 769 global CEOs from 40 countries chose excellence of execution as their top challenge.

Okay, so we get the part about execution. But why agility again? Let's return to the middle of the meltdown:

- "True champions have the capacity for both agility and absorption." That's the top line conclusion from a recent (February 2009) *Harvard Business Review* article, "How to Thrive in Turbulent Markets." The article outlines the concept of "agile absorption," also citing a recent McKinsey & Company survey that found that 9 out of 10 executives ranked organizational agility *as both critical to business success and growing in importance over time.*

That's all very good, but still, there really isn't any new news in these surveys, reports, and articles! We have always known these things as they are all so intuitive. Blinding flashes of the obvious, even! If that is the case, why is it that we struggle so much to translate this intuition into reality in our businesses? Why are we so often disappointed with our efforts to do so? What is getting lost in translation?

Lost in Translation?

We must understand how and where things get lost in translation. By understanding how we can more fully fill our role *In the Driving Seat* of organizational agility, we will become stronger at translating strategy and execution into traction. In times of more turbulence, more uncertainty, and more volatility, we must be able to translate more strategy and more execution into more traction, between the rubber and the road. That is the only place where it counts and is where we keep cash as king in our businesses.

By the time we are done, our strategic framework, system, and tools will help you diagnose the source of any wheel$pin in your business and how to treat it to get back into traction. The challenge pivots on the efficacy of the framework for that diagnostic assessment and prescriptive treatment plan.

In addition to the turmoil created by the 2010 safety recalls, it has been quite a wild ride during recent years with the Toyota dealership on whose board I serve. First, the oil price spikes of 2008 created a shift away from large SUVs and trucks toward smaller vehicles and hybrids. Second, there was the recession of 2009, and third, the recalls of 2010. Fourth, the supply-chain disruption of 2011, in the aftermath of the earthquake and tsunami in Japan. Normally we have more than 300 new vehicles in inventory on the lot and we got as low as having less than 100. That's a major, life threatening upset to our business, every year for the last four years! We know there will be something else next year which will be our 2012 challenge, or before, and so on. We expect it. It's situation normal. Potentially whitewater all the way, and no shortage of monthly performance and peer group benchmarking data from Toyota to emphasize the point. Instead, through the ongoing process, discipline, and cycle of diagnosis and treatment which we are exploring, in pretty much every downswing, our rankings have gone up. Our organizational agility is paying off, not least of all in terms of cash flow. As a result, we have been taking the opportunity to add to our portfolio of real estate, service operations, and dealership franchises. We are on a roll, and the leadership team is "getting an A."

As a result of progressively exploring the concepts, models, and tools, you too will understand what it takes to "get an A" these days, as a great CEO, executive, and manager *In the Driving Seat* of organizational agility, being ready, willing, and able. Our challenge is to translate the intuitive concept of organizational agility into a whole solution for the whole problem of the whole three-dimensional challenge, with nothing getting lost in translation. It's about fully filling the void we described in Chapter 1. We will begin by implanting a new chassis of business acumen, uniquely integrated, aligned, and attuned with the challenge of these increasingly turbulent, uncertain, and volatile times.

As quoted from Richard Normann earlier in this chapter, we are exploring the interplay of two realms:

• **The Mental Realm:** "investigating the mental, symbolizing processes of the collective mind, which allow institutions to change themselves and function in this new context." This is about a new mindset of business acumen required for success these days, integrated, aligned, and attuned with the new normal of volatility, uncertainty, and turbulence. This new mindset calls up a new combination of intelligences needed to "get an A" as executives these days.

• **The Business Realm:** "looking at the changing logic of today's business context and logic of value creation, expressed in opportunities for dramatic reconfiguration of business systems." This is about implanting a new chassis into our business infrastructure, integrated, aligned, and attuned with this new mindset, around which to reassemble our business vehicle to be fit for the journey challenge.

Fully filling our role *In the Driving Seat* of organizational agility requires an integration, alignment, and attunement of these two realms, a *new mindset* for the mental realm and a *new chassis* for the business realm.

In the next chapter we will begin to build out this new chassis, starting by looking more closely at what agility is, and what it is not.

Chapter 2 Summary

Why is organizational agility increasingly crucial? Because you ain't seen nothing yet! With increasing uncertainty, turbulence, and volatility, we have less and less that we can count on. The only certainty is uncertainty. So, buckle up! We must expect the unexpected. We must be comfortable being uncomfortable. That's the new normal! When there is less and less we can count on with any certainty, we must be able to count more and more on our organizational agility to cope, no matter what. That requires a new mindset of business acumen and a new chassis for our business vehicle, integrated, aligned, and attuned with the changed nature of our challenge.

Things to Think About

- *Think about* the increasing uncertainty, turbulence, and volatility you are experiencing in your business and/or your role in your business.
- *Think about* the demands this places on your agility to cope as an organization and as an executive.
- *Think about* the higher order strengths of journey orientation you must develop to be successful in your current role and to have a successful career.

Questions to Ponder

- *Ask yourself* how real time is your organization or the part of the organization you are responsible for?
- *Ask yourself* when was the last time you experienced agility and when was the last time you experienced a lack of agility?
- *Ask yourself* where agility comes from, or not?

Decisions to Make

- *Decide* that agility is mission critical for your organization and career.
- *Decide* to go on the master's journey to develop this master competency and bring your team with you.

Actions to Take

- *Declare* your intention at your next team meeting, explain why and what the benefits will be.

What Is Organizational Agility?

"Times of growth are beset with difficulties. But these difficulties arise from the profusion of all that is struggling to attain form. Everything is in motion. Therefore, if one perseveres, there is great prospect of success."

–The I Ching

Are you driving things, or are things driving you? Organizational agility comes from us being *In the Driving Seat* of things, not letting things be *In the Driving Seat* of us. If we let them, the volatility, uncertainty, and turbulence of things these days will drive us crazy. It will drive us up the wall. It will drive us around the bend! So much so that, if we aren't careful, life can easily feel like a constant whitewater ride. In that state of things, it controls us, and we don't control it.

But it doesn't have to be that way. We can get back up on terra firma, onto dry land, and claw our way back into the driving seat of things. While it may not feel like it at times, it is a choice that we make, of whitewater or driving seat. It is a choice that we make, in the form of our investment in compounding our interest, or not, in developing our organizational agility.

Until you started reading this book, it may not have been a very conscious choice, but it is a choice, nevertheless. We make that choice through thinking and acting or, more likely, through a lack of thinking and acting. We must choose differently and more consciously, thinking and acting differently, to be *In the Driving Seat* of things and not let things be *In the Driving Seat* of us.

Being in a state of a constant whitewater is one way to travel, but it can be very stressful, painful, and expensive, both financially and nonfinancially. Choosing differently and more consciously to master organizational agility will allow us progressively to feel more composed, confident, and courageous, with less stress, more balance, and better perspective.

Choosing differently and more consciously involves a new mindset and a new chassis, around which to reframe our approach to translating strategy and execution into traction. It's about persevering in driving a profusion of new behaviors of thinking and acting. The quote from I Ching at the head of this chapter puts it well: *"Times of growth are beset with difficulties. But these difficulties arise from the profusion of all that is struggling to attain form. Everything is in motion. Therefore, if one perseveres, there is great prospect of success."*

There is such a profusion of things in motion in business these days that it is very difficult to be *In the Driving Seat* of it all. We have to shape new forms and behaviors of thinking and acting, persevering with everything, struggling to attain form. In my experience, many CEOs, executives, and managers don't persevere with these new behaviors long enough. Therefore, if we are in the minority who do persevere, there is the prospect of great success. As we discussed in Chapter 1, it is a long and arduous journey to mastery of this "master competency"; it is about persevering on that journey to mastery of this master competency!

As a result, organizational agility is at the core of the sorting out anew. It sorts out the minority from the majority, the winners from the losers, the first from the worst, and the best from the rest. Choosing differently and more consciously to be in the minority requires us to have a greater understanding of what agility is, and what it is not. That is what we will further explore in this chapter, extending our integration, alignment and attunement process from a new mindset and a new chassis to a new framework of the higher-order executive strengths of journey orientation, integrated, aligned and attuned with the anatomy of dynamic complexity.

Together, this new mindset, new chassis, and new framework, inform new behaviors of thinking and acting for organizational agility, reframing our approach to translating strategy and execution into traction. Toward the end of the last chapter, we were talking about the theory of evolution by natural selection and how species adapt to their environment by evolving their DNA and their resulting anatomy. This book is about you evolving your organizational agility DNA and your resulting anatomy.

To delve further into the DNA of organizational agility, we must understand the anatomy of dynamic complexity at the four different levels in our equation for the higher-order executive strengths of journey orientation. This creates our new framework:

Higher Order Executive Strengths of Journey-Orientation:	Understanding the Anatomy of Dynamic Complexity:

+ Execution Excellence .... the anatomy of the **Vehicle** fit for the journey challenge.

+ Executive Intelligence, Intuition & Resilience .... the anatomy of the **Journey** and how it unfolds real-time.

+ Path-Finding ....the anatomy of the **Road** and paths of least resistance.

Bottom-line

= Organizational Agility .... the anatomy of **Breakthrough Leadership & Architecting Breakthrough Journeys.**

our ability to deal with rapidly changing circumstances, while out-executing our competition and stakeholder expectations (of customers, employees, suppliers and shareholders)

ordinary people achieving extraordinary things, making possible tomorrow, what seems impossible today

As you will see in the above framework, we have included some definitions:

Organizational Agility:
our ability to deal with rapidly changing circumstances,
while out-executing our competition and stakeholder expectations
(of customers, employees, suppliers, and shareholders).

Breakthrough Leadership
(and Architecting Breakthrough Journeys):
ordinary people achieving extraordinary things,
making possible tomorrow what seems impossible today.

These two definitions are highly interrelated. To understand and leverage the journey-oriented, higher-order executive strengths of organizational agility, we must understand the anatomy of dynamic complexity involved in breakthrough leadership and architecting breakthrough journeys. As we progress, we will compound our understanding of these definitions and our new framework. It will evolve into the clear strategic framework, system, and tools we need to be *In the Driving Seat* of things.

However, to begin to understand the DNA and anatomy of what organizational agility is, let's first understand what it isn't! Let's start by considering the opposite of agility—*fragility*.

Fragility

Often, when I ask, "What's the opposite of agility?" the answer I get back is "rigidity" or something like that. That's a great start in understanding what agility isn't. You see, to hold "agility" and "rigidity" in mind as opposites is a mental trap which many executives fall into. Let me explain:

- Rigidity means very structured, tightly organized, ordered, controlled, and hands-on; we might even say bureaucratic. We know that's bad, and we don't want that!

- So, let's toggle back to where we started. As the opposite of rigidity, agility must therefore mean very unstructured and very loosely organized, unordered chaos, uncontrolled and hands-off, we might even say seat-of-the-pants.

- Right? Wrong! That's equally bad and we don't want that either!

Confused? Don't worry. To help us think this through some more, let's look at the spectrum we have laid out so far:

"Rigidity"		"Agility"
Structured		Unstructured
Tight		Loose
Order		Chaos
Controlled		Uncontrolled
Hands-On		Hands-Off
Bureaucratic	"or"	*Seat-of-the-Pants*

Unconsciously, we have lapsed into "or" thinking, and we are flip flopping backwards and forwards. We are defaulting into holding in mind structured and unstructured, tight and loose, order and chaos, controlled and uncontrolled, and hands-on and hands off as mutually exclusive opposites, from which must choose one or the other proposition.

In my experience, many entrepreneurs are often unconsciously stuck defining agility incorrectly. Fearing the rigidity of bureaucracy, they unconsciously default into a seat-of-the-pants, unstructured, and loose approach, incorrectly believing this to be agility. It isn't! This so easily decays into a constant state of chaos, leaving the organization fragile, not agile.

That's fragility, not agility! That fragility often causes expensive consequences with our stakeholder groups, which are mentioned in our definition of organizational agility, as follows:

- **Customers**: losing our best, most discerning, and most profitable customers, who experience our customer service as chaotic;

- **Employees**: losing our most talented employees, who experience our work environment as chaotic;

- **Suppliers**: losing our most supportive suppliers, who experience our supply chain relationship as chaotic;

- **Shareholders**: losing the trust and belief of our shareholders, and debt holders, who experience our strategy and execution as chaotic.

This can easily put our business into a descent, along the lines of our Eastern Airlines story. Imperceptible at first, followed by a perceptible descent, often followed by a nosedive, followed by a tailspin, followed by a smoking hole in the ground! Think about the Eastern Airlines scenarios we have seen in business lately, which we discussed in Chapter 1.

Agility is not an "or" proposition. It is an "and" proposition, of both ends of the spectrum, which are not mutually exclusive opposites. Creative approaches can give us the best of both worlds. When we hold this in mind, our spectrum of thinking evolves to looking like this:

Fragility	**Agility**	*Fragility*
Structured		Unstructured
Tight		Loose
Order	..."Cha-ordic"..	Chaos
Controlled		Uncontrolled
Hands-On		Hands-Off
Bureaucratic	"and"	*Seat-of-the-Pants*

Agility is an "and" proposition of structured *and* unstructured, tight *and* loose, order *and* chaos, controlled *and* uncontrolled, and hands-on *and* hands-off, all at the same time. Indeed, as we saw in the quotation at the head of Chapter 2, Dee Hock coined the term "cha-ordic" as the "and" proposition of chaos *and* order, asserting that we live in the "cha-ordic age." I couldn't agree more.

Being too much of one end of the spectrum and not enough of the other results in fragility, which is the opposite of agility, either way around:

• Being too unstructured, loose, chaotic, uncontrolled, and hands-off leaves our organization fragile, not agile.
• Being too structured, tight, ordered, controlled, and hands-on leaves our organization fragile, not agile.
• These two different kinds of fragility can be equally damaging. We will equally lose our best customers, most talented employees, most supportive suppliers, and the trust and belief of our shareholders and debt holders, whether we are too chaotic and seat-of-the-pants or too rigid and bureaucratic. Neither works these days.

The "and" proposition of this spectrum is a crucial part of our mindset for organizational agility. Organizational agility comes from mastering the challenge of the "and," as a paradoxical blend of all these elements and more.

Mastering the Challenge of the "and"

In his 2007 book, *The Opposable Mind: How Successful Leaders Win Through Integrative Thinking*, Roger Martin puts it well: "The leaders I have studied share at least one trait, aside from their talent for innovation and long-term business success. They have the predisposition and the capacity to hold two diametrically opposing ideas in their heads. And then, without panicking or simply settling for one alternative or the other, they're able to produce a synthesis that is superior to either opposing idea. Integrative thinking is my term for this processor—more precisely, this discipline of consideration and synthesis—that is the hallmark of exceptional businesses and the people who run them."

That is the hallmark of exceptional businesses and the people who run them! Roger Martin explores this further:

"The skill with which these thinkers held two opposing ideas in fruitful tension reminded me of the way other highly skilled people use their hands. Human beings, it's well known, are distinguished from nearly every other creature by a physical feature known as the opposable thumb. Thanks to the tension we can create by opposing the thumb and fingers, we can do marvelous things that no other creature can do—write, thread a needle, carve a diamond, paint a picture, guide a catheter up through an artery to unblock it. All those actions would be impossible without the crucial tension between the thumb and fingers.

Evolution provided human beings with a valuable potential advantage. But that potential would have gone to waste if our species had not exploited it by using it in ever more sophisticated ways. When we set out to learn to write or to sew, paint, or golf, we practice using our opposable thumbs, training both the key muscles involved and the brain that controls them. Without exploring the possibilities of opposition, we wouldn't have developed either its physical properties or the cognition that accompanies and animates it.

Similarly, we were born with an opposable mind we can use to hold two conflicting ideas in constructive tension. We can use that tension to think our way through to a new and superior idea. Were we able to hold only one thought or idea in our heads at a time, we wouldn't have access to the insights that the opposable mind can produce. And just as we can develop and refine the skill with which we employ our opposable thumbs to perform tasks that once seemed impossible, I'm convinced we can also, with patient practice, develop the ability to use our opposable minds to unlock solutions to problems that seem to resist every effort to solve them."

–Roger Martin, 2009, *The Opposable Mind: How Successful Leaders Win Through Integrative Thinking*

To read more, visit www.mydrivingseat.com/booklinks booklink #9

We must develop our ability to use our opposable minds to unlock solutions to problems that seem to resist every effort to solve them! The problem of organizational agility certainly falls into that category for many CEOs, executives, and managers, resisting their every effort to solve it. Tapping into the integrative thinking of our opposable minds, we are exploring the paradoxical blend of all the elements of agility, which we have begun considering in our spectrum, and many more. We are integrating them into a unique framework, unlocking the solution to the seemingly unsolvable problem of organizational agility. That's what mastering the challenge of the "and" is all about. As an example, let's consider the integrative thinking and design of a modern jet fighter plane:

The Integrative Thinking and Design of a Modern Jet Fighter Plane

The airframe of a modern jet fighter plane (such as the F-22 or the F-35) is not designed with gliding in mind. Unlike other aircraft for which the airframe is structured for gliding, a modern jet fighter is designed to be implicitly unstable and in a state of disequilibrium. If you turn everything off, it crashes. Plain and simple.

What keeps it in the air under normal circumstances? The fly-by-wire computers, keeping it stable by making micro-adjustments many times a second to cope with the disequilibrium.

This integrative thinking of being very unstable (an airframe not structured for gliding) and stable (the fly by wire computers) all at the same time is what gives modern jet fighters their immense agility. When we want to turn hard right, we can do so, very easily and very rapidly, tapping into the aircraft's implicit instability and disequilibrium. There is less inertia to overcome than in an aircraft which is designed to glide and which, therefore, has more implicit stability.

A modern jet fighter is designed as a cha-ordic "and" proposition, being a paradoxical blend of stable and unstable, all at the same time. Being more unstable (fly-by-wire computers which aren't up to the job) or more stable (more gliding inertia to overcome) would result in fragility, either way around! Agility comes from a balanced, optimized blend, right down the middle.

To read more, visit www.mydrivingseat.com/booklinks booklink #10

Drawing upon this example of a modern jet fighter plane, our agility spectrum has evolved to look like this:

Fragility	**Agility**	*Fragility*
Stable/Equilibrium		**Unstable/Disequilibrium**
Structured		Unstructured
Tight		Loose
Order ...."Cha-ordic"........................ Chaos		
Controlled		Uncontrolled
Hands-On		Hands-Off
Bureaucratic	*"and"*	*Seat-of-the-Pants*

Agility is an "and" proposition of this spectrum, right down the middle. Being too far at one end or the other, either way around, results in fragility, not agility!

I was once working with a husband and wife, who were CEO and chairman, respectively, of a $50 million manufacturing company. The husband was the entrepreneur, but it was the wife who asked me to work with them. They had been investing in many of the parts of execution excellence and organizational agility (leadership development, team building and culture, etc.) but weren't getting the payback in terms of the traction they were hoping for from the whole. There was a frustrating element of wheel$pin and they weren't sure why.

I was doing an initial orientation briefing with some of the core concepts, models, and tools, meeting the husband for the first time. I was just getting to the infrastructural part of systems, processes, and structures (which we will review in later chapters) when the husband abruptly stopped me in my tracks saying, "You clearly don't understand!" He carried on by saying, "We don't need more structure in this business. If that's where you are going with this, we can stop right now. We just need people to be more accountable around here."

Bingo! That's the classic entrepreneur's mindset. We had arrived at a moment of truth, a gate to get through, and everything hinged upon it. He had pretty much told me everything I needed to know:

• His knee-jerk reaction to structure is a telltale sign that we are probably dealing with someone with an "or" mentality of agility. People with an "or" mentality of agility are stuck at the loose, seat of the pants end of the spectrum, because of an acute aversion to the tight, bureaucratic end of the spectrum. They don't have an "and" concept of agility that gives us the best of both worlds.

• The use of the word "just" is very often another tell-tale sign that we are probably dealing more in stupid simplicity (remember our discussion in Chapter 1) rather than elegant simplicity, ignoring complexity rather than embedding complexity.

• His focus on just needing "people to be more accountable around here" is a clue that he is more focused on the "what" of things than facilitating the "how" of things.

On that last point, I knew he happened to be an ex-stockbroker. So I said that pinning his hopes on "we just need people to be more accountable around here" was similar to a stockbroker pinning his hopes on "we just need to buy lower and sell higher!" Yes, you and every other stockbroker on the planet! There is just the small matter of the "how?"

I asked if he would agree that for any stockbroker to outperform others on a sustained basis (beyond just dumb luck), that person would have to be using better technology, better systems, and better processes, together with other infrastructural components, and that a seat of the pants approach just wouldn't cut it. After a few tries, he somewhat reluctantly started to agree and let me carry on with the briefing.

Six months later, in an offsite team session of 18 of his executives and managers, he made a point of standing up and declaring publicly, "I have had an epiphany!" He continued, saying, "We need more structure in this business." He had shifted from unconsciously having an "or" concept of agility to understanding and consciously having an "and" concept of agility. In continuing the process, we worked to help them master the challenge of the "and," developing their execution excellence, organizational agility, and translating more strategy and more execution into more traction.

On another occasion, I had been working for some time with the president of a $100 million wholesale distribution business, and she was progressing very well up the learning curve of execution excellence and organizational agility. The trouble was that the business had been in a seat of the pants survival mode for a long time, due to the economic crisis, consumed with fighting fires and struggling to find a path to turn things around and get back to thriving. In an attempt to drive top line growth, the company initiated a host of sales and marketing initiatives with very mixed results. It was a frustrating and exhausting time, which was taking its toll on the president and her owner/CEO.

The president sensed the potential to adopt more agile methods and, despite time and money being in very short supply, she managed to get her owner/CEO's agreement to schedule a four hour block of quality time for an orientation briefing. As I started to talk about the concept of agility, the CEO immediately interjected, saying, "Oh, I do that very well," and proceeded to tell me how agile his average day, week, and month was. That's a common and understandable misconception of agility that I often encounter. Managers, executives, and CEOs often tell me how they are always zipping around here and there, zigging and zagging from one thing to the next, touching a lot of different things all day, week, and month.

I went to the flipchart and said, "Okay, great, if we start from that definition of agility, then what's the opposite of agility?" And so on; you know the how the rest of that goes! Once I had laid out the spectrum, which we have been reviewing earlier in this chapter, and elaborated on it with the fighter jet analogy, the light bulb came on for him. Given my use of an aviation analogy, he even added the term "seagull management" to the loose, chaotic end of the spectrum. You know the one: swoop in, poop all over everyone, and then fly away into the distance again! When I elaborated further, by overlaying the three-dimensional challenge of the "and" proposition of detail complexity and dynamic complexity (which we reviewed in Chapter 1), he started to get excited and relieved.

You see, a few years previously, the company had undertaken a major strategic planning and implementation process, along conventional and traditional lines. It had ended up with initiatives and spreadsheets up to everyone's eyebrows, all of which had become rapidly and progressively irrelevant and redundant, as the landscape had shifted. The process had attracted more and more derogatory remarks around the business, not least of all from him. He was very jaded about the whole process as being overly planned and, as a reaction to the fear of that happening again, was lapsing into a mode of being underplanned. Flip-flopping! Which brings us to the spectrum looking like this:

Fragility	**Agility**	Fragility
Stable/Equilibrium		**Unstable/Disequilibrium**
Structured		Unstructured
Tight		Loose
Order ...."Cha-ordic"........................ Chaos		
Controlled		Uncontrolled
Hands-On		Hands-Off
Overly planned		Under planned
Bureaucratic	*"and"*	*Seat-of-the-Pants*

When the CEO realized that I wasn't about to recommend a repeat performance, having a middle of the road, agile approach in mind, not overly planned and not underplanned, he was visibly relieved and started to relax. He had shifted from unconsciously having an "or" concept of agility to understanding and consciously having an "and" concept of agility. In continuing the process, we worked to help the company master the challenge of the "and," developing its execution excellence and organizational agility, and translating more strategy and more execution into more traction. The president had been given license to drive more agile approaches, navigating a middle road in our spectrum, and she used that new driving license very well to establish a new trajectory of profitable growth.

Bringing Things to the Balance Point and Not Beyond

I used to work for an inspiring corporate CEO who was a great leader who, after coming on board about a year after I joined the company, transformed us from being a $500 million loose conglomerate into a $1 billion aligned and attuned corporation. We made it (albeit briefly because of the technology bubble bursting in 2000 and 2001) into the top 100 public companies on the U.K. stock market. As we went in, Rolls Royce fell out! As part of that journey, he promoted me to run the aerospace division and my boss to run the systems group. This was one of the best phases of my career journey, working with these two inspiring leaders.

When I would talk about my strategy, execution and traction plan for the division, including mentioning some process improvements I was rolling out, even the CEO had an automatic response of reminding me that "we don't want bureaucracy!"

So I would ask him, "Do you want me to have a reliable budget?" "Yes, absolutely!" "Do you want me to be predictably hitting my numbers?" "Yes, absolutely!" "Do you want me to have my finger on the pulse enough to be able to assess quickly and accurately upsides and downsides and do frequent forecasts, reflecting the very latest situation?" "Yes, absolutely!" Of course, his answer was "Yes, absolutely" to all of these questions!

So, then I would explain that I had to improve some of our core processes across the division to be able deliver on those promises. Of course, not least of all and most critically, I also had to improve our core business development and innovation processes. Without those I wouldn't be able to deliver the desired trajectory of profit and growth which he wanted my year-to-year budgets and three year business plans to reflect.

I gradually oriented him to the "and" concept of agility, which I was evolving across my division, and that my purpose was to bring our agility to the balance point of the "and," and not beyond.

Not too structured and not too unstructured, not too tight and not too loose, not too much order and not too much chaos, not too controlled and not too uncontrolled, and not too hands-on and not too hands-off.

To the balance point and not beyond! When I am talking with CEOs, executives, or managers who live at the seat of the pants end of the spectrum, the first time I remotely mention anything about structure, they panic. They assume that I am trying to take them to the other end of the spectrum. I educate them: no, just to the balance point and not beyond. When I am talking to CEOs, executives, or managers who live at the bureaucratic end of the spectrum, the first time I remotely mention anything about loosening things up, they panic. They assume that I am trying to take them to the other end of the spectrum. I educate them: no, just to the balance point and not beyond.

For organizational agility, we must bring our business, organization, and team to the balance point and not beyond. We must shift from an unconscious "or" concept of agility to consciously having an "and" concept of agility, just like a modern jet fighter plane. It's about mastering the challenge of the "and" by navigating a middle road.

Navigating a Middle Road

There are many "and" propositions to bring to the balance point and not beyond. We have touched upon a few so far including tight and loose, structured and unstructured, ordered and chaotic, controlled and uncontrolled, hands-on and hands-off. We must master the challenge of the "and" by navigating a middle road of these and many other "and" propositions, including:

Structured		**Unstructured**
Tight		**Loose**
Ordered		**Chaotic**
Controlled		**Uncontrolled**
Hands-on		**Hands-off**
Overly-Planned	*and*	**Underly-Planned**
Operations Management	*and*	**Strategic Leadership**
Profitability	*and*	**Growth**
Short-Term	*and*	**Long-Term**
Convergence	*and*	**Divergence**
Left Brain	*and*	**Right Brain**

What I hear all the time from my clients and from my Vistage members is: "How am I supposed to be strategic and operational, all at the same time?" "How am I supposed to be a leader and a manager, all at the same time?" "How am I supposed to balance profitability and growth, short term and long term, all at the same time?" It's not easy, balancing these and other "and" propositions, all at the same time!

Among other things, we also have to balance the divergence and convergence of our focus, all at the same time. Remembering our Eastern Airlines story from Chapter 1, the convergence of our focus is about fixing bulbs, and the divergence of our focus is about flying the plane. Focus is an "and" proposition of both convergence and divergence, which we will explore further.

Last but not least, many of these "and" propositions are facilitated by having our left brain and our right brain engaged as an "and" proposition, tapping into the power of our opposable mind and integrative thinking. It's a whole brain proposition. In his 2005 book, *A Whole New Mind: Moving from the Information Age to the Conceptual Age*, Daniel Pink puts it well:

> "We are moving from an economy and a society built on the logical, linear, computer-like capabilities of the Information Age to an economy built on the inventive, empathetic, big-picture capabilities of what's rising in its place, the Conceptual Age. Today, the defining skills of the previous era—the "left brain" capabilities that powered the Information Age—are necessary but no longer sufficient. The "right brain" qualities of inventiveness, empathy, joyfulness, and meaning increasing will determine who flourishes and who flounders. For individuals, families, and organizations, professional success and personal fulfillment now require a whole new mind.
>
> Left-brain-style thinking used to be the driver and the right-brain-style thinking the passenger. Now R-Directed thinking is suddenly grabbing the wheel, stepping on the gas, and determining where we're going and how we will get there. L-Directed aptitudes are still necessary. But they're no longer sufficient."
>
> –Daniel Pink, 2005, *A Whole New Mind: Moving from the Information Age to the Conceptual Age*
>
> To read more, visit www.mydrivingseat.com/booklinks booklink #11

Left-brain-style thinking used to be the driver and right-brain-style thinking used to be the passenger! But now the right brain is grabbing the wheel, stepping on the gas, and determining where we are going and how we will get there. The left brain is no longer solely sufficient. We need both, combined as a whole new mind, *In the Driving Seat*. What is each side of the brain good at?

- **The left brain** is linear, logical, and analytical, focused on the parts, detail-complexity, convergence, and is good at fixing bulbs.

- **The right brain** is nonlinear, intuitive, creative, focused on the whole, dynamic-complexity, divergence, and is good at flying the plane.

Being half-brained, one way or the other, isn't going to work well! Not least of all, to avoid Eastern Airlines scenarios in our future, we need our whole brain engaged in fixing bulbs and flying the plane! As Daniel Pink goes on to say, "*After a few generations in the [predominantly left-brained] Information Age, these [right-brained] muscles have atrophied. The challenge is to work them back into shape.*" Being *In the Driving Seat* of organizational agility has become a whole brain, whole person, and whole vehicle challenge, in the three dimensions we have been exploring so far in this book, of mastering detail complexity and dynamic complexity. With wave after wave of dynamic complexity washing over us, our right brain can no longer be a passenger. It must be grabbing the wheel and stepping on the gas, at least equally to our left brain. We need the "and" proposition of our whole brain *In the Driving Seat.*

BONUS

GET   3

http://bit.ly/o7ZGna

Mastering the challenge of all these "and" propositions, and more, can be overwhelming, especially if we are trying consciously to hold them all in mind predominantly in the static plane of thinking of detail complexity, using our static skills. When the going gets tough, we can easily and unconsciously lose the plot, veering off track into the stupid simplicity of "or" thinking rather than the elegant simplicity of "and" thinking. We also need to hold them in mind in the dynamic plane of thinking of dynamic complexity, developing our dynamic skills. Then we have a much better chance of staying with the plot, of navigating a middle road, and mastering the challenge of the "and."

That's the power of expanding our mindset to include the third and longitudinal dimension of the journey orientation, just as we do when we are *In the Driving Seat* of our car. We are able to tap into the power of our opposable mind and integrative thinking, navigating a middle road of all these "and" propositions, and more, with elegant simplicity.

Let's think about it some more. *In the Driving Seat* of our car, we are able to be strategic and operational, leaders and managers, long-term and short-term oriented, all at the same time, hardly giving it a second thought, at the same time as changing the channel on the radio, making a cell phone call (hopefully hands-free), talking to a passenger, and thinking about life, usually arriving at our desired destination, safely, on time and ready for what's next. We do it in a way that just comes naturally, not too structured and not too unstructured, not too tight and not too loose, not too much order and not too much chaos, not too controlled and not too uncontrolled, and not too hands-on and not too hands-off. It's an unfolding flow of divergence and convergence, right brain and left brain, all at the same time. Amazing!

So we know we can do this! We do it every day when we drive our car. What happens then, when we park in the lot outside our office and walk inside? Where do these natural abilities go? How come we struggle so much with these "and" propositions when we are *In the Driving Seat* of our business, compared to being *In the Driving Seat* of our car?

Here's one reason why. *In the Driving Seat* of our car, we cannot help but be oriented to the longitudinal dimension of journey orientation, which is in natural alignment with the corpus callosum of our brain! What's that? The corpus callosum is that white matter structure in the longitudinal fissure between the left and right hemispheres of our brain (actually, the cerebral cortex upper part of our brain, to be more exact). It facilitates communication between the two hemispheres of our brain, and much of the communication in the brain is conducted across it. Naturally aligned with the longitudinal dimension of journey orientation, the corpus callosum facilitates our opposable mind, integrative thinking, and whole brain *In the Driving Seat* of our car. That natural alignment with the longitudinal dimension of journey orientation is part of why being *In the Driving Seat* of our car comes so naturally.

In similar ways, it can also help the challenge of being *In the Driving Seat* of our business come more naturally. Our corpus callosum is the start of a process of integration, alignment, and attunement for organizational agility, from gray matter to gray matter.

From Gray Matter to Gray Matter

From the gray matter of our brain to the gray matter of the asphalt, between the rubber and the road, that's the end to end process of integration, alignment, and attunement we need for the challenge of dynamic complexity these days:

• From our corpus callosum, aligned with the longitudinal dimension of journey orientation and facilitating the communication between our left brain and right brain, tapping into the power of our opposable mind, integrative thinking, and our whole brain;

• Through the integration, alignment, and attunement of a new mindset with the longitudinal dimension of journey orientation, facilitating the elegant simplicity for navigating a middle road of all the "and" propositions we need to hold in mind;

• Through the integration, alignment, and attunement of a new chassis of business acumen, around which we must reassemble the parts and the whole of our business vehicle to be fit for the journey challenge;

• Through the integration, alignment, and attunement with the longitudinal dimension of journey orientation, around which we must reframe our approach to translating strategy and execution into traction;

• Through the integration, alignment, and attunement with a new strategic framework, system, and toolbox, for the higher-order executive strengths of journey orientation we need these days;

• Through the integration, alignment, and attunement of the whole business with journey orientation, educating our executives, managers, and employees, broadly and deeply across our organization;

• Down to traction, between the rubber and the road, on our desired journey, path, and trajectory of profit and growth.

From a new mindset, through a new chassis of business acumen, through a new framework of the higher-order executive strengths of journey orientation, translating strategy and execution into traction between the rubber and the road! Being *In the Driving Seat* of organizational agility requires a process of integration, alignment and attunement with the challenges of dynamic complexity, from gray matter to gray matter. From the gray matter of our brains to the gray matter of the asphalt, in integration, alignment and attunement with the longitudinal dimension of journey orientation. From our corpus callosum to the road we are on, that is what it takes to be dealing in agility these days.

Dealing in Agility

Let's return to our definition of organizational agility from earlier in this chapter:

Organizational Agility:
our ability to deal with rapidly changing circumstances,
while out-executing our competition and stakeholder expectations
(of customers, employees, suppliers, and shareholders). Let's dissect this to
understand it further and review our progress in this book so far:

"Our ability to deal"

This book is about dealing in agility and being ready, willing, and able to do so. It's about our ability to deal in agility, together with our readiness and willingness. It's about having a new mindset, the motivation, and the means. Our new framework of the higher-order executive strengths of journey orientation introduces a concept suite, model set, and toolbox providing the means. For agility not to be an ordeal in your business, it needs to be an "and-deal." As we reviewed earlier in this chapter, dealing in agility is about mastering the challenge of the "and," as a three-dimensional challenge, and having the new chassis of business acumen we need for that. Overall, dealing in agility is about an end-to-end process of integration, alignment and attunement, from gray matter to gray matter, broadly and deeply throughout the organization.

"With rapidly changing circumstances"

As we reviewed in Chapter 2, we live in a new normal of unprecedented volatility, uncertainty, and turbulence, and it's only going to get worse. The speed of business, the pace of change, the diversity and the complexity of things are accelerating all the time. One of the most challenging "and" propositions we must be ready, willing, and able to deal with is that of detail-complexity and dynamic-complexity. With wave after wave of dynamic complexity washing over us, business has become much more like an unfolding dynamic journey on a shifting landscape. To deal with that, we must achieve integration, alignment and attunement with the longitudinal dimension of journey orientation and the challenges of dynamic complexity.

"While out-executing our competition"

A core part of organizational agility is about defogging our understanding of execution excellence. We must be ready, willing, and able to execute better, translating more strategy and more execution into more traction, to stay ahead of our competition. It's all about out-executing the other guys. It's like that well-known story of two guys in the middle of the jungle who get chased by a tiger. One stops to put on his running shoes, to the other's amazement, who says, "why are you stopping, we have to outrun the tiger!" The guy lacing up his shoes says, "Oh, I don't need to outrun the tiger, I just need to out run you!"

"And stakeholder expectations"

It's not just about outrunning and out-executing our competition, but also it's about staying ahead of the expectations of our different categories of stakeholders:

• **Our customers**, so that we get to keep the best and most profitable ones: Are we wowing and delighting them, ahead of their ever increasing expectations and other options, or are we really starting to test their loyalty by being behind the power curve? In particular, during a recession, when competitors are scrambling for business and offering attention grabbing prices.

• **Our employees**, so that we get to keep our best talent: Are we satisfying their insatiable desire for learning and growth, career opportunities, and their belief and hope about the future, or are we allowing a growing crisis of confidence? In particular, as we emerge from a recession, we risk our best talent going down the street to a competitor as soon as they possibly can.

• **Our suppliers**, so that we get preferential service, pricing, and support from the best ones: Are we partnering with them in the right mode, or are we, to some degree, treating them like second class citizens? We all know what that feels like when we are on the receiving end of that from our customers.

• **Our shareholders**, so that our perceived market capitalization and share price stay high (whether we are a publicly quoted company or not, it is still a matter of perception of value, worth, and belief in the future potential) with our equity holders and our debt holders: How many businesses have had their lines of credit pulled or their loans called by the bank recently because of a loss of confidence?

When we stay ahead of our stakeholder expectations, we can place more trust in their loyalty. When we start taking them for granted, we risk them walking down the street in pursuit of better options!

As we reviewed in Chapter 2, organizational agility is often the core differentiator, and sometimes the only differentiator, between the best and the rest. We know it when we see it, and we know it when we don't. In my experience, the biggest difference is that, in one case, a company is addressing the whole problem and the whole solution of organizational agility, and, in the other case, it is only addressing some of the parts of the problem and parts of the solution. As a result, a lot is lost in translation, and organizational agility becomes an ordeal.

As a result, the company suffers the ordeal of lurching from one crisis to another, in a constant state of whitewater while experiencing all kinds of Eastern Airlines scenarios. Or maybe just the ordeal of not translating as much strategy and as much execution into as much traction as their competition, so they are losing market share.

For agility not to be an ordeal in your business, it needs to be an "and-deal" for which we need an end-to-end process of integration, alignment and attunement with the journey-oriented challenge of dynamic complexity, from gray matter to gray matter. The final part of that process is a new framework of the higher-order executive strengths of journey orientation, addressing the anatomy of dynamic complexity at four different levels. As we quoted from C.K. Prahalad in Chapter 2, we need *"a clear strategic framework and system"* for the new normal of unprecedented volatility, uncertainty, and turbulence.

A Clear Strategic Framework and System

Now let's return to our new framework of the higher-order executive strengths of journey orientation. In our process of integration, alignment and attunement, from gray matter to gray matter (from our corpus callosum to the asphalt), the longitudinal dimension of journey orientation is about becoming aligned and attuned with the challenge of dynamic complexity. To do that, we must unbundle and understand the anatomy of dynamic complexity at four different levels, which correspond with our equation of the higher order strengths:

Higher Order Executive Strengths of Journey-Orientation:	Understanding the Anatomy of Dynamic Complexity:

+ Execution Excellence .... the anatomy of the **Vehicle** fit for the journey challenge.

+ Executive Intelligence, Intuition & Resilience .... the anatomy of the **Journey** and how it unfolds real-time.

+ Path-Finding ....the anatomy of the **Road** and paths of least resistance.

Bottom-line

= Organizational Agility .... the anatomy of **Breakthrough Leadership & Architecting Breakthrough Journeys.**

our ability to deal with rapidly changing circumstances, while out-executing our competition and stakeholder expectations (of customers, employees, suppliers and shareholders)	*ordinary people achieving extraordinary things, making possible tomorrow, what seems impossible today*

As we bring our process of integration, alignment and attunement down to the gray matter of the asphalt, we can best understand the anatomy of dynamic complexity first at the three different levels of *the vehicle, the journey,* and *the road.*

• **The vehicle:** We must understand the anatomy of the business vehicle we need to be fit for the journey challenge of dynamic complexity. The higher-order executive strength of journey orientation that addresses this level in the anatomy of dynamic complexity is Execution Excellence. We began discussing this in Chapter 1. You will recall, when asking, "Why Execution Excellence?" we mentioned, "A leader who executes assembles an architecture of execution." In Chapter 5, we will review an integrated model for exactly that, a unifying architecture of execution.

• **The journey:** We must understand the anatomy of a journey, at a microscopic level, not just a macroscopic level, and how it unfolds in real time. The higher-order executive strength of journey orientation that addresses this level in the anatomy of dynamic complexity is Executive Intelligence, Intuition, and Resilience. We began discussing this in Chapter 1. You will recall, when asking, "Why Executive Intelligence, Intuition, and

Resilience?" we mentioned, "What we are talking about is an internalized set of skills, those that finally make explicit the elusive concept of business acumen." In Chapter 4, we will review an integrated model for this strength.

• **The road:** We must understand the anatomy of the road and how we find paths of least resistance. The higher-order executive strength of journey orientation which addresses this level in the anatomy of dynamic complexity is Pathfinding. We began discussing this in Chapter 1. You will recall when asking, "Why Pathfinding?" we mentioned that "new pathways come into view, bringing possibility to life, and extraordinary accomplishment becomes an everyday occurrence." In Chapter 5, we will review an integrated model for this strength.

Together, these three levels in the anatomy of dynamic complexity and the corresponding higher-order executive strength of journey orientation add up to a bottom line of *organizational agility* and the anatomy of *breakthrough leadership and architecting breakthrough journeys*. We already revisited our definition of organizational agility earlier in this chapter, so now let's do the same with our definition of breakthrough leadership and architecting breakthrough journeys:

Breakthrough Leadership
(and Architecting Breakthrough Journeys):
ordinary people achieving extraordinary things,
making possible tomorrow what seems impossible today.

Breakthrough leadership is about ordinary people achieving extraordinary things and architecting breakthrough journeys. It's not about having more than your fair share of extraordinary people. It's about ordinary people, like you and me, coming together with the agility we need to make possible tomorrow what seems impossible today. It's about bringing possibility to life, and extraordinary accomplishment becoming an everyday experience.

That doesn't happen by accident! It happens by design! In my experience, many CEOs, executives, and managers are not ready, willing, or able to invest sufficient design intention into this, staying the course, going the distance, and seeing it through long enough to master it. They become overwhelmed by the anatomy of dynamic complexity involved and the higher-order executive strengths required. Being ready, willing, and able to be a breakthrough leader, who is architecting breakthrough journeys, is complicated. In particular, it is a dynamic complexity challenge, requiring these multiple higher order executive strengths of journey orientation, which we are exploring.

In his 2002 book, *The Heart of Change* (which I believe could equally have been entitled, *Breakthrough Leadership*, as that is my sense of the core of what this book is about), John Kotter puts it well:

> "In a turbulent world, the requirement for change is ongoing. Imagine needing to keep urgency up and complacency, fear and anger down all the time and throughout the organization. Imagine needing to have groups guiding change efforts all the time and throughout the enterprise. Imagine the demand to develop visions and strategies for all the changes, to communicate volumes of information to everyone, to keep batting obstacles out of the way throughout the organization. To succeed in that world, how many people in an enterprise must see change as a part of their jobs? How many of us must understand change well enough to help with the waves of new product lines, mergers, reorganizations, the e-world, process reengineering, or leaps of any kind? How many of us need some minimum capability [of breakthrough leadership]? Reasonable people can argue about what these numbers should be, but the figures surely are very large. Most organizations have less than half of what they need today and many enterprises have only a fraction."
>
> –John Kotter, 2002, *The Heart of Change*

Imagine! You probably don't have to work very hard at imagining, as it is probably very reflective of your reality and the dynamic complexity challenge you face every day. In other words, breakthrough leadership and architecting breakthrough journeys are a dynamic complexity challenge, requiring multiple, higher-order executive strengths. No wonder things so easily decay into being a constant whitewater ride with all kinds of Eastern Airlines scenarios—there are so many bulbs to fix we can easily lose the plot of flying the plane! Most organizations have less than half of the breakthrough leadership they need today, and many enterprises have only a fraction. Organizationally, we aren't ready, willing, and able, with the agility we need.

In December 2001, the *Harvard Business Review* devoted its first special edition in 79 years to the subject of Breakthrough Leadership, calling it the "most perplexing and urgent management challenge." They went on to say:

"The term 'breakthrough leadership', as we define it, is multivalent—it points in several directions at once. Certainly it involves breaking through old habits of thinking to uncover fresh solutions to perennial problems. It also means breaking through the interpersonal barriers that we all erect against genuine human contact. It's leadership that breaks through the cynicism that many people feel about their jobs and helps them find meaning and purpose in what they do. And it breaks through the limits imposed by our own doubts and fears to achieve more than we believed possible. Those who would lead these voyages of inner and outer discovery face extraordinary demands on their time, energy and intellectual capacities. The emotional demands are just as daunting."

–Harvard Business Review, December 2001

Those who would lead these voyages of inner and outer discovery face extraordinary demands on their time, energy, and intellectual capacities. The emotional intelligence demands are just as daunting. In other words, breakthrough leadership places extraordinary demands upon our strengths and intelligences, intellectual, emotional, and otherwise.

It has been a thrill to serve, for the past several years, on the board of Junior Achievement San Diego, which is a not-for-profit dedicated to teaching our youth about financial literacy, workforce readiness, and entrepreneurship. About five years ago, we started a strategy and execution process, using the concepts, models, and tools we are exploring. At the first session with the board, the CEO and her right-hand person came up to me at a break, asking how they would position a fledgling, game-changing idea with the board, in a way that would generate traction, not wheel$pin. They wanted the board to consider making a big leap to build a BizTown in San Diego, when there was only a handful in the whole country at that time.

The McGrath Family JA BizTown in San Diego is a 10,000 square foot mini-city in which kids discover how free enterprise really works. There are 19 life-size businesses, a non-profit organization and a city hall. Every day, 150 new students become business owners, make financial decisions, explore philanthropy, and pay taxes. Teachers spend four weeks teaching the curriculum. Students learn principles like economics, good citizenship, and money management. Each business offers the students the opportunity to work as CEO, CFO, or in a specific business job. Students apply for the job that interests them. Once they are assigned to a job, students spend time with the other employees in their business to develop their business operating budget,

apply for a bank loan, create advertising, and develop their marketing strategies. After
the curriculum has been taught, the students come to the McGrath Family JA BizTown
to become "grown-ups" for one day to put into practice all of the principles they have
been learning in the classroom.

> "The students are in charge and they work in a life-sized interactive city that
> is designed to reflect San Diego in the businesses, landscape, and architecture.
> In front of City Hall, the mayor gives a speech reminding the citizens of the
> laws of the village and encouraging everyone to exercise their civic duty by
> voting. Students check the business break schedule to know when they are
> allowed to leave work, visit the bank, and become a consumer in the city.
> The students leave the village personally successful after spending the day
> working hard at their jobs. They also leave with a greater understanding of the
> value of a dollar, the importance of team work, and how to be a contributing
> citizen in the community. The time spent at the village is only one day, but the
> impact that this experiential learning has will last a life time!"
>
> –Source: Junior Achievement San Diego

It's all part of JA's mission to teach kindergarten through 12th grade kids
about the free enterprise system, to inspire and prepare young people to succeed
in a global economy, and, in particular, to enrich the experiential learning for fifth
graders. I wish I could have benefited from those kinds of learning experiences
at that age. My translation: Junior Achievement gives an early introduction to the
dynamic complexity and detail complexity of business, which readily translates
from "junior" achievement to "senior" achievement. It's a shame that some of our
"senior" managers and "senior" executives typically don't get much of these kinds of
immersion learning experiences.

But the CEO was concerned that this would be a big endeavor, which would test
the agility of the organization like never before. It involved a large capital commitment
and fundraising campaign, together with a quantum shift of dynamic complexity and
detail complexity, not only building the facility but then operating it. In particular, the
CEO was concerned about navigating the middle road of the "and" proposition we
have been exploring, given the not-for-profit nature of the organization. With such a
reliance on volunteers at the board level and with only a relatively small staff, there is
a small margin for error between agility and fragility.

I said we should weave it into our process and let things unfold from there, which we did. About three years later we were doing another of our annual strategic review sessions inside our brand new McGrath Family JA BizTown, which was fully operational and open for business as a new flagship for JA San Diego. What a thrill, to be facilitating a session in our ongoing process that was a result of the process. We are on a roll, so much so that we are already looking at taking things to the next level with another program for 8th and 9th grade students called Finance Park. The leadership team is "getting an A" with the strengths and intelligences required.

Strengths and Intelligences

The complexities of organizational agility call up new aspects of our intelligence, underlying the higher-order executive strengths of journey orientation we need. In recent times, Daniel Goleman has been one of the leading authors helping us unbundle and understand a contemporary view of the different intelligences which we need as executives these days:

EQ: Emotional Quotient

Daniel Goleman's earliest work was on emotional intelligence and competence, defining EQ as "the ability to accurately identify and understand one's own emotional reactions and those of others. It also includes the ability to regulate one's emotions and use them to make good decisions and act effectively." Essentially, EQ is a non-cognitive intelligence, whereas IQ (Intelligence Quotient) is a cognitive intelligence.

Business Intelligence (Let's call it BQ)

This is a lesser-known intelligence, which Daniel Goleman touched upon in the 2002 book, *Business: The Ultimate Resource*, saying, "Could there be a business intelligence—a set of abilities that distinguish those truly outstanding in the world of commerce? Could business intelligence be the mark of outstanding individual performers, as well as the building block of the best performing companies?" He goes on to ask:

> "What special talents allow some people to build a flourishing business from nothing, while others—though given every advantage of background, and preparation at the best business schools—run a business into the ground? What abilities allow one person to take a mediocre company and transform it into an industry leader, while others turn great companies into mediocre ones?

The sum of what everybody in a company knows and knows how to do—its aggregate business intelligence—gives a company much of its competitive edge—if it can mobilize that expertise well. Today's business reality poses a paradox: the challenge of reconciling information overload with lightning-fast decision making.

Business intelligence, literacy or wisdom are themselves useless unless we can translate them into action. It is only in the day to day demonstration of wise efforts that business intelligence proves its worth."

–Daniel Goleman, 2002, *Business: The Ultimate Resource*

In our process of integration, alignment and attunement, from gray matter to gray matter, that's what our new chassis of business acumen is about. It's about knowing how to combine and translate our business intelligence, literacy, and wisdom into the actions of day to day, wise efforts. In other words, traction!

Others have also written about other intelligences:

Adversity Quotient (Let's call it AQ)

In his 1999 book, *Adversity Quotient: Turning Obstacles into Opportunities*, Paul Stoltz relates to this as "the science of human resilience. People who successfully apply AQ perform optimally in the face of adversity—the challenges that confront us each day. A high-AQ workforce translates to increased capacity, productivity, and innovation, as well as lower attrition and higher retention."

IQ: Intelligence Quotient

As we touched upon in Chapter 1, Justin Menkes brought IQ back into the foreground in his 2005 book, *Executive Intelligence: What All Great Leaders Have*, saying, "the granular stuff of business is critical thinking—the skilled, active interpretation and evaluation of observations, communications, information, and argumentation as a guide to thought and action." He goes on:

"In other words, critical-thinking ability determines how skillfully someone gathers, processes, and applies information in order to identify the best way to reach a particular goal or navigate a complex situation.

In 2004, two of the most respected researchers in assessment methodologies, Professors Frank Schmidt of the University of Iowa and John Hunter of Michigan State University published a comprehensive study comparing the predictive power of IQ tests to that of other assessment methodologies. Combining the results of 515 independent studies involving over 100,000 employees, they declared that cognitive ability (IQ) tests predict occupational performance better than any other ability, trait, or disposition, and better than job experience.

Though IQ tests are powerfully predictive, these instruments have too many shortcomings to be used with a modern managerial population. Instead of correcting the problems with intelligence testing we have gone completely in the other direction. The key to solving this problem is to bring the concept of intelligence back into the business arena in acceptable form."

–Justin Menkes, 2005, *Executive Intelligence:*
What All Great Leaders Have

Mapping these intelligences into our new framework of strengths and understandings, the equation becomes:

Higher Order Executive Strengths of Journey-Orientation:

Understanding the Anatomy of Dynamic Complexity:

+ Execution Excellence .... **XQ** .... the anatomy of the **Vehicle** fit for the journey challenge.

+ Executive Intelligence, Intuition & Resilience .... **EQ (IQ)** .... the anatomy of the **Journey** and how it unfolds real-time.

+ Path-Finding .... **PQ** .... the anatomy of the **Road** and paths of least resistance.

Bottom-line   XQ + EQ (IQ) + PQ = BQ (AQ)

= Organizational Agility .... **BQ (AQ)** .... the anatomy of **Breakthrough Leadership & Architecting Breakthrough Journeys.**

our ability to deal with rapidly changing circumstances, while out-executing our competition and stakeholder expectations (of customers, employees, suppliers and shareholders)

ordinary people achieving extraordinary things, making possible tomorrow, what seems impossible today

These intelligences are the foundations for the higher-order executive strengths of journey orientation. Further to those we have discussed, XQ and PQ are two additional intelligences, at the heart of our work in this book.

XQ is that eXecution "X-factor," which some people have and some people don't, when it comes to execution excellence. They just seem to get it, knowing how to get the parts to come together as a whole, whereas others don't have the foggiest idea, even though they might think they do. That's what we typically mean by an "x-factor": We know it when we see it, and we know it when we don't, but we are not really sure what "it" is. We will demystify what "it" is in Chapter 5, as we review our model for the journey-oriented, higher-order executive strength of Execution Excellence. It separates the haves from the have-nots, those who can from those who can't, those who are engaged in the traction of business from those who are engaged in the wheel$pin of busyness. We will help you develop your underlying intelligence of XQ.

PQ is an intelligence and competence relating to pathfinding and the mental agility required for that. As we mentioned in Chapter 2, Justin Menkes calls it "an uncanny sense of direction… a highly developed intuition for the analytic path that will get them to their destination." These days, it's not about road mapping, as dynamic complexity is such that, as soon as the ink is dry on a road map, the landscape has shifted and it is out of date! Instead, it's a constant process of pathfinding—finding a path through, no matter how the landscape shifts. As we will discuss further, this requires the simultaneous divergence and convergence of our focus, which tests our mental agility, opposable mind, integrative thinking, and whole brain approach, to avoid being overwhelmed and to prevail. We will demystify this in Chapters 4 and 5. It separates the haves from the have-nots, those who can from those who can't, those who are engaged in the traction of business from those who are engaged in the wheel$pin of busyness. We will help you develop your underlying intelligence of PQ.

So our bottom line equation of intelligences becomes:

$$\mathbf{XQ} + \mathbf{EQ}\ (IQ) + \mathbf{PQ} = \mathbf{BQ}\ (AQ)$$

EQ (IQ) are the emotional (noncognitive) and intellectual (cognitive) intelligences and competences. My experience is that the EQ challenge is uppermost and foremost and that it is underpinned by our IQ. BQ (AQ) is the business intelligence and adversity quotient components. My experience is that the BQ challenge is uppermost and foremost and that it is underpinned by our AQ.

My equation of these intelligences and my associated executive strengths and agility were most tested during the three-year period from 1999 to 2001, when I experienced what Warren Bennis and Robert Thomas later called a "crucible of leadership" (*Harvard Business Review*, September 2002, "Crucibles of Leadership").

"Crucible:
A Severe Test of Patience or Belief; A Trial
A place, time, or situation characterized by the confluence of powerful intellectual, social, economic, or political forces.

For the (40) leaders we interviewed, the crucible experience was a trial and a test, a point of deep self-reflection that forced them to question who they were and what mattered to them. It required them to examine their values, question their assumptions, hone their judgment. And, invariably, they emerged from the crucible stronger and more sure of themselves and their purpose changed in some fundamental way.

A crucible is, by definition, a transformative experience, through which an individual comes to a new or an altered sense of identity."

–Warren Bennis and Robert Thomas, September 2002,
"Crucibles of Leadership," *Harvard Business Review*

I had been running my aerospace division for two years and had created good traction in uplifting and expanding the business model, integrating and globalizing the business units, and orienting everything to a new growth path and vision, which the corporation was behind. We had acquired three companies in North America, two in the United States and one in Canada, bringing new software solutions, and some hardware, to our portfolio. We were building a new, paradigm shifting, integrated systems and solutions set called AIS (Aviation Information Solutions), which was gaining a great deal of interest.

AIS allowed commercial airlines to move large amounts of data on and off aircraft at the gate environment, between ground based enterprise software systems and aircraft based applications for the cabin and cockpit crew, increasingly on electronic devices as a replacement for paper. Ultimately, for instance, replacing the pilots' flight bag/manuals with electronic equivalents.

Things were going pretty well, and then the wheels started coming off!

I had to part ways with the president of my Wichita, Kansas, facility, after recruiting him only a year earlier. He just hadn't worked out, I had lost my ability to trust him to do what he said he was going to do, and I didn't sense that he had the leadership capabilities and capacities we needed. As a result, the business was beginning to spiral downward. I didn't have a strong enough internal candidate and, rather than take a risk on another person, I decided to move there myself from the U.K. and wear a second hat of running that business for a while, to get things turned around and back on an upward spiral.

In parallel, a business we had acquired in San Diego, about a year earlier, had started to get into real trouble. Major military contracts, which had attracted us to the business, had been canceled, and where we were subcontracted with our specialist software through major prime contractors, they were being cancelled, through no fault of ours. The business was beginning to hemorrhage. At that point in the parent company's history, it was the largest acquisition we had ever made, so they were breathing down my neck as this was share price sensitive. We had recruited a president into the business the previous year, to transition from the prior owner/managers, and he was struggling. Things were going from bad to worse. So, after relocating my family to Wichita, Kansas, and starting to run that business, I also started spending a lot of time in San Diego, to help brew up a breakthrough plan.

After about six months of that, I sensed the new president didn't have the leadership capabilities and capacities we needed and also had to part ways with him. Fortunately, in parallel with all of this, I had acquired a business in Minneapolis with a great president, who I sensed did have the leadership capabilities and capacities we needed. He offered to relocate to Wichita, to take over running that business and run Minneapolis as a satellite. That made great sense, and I took him up on it. I set about relocating to San Diego to do the same there as I had done in Wichita. Because the housing market had softened in Wichita, it took us about a year to sell the house, and during that time, I commuted to San Diego.

In parallel, one of my presidents in the U.K. left. She hadn't really ever been totally aligned with integrating, globalizing, and innovating the division, and so it was always just a matter of time. Except, it probably couldn't have come at a worse time. Fortunately, I had another great president in the U.K., with the leadership capabilities and capacities needed, and he wore a second hat of running that business too.

So we got our bases covered, with organizational agility, kind of! In the middle of all of this, we were dealing with Y2K (remember that?), which was stressing and straining our agility even more, and we managed to get through it. Meanwhile, the corporation had made huge investments in telecommunications acquisitions from 1998 to early 2000 (massively eclipsing San Diego as the previous largest), repositioning itself in that space for a higher price/earnings ratio. Sure enough, our share price peaked at about £7, compared to £1 when I had joined in 1994 (on a like for like basis after stock splits, etc.).

You remember well what happened next, in March 2000. On March 10, the NASDAQ Composite Index peaked at 5,048.62, more than double its value just one year before. On March 13, due to a large premarket selloff, it opened down 4%. By March 15, it was down 10%. What followed was a long slide, as the whole dot com, IT, and telecoms bubble burst (with the NASDAQ finally bottoming out on October 9, 2002, at 1114.11). From its peak of about £7, our share price ultimately plummeted to about 7 pence!

While all of this was unfolding in 2000, I was finally able to sell my house in Wichita and relocate my family to San Diego during the summer. I set about shifting up into a next gear in turning the business around. I was having to make presentations to the corporate board several times a year and was under a great deal of pressure, not least of all because they were under a great deal of pressure with the slippery slope our share price was on. I knew the currency I was dealing in was their belief in my belief that I could prevail, that we had the organizational agility to prevail. We were being very agile and had enough good stuff going on to sustain their belief: We were bidding major projects at major airlines globally and were attracting great interest from much larger systems integrators like Rockwell Collins, Honeywell, and Teledyne. Even GE and Boeing decided to get into the AIS space and were in active discussions with us. We actually ended up formalizing a teaming agreement with Boeing for one of the airlines we were bidding to. Then the airlines started to struggle in the prevailing economic environment. Some of the potential large projects we were bidding on got deferred and/or canceled.

We began to lose traction, the corporation's share price was in the doldrums, and there was no appetite to continue to invest in us. But we had created something of great value, as perceived by the much bigger players we were in teaming discussions with. So we shifted gears into selling the division, actually bolting on some other parts from associated businesses in the corporation. It was early/mid 2001. We worked with Morgan Stanley, put the prospectus together, and did a first round of presentations in New York. Most of the big players were at the table showing keen interest.

Then 9/11 happened. Nobody wanted to buy aerospace after 9/11. We managed to salvage some interest as we approached the end of year holiday season, but most of that fell away at the start of January. We actually ended up selling a part of the division to Curtiss Wright (what a coincidence, to sell to the company that started it all and grew out of the Wright Brothers' endeavors and first manned flight) and then later to Teledyne. The rest ended up as a private equity backed management buyout after I had left.

I had managed to secure a green card in July before 9/11, thank goodness, as the Immigration and Naturalization Service (INS) pretty much closed up shop immediately after 9/11, and I was three years into my four-year work permit. I now had options and, through an unpredictable sequence of events, had ended up living in one of our top three places on the planet (I had been to a conference in San Diego in the early 1990s; my brother was in Sydney, Australia, where I had been a couple of times on business; and my wife and I had spent four months in Vancouver, Canada, before we were married, on exchange for a semester from my MBA at London Business School). So we decided I would take the leap from the corporate world and do my own thing, so that we could stick around and be masters of our own destiny (and where we chose to live). And so the next chapter of my journey commenced.

That three year period from 1999 to 2001 certainly was a leadership crucible experience for me. Warren Bennis and Robert Thomas defined a crucible as "a severe test of patience or belief; a trial. A place, time, or situation characterized by the confluence of powerful intellectual, social, economic, or political forces."

Looking back now, I realize how transformative those three years were, as a culminating phase of the evolutionary path of my learning journey to that point. It was a trial and a test that caused me to reflect upon the leadership capabilities and capacities that I had, some of my team had, and some didn't. It caused me to reflect on my sense of void for the help and support that CEOs, executives, and managers need to go on those kinds of journeys, and my passion for filling that void. It caused me to question my sense of identity, my core values, and what I stood for. As a result of those experiences, I became surer of myself, in some fundamentally changed way, and my agility to cope, no matter what. I was more conscious of my strengths and intelligences to do so, as the equation of my **XQ**, **EQ** (IQ), **PQ** and **BQ** (AQ), which we have been reviewing in this chapter:

$$\mathbf{XQ} + \mathbf{EQ}\ (IQ) + \mathbf{PQ} = \mathbf{BQ}\ (AQ)$$

These intelligences are at the heart of our new framework of the journey-oriented strengths and understandings of the anatomy of dynamic complexity. We can develop these intelligences, strengths, and understandings *In the Driving Seat* of our businesses, just like we can in the driving seat of our cars. It's not going to happen by accident, and it's not going to happen the first time we go out for a spin. It is like learning to drive again and mastering driving at an advanced level. If we are willing to go on that mastery journey *In the Driving Seat* of our business, or our role in our business, we will have the organizational agility we need when we need it.

Chapter 3 Summary

What is organizational agility, and what is it not? My experience is that there can be a great deal of confusion about that, and many CEOs, executives, and managers are prone to holding it as an "or" proposition not an "and" proposition. As a result, we are not mastering the challenge of "and," bringing things to the balance point, and navigating a middle road. Our organizational agility is suffering as a result and is an ordeal in our business, not an "and deal." To change that, we must develop our strengths, understandings, and intelligences, as a process of integration, alignment and attunement, from gray matter to gray matter.

Things to Think About

◆ *Think about* the balance you are striking in your business on the "bureaucratic" versus "seat-of-the-pants" spectrum.

◆ *Think about* how well you are finding the middle and the agility or fragility you are experiencing as a result.

◆ *Think about* the strengths, understandings, and intelligences you need to develop, enterprise wide and enterprise deep.

Questions to Ponder

◉ *Ask yourself* where you are on the agility/fragility spectrum in bringing things to the balance point and how you will navigate a middle road of "and" propositions.

◉ *Ask yourself* how to promote the integrative thinking, opposable mind, and whole-brained approach necessary.

Decisions to Make

◗ *Decide* that you can no longer tolerate an "or" mentality from your team.

◗ *Decide* that you will progressively achieve integration, alignment and attunement, from gray matter to gray matter, enterprise wide and enterprise deep.

Actions to Take

◀ *Point out* "or" thinking when you hear it or see it and facilitate/coach "and" thinking instead.

When Do We Need Organizational Agility, And When Do We Have It?

When you need a friend, it's too late to make one!
Be making friends with organizational agility
before it's too late!

Twenty-twenty Hindsight is a Wonderful Thing!

When things have melted down and we are swept up in the whitewater ride of a crisis, it's easy to have hindsight of what we might have done to avoid it. Or, at least, be in better shape to deal with it. Just ask BP! Just ask Toyota! Twenty-twenty hindsight is a wonderful thing. How many times do we hear people saying something like, "Oh, we didn't think of that," or "Oh, we didn't see that coming," or "Boy, oh boy, I wish we had spent more time thinking about that!"

In business and in life, we will always learn from hindsight. But it can be incredibly painful and expensive, both financially and non financially, in terms of stress and frustration. So, in addition to learning from hindsight, I would rather we learn as much as possible from insight and from foresight, as it is typically much less painful and expensive!

Hindsight: what has just happened and how did things unfold in the past, *to arrive at this point*?

Insight: what is happening *right now* in the present?

Foresight: what is likely to happen next and how might things unfold *from* here in the future?

Think about the 20/20 hindsight we gained from our Eastern Airlines story and from Toyota and BP, among many other similar scenarios, and how painful and expensive that was. For organizational agility, we must be aligned and attuned with the longitudinal dimension of journey orientation, as a continuum of the past, the present, and the future. To avoid the additional pain and expense of learning from hindsight, we must learn as much as we can from insight in the present and foresight about the future. When we experience hindsight, it is telling us that there are some things which we might have learned, less painfully and less expensively, from insight and from foresight! When hindsight shows up, it's already too late!

As the saying goes, "When you need a friend, it's too late to make one!" I want you to make friends with organizational agility before it's too late. When do we need to make friends with organizational agility?

- When we are heading into a recession;
- When we are finding bottom in a recession;

- When we are emerging from a recession;

- When we are in a growth mode;

- When we are undergoing key transitions or transformations, such as large-scale change programs (software deployments, restructurings, changing incentive programs, etc.), mergers, acquisitions and alliances, diversifications and expansions;

- When problems or opportunities show up out of the blue;

- When Murphy's Law shows up, and "what can go wrong will go wrong";

- When we most expect to need it;

- When we least expect to need it;

- When the unexpected happens.

In their 2007 book, *Managing the Unexpected: Resilient Performance in an Age of Uncertainty*, Karl Weick and Kathleen Sutcliffe say: "Unexpected events often audit our resilience. They affect how much we stretch without breaking and then how well we recover. Some of those audits are mild. But others are brutal. Unrecognized mild audits often turn brutal. Most organizations experience unexpected events all the time. These dynamic and uncertain times raise the questions of how and why some organizations are much more capable than others of maintaining function and structure in the face of drastic change and of bouncing back in a stronger position to tackle future challenges."

Returning to our Eastern Airlines story, the pilots' agility got audited in the cockpit that day, initially only mildly—it was just a malfunctioning bulb. But that mild audit turned brutal, in particular at 150 feet with a few seconds left. Tragically, they failed the audit. BP's agility got audited, initially only mildly—there were just some early issues and causes for concern. But that mild audit turned brutal, at 8:00 p.m. on April 20, 2010, with one hour and 49 minutes left. Toyota's agility got audited, initially only mildly—there were a few isolated incidents, reports, and enquiries. But that mild audit turned brutal with the torrent of media coverage and the crisis of public confidence. Karl Weick and Kathleen Sutcliffe go on to say:

> "This book is based on examination of the ways people and organizations organize for high performance where the potential for error and disaster is overwhelming: nuclear aircraft carriers, air traffic control systems, aircraft operations systems, hostage negotiation teams, emergency medical treatment

teams, nuclear power generation plants, continuous processing firms and wild-land firefighting crews. These diverse organizations share a singular demand: they have no choice but to function reliably. If reliability is compromised, severe harm results. We call them High Reliability Organizations (HROs), which operate under very trying conditions all the time and yet manage to have fewer than their... [fair] share of accidents.

HROs practice a form of organizing that reduces the brutality of audits and speeds up the process of recovering. We attribute the success of **HROs** in managing the unexpected to their determined efforts to **act** *mindfully*. By this we mean that they organize themselves in such a way that they are better able to notice the unexpected in the making and halt its development. If they have difficulty halting the development of the unexpected, they focus on containing it. And if the unexpected breaks through the containment, they focus on resilience and swift restoration of system functioning.

HRO environments unfold rapidly, and errors propagate quickly. Understanding is never perfect, and people are under pressure to make wise choices with insufficient information. But whose environment isn't like that?"

–Karl Weick and Kathleen Sutcliffe, 2007, *Managing the Unexpected:*
Resilient Performance in an Age of Uncertainty
To read more, visit: www.mydrivingseat.com/booklinks booklink #12

Whose environment isn't like that? These days, all of us are operating in that kind of environment, to some degree! When unexpected events audit our organization, sometimes mildly and sometimes brutally, how well does our agility pass the test? Are we able to be on our toes, acting mindfully as a high-reliability organization, or are we caught flat-footed as a medium-to-low reliability organization?

You snooze, you lose! We can't be asleep at the wheel, to any degree. We must be fully awake and fully mindful of what it takes to master the whole challenge, the whole problem, and the whole solution these days. We must make friends with agility before it's too late, by becoming more mindful as individuals, teams, and organizations, as a process of integration, alignment and attunement, from gray matter to gray matter. We must become higher reliability organizations, with the organizational agility to cope, no matter what.

When you need a friend it's too late to make one! Making friends with organizational agility is about expecting the unexpected and acting mindfully. It's about being ready, willing, and able to pass the test when our agility next gets audited, sometimes mildly and sometimes brutally. It's uncomfortable to be mindful of those kinds of scenarios, in which our agility gets really tested. Making friends with agility is about getting comfortable with being uncomfortable.

More than just being mindful, expecting the unexpected and being comfortable being uncomfortable, agility is about being productively paranoid.

Only the Paranoid Survive

"Sooner or later, something fundamental in your business world will change. I'm often credited with the motto, 'Only the paranoid survive.' I have no idea when I first said this, but the fact remains that, when it comes to business, I believe in the value of paranoia. Business success contains the seeds of its own destruction."

–Andy Grove, 1996, *Only the Paranoid Survive: How to Identify and Exploit the Crisis Points that Challenge Every Business*

I want you to be productively paranoid! I don't want you to be unproductively so, analysis-paralysis like – paralyzed by the need to analyze every last aspect and detail before we are ready to make a decision. That wouldn't be agility; it would be fragility. Being productively paranoid is about being ever ready, ever willing, and ever able to cope with anything that might happen, making friends with organizational agility before we need it. We do that, as a mindful process of integration, alignment and attunement, from gray matter to gray matter, by developing our new journey-oriented framework of understandings, strengths, and intelligences:

<u>Higher Order Executive Strengths</u>
<u>of Journey-Orientation:</u>

<u>Understanding the Anatomy</u>
<u>of Dynamic Complexity:</u>

+ Execution Excellence .... the anatomy of the **Vehicle** fit for the journey challenge.

+ Executive Intelligence, Intuition & Resilience .... **EQ (IQ)** .... the anatomy of the **Journey** and how it unfolds real-time.

+ Path-Finding ....the anatomy of the **Road** and paths of least resistance.

Bottom-line	XQ + EQ (IQ) + PQ = BQ (AQ)

= Organizational Agility .... **BQ (AQ)** .... the anatomy of **Breakthrough Leadership** & **Architecting Breakthrough Journeys.**

our ability to deal with rapidly changing circumstances, while out-executing our competition and stakeholder expectations (of customers, employees, suppliers and shareholders)

ordinary people achieving extraordinary things, making possible tomorrow, what seems impossible today

We will be reviewing these strengths in the coming chapters, together with the associated models and tools for each. We will start here with the middle level in our framework for *understanding the anatomy of a journey and how a journey unfolds in real time,* and the associated journey-oriented, higher order executive strength of *Executive Intelligence, Intuition, and Resilience.* Calling upon the foundations of our emotional intelligence (EQ) and our cognitive intelligence (IQ), this understanding and strength is at the heart of being ready, willing, and able—expecting the unexpected, being comfortable with being uncomfortable, and being productively paranoid. Let me explain.

We all have a macroscopic understanding of a journey, in a getting from A to B kind of way—where are we now (A), where do we want to be (B), and how do we get there from here? However, because of the increasing dynamic complexity we experience these days, we need a much more microscopic, granular understanding of a journey and how it unfolds in real time. Justin Menkes puts it well:

> "The granular stuff of business is critical thinking—the skilled, active interpretation and evaluation of observations, communications, information,

and argumentation as a guide to thought and action. In other words, critical-thinking ability determines how skillfully someone gathers, processes, and applies information in order to identify the best way to reach a particular goal or navigate a complex situation."

–Justin Menkes, 2005, *Executive Intelligence*

In my experience, a lack of appreciation for this granular, microscopic under-standing of a journey is why so much of our intuition about organizational agility gets lost in translation; remember, that's where we started in Chapter 1, asking why so much of this gets "lost in translation." In our mindful process of integration, alignment and attunement, from gray matter to gray matter, this middle level in our framework can easily be an oil slick, causing wheel$pin in translating strategy and execution into traction. That is why we are going to start here.

The Anatomy of a Journey and How it Unfolds in Real Time

Back in the summer of 2001, my wife and I were going back to the U.K. for a wedding, in a place called Hazelwood. We had received the invitation about nine months prior and had begun planning our trip. We began thinking about all the different aspects of it—flights, cars, hotels, kids, family and friends, dates we were coming and going. We began asking questions of ourselves about our preferences and how we wanted to spend our time, to fit everything in. We began making decisions and taking actions to line up everything the way we wanted it.

We were living in San Diego, where we still live today. Back then, British Airways had just put on a direct flight from San Diego to London Gatwick airport using a Boeing 777, and it just so happened that my corporate head office was right outside of Gatwick. So, after discussing it with my wife, we agreed that we would fly over on a Monday, and I would do a week's worth of work in the corporate head office, with my wife and two boys continuing on to Scotland to stay with her parents. I would fly up Thursday night, and we would drive away Friday morning, leaving the boys with my wife's parents. We would get to the wedding for the rendezvous dinner Friday evening, before the ceremonies on Saturday. Sounds like a plan!

So, sure enough, we flew over on Monday, I did my week's worth of work, and flew up Thursday night. By the time my wife picked me up and got us back to her parents' place, it was about 9 p.m. I had a single malt scotch whiskey by my side, and

I turned to my wife and said, "So, do we have a plan then?" She said, "sure," picked up a road atlas of Great Britain and turned to the overview page. She had put a sticker on the map with an arrow pointing at Hazelwood, on which she had also made a few notes for herself, which she then referred to. She said, "It's about 300 miles. So I figure we can leave at 9 a.m. and drive over to Leeds, getting there at 11 a.m." Leeds is a big city in the northeast of England that is about halfway to Hazelwood from where we were in Scotland. She continued, saying, "We can have lunch in Leeds, buy a wedding present, and leave at about 2 p.m. We can then drive south to Hazelwood, arriving at about 4 p.m., giving us time to get showered and changed, in time for the rendezvous dinner at 5:30 p.m." "Sounds good," I said.

So, sure enough, the following morning we kissed the kids goodbye, jumped in the rental car, and drove away. We were right on time at 9 a.m. Now, I had been traveling the world like a maniac, running the aerospace division of the British corporation I worked for, and my wife and I hadn't spent much time alone together recently. There we were, heading out for a great weekend, without any kids fighting it out in the back seat! We started to talk, catch up, and have a great conversation. It felt really good and we were traveling really well.

We got to Leeds right on time at 11 a.m. We parked the car, walked into town, came across a department store, went inside and found exactly the present we were looking for—an English wicker picnic basket, with nice English china and cutlery inside. We even had time to have a brass plate engraved and put on top! We went a little further into town and found a little French restaurant, in which we had a lovely lunch. We continued having a great conversation. Things were feeling really good. We were traveling really well.

We got back to the car right on time at 2 p.m. and started driving south out of Leeds. We had about 100 miles of freeway to go and then about 25 miles cross country, on English country roads and lanes, and it was a bit of a tricky navigation, and my wife is navigationally challenged! However, on this occasion, she flawlessly navigated us to the heart of Hazelwood. All the way there, we continued having a great conversation. Things were feeling really good. We were travelling really well.

Hazelwood is a small cross-roads village. We came up to the cross-roads, I looked at my watch and it was approaching 4 p.m., right on time. I turned to my wife again and asked, "So where's the hotel then?" She said, "Hey, give me a break, I got us to the heart of Hazelwood, it's a small cross-roads village and I'm sure we'll be able to find the hotel." "Fair enough," I said, "let's drive this way through the cross-roads and, if we don't find it, we'll come back and drive the other way." So that is what we did.

After about five minutes, we hadn't found the hotel, so we turned around and were returning to the cross-roads when we passed a woman walking along the road. We pulled over and asked her, "Excuse me, we are coming to a wedding at the Hazelwood Manor or the Hazelwood Castle hotel, the invitation is in the trunk, can you tell us where that is please?" She looked slightly puzzled and said, "I'm sorry, that doesn't ring a bell." "No problem," I said, "if you could tell us where the big hotel is in the village, I'm sure that will be it." To which, looking even more puzzled, she said, "I'm sorry, there isn't anything like that around here." I thanked her for her help, and she continued on her way.

Puzzlement had shifted to my face! There were some sparks going off in the back of my brain! I turned back to my wife and said, "Um, you know when you put that sticker on the map pointing at Hazelwood, how did you determine that this is the right Hazelwood?"

Now, I love my wife dearly, and we are still married. In fact we are celebrating 20 years this year. She said that she looked up the index of the map, there was only one entry for Hazelwood, and this was it. Now there were a lot of sparks going off in the back of my brain! I was thinking about how many Hazelwoods there might be in Great Britain one level of resolution below the resolution of this map. It could be anywhere! For instance, there are several San Diegos in the United States that aren't the one I live in.

I got on my cell phone, was fortunate to get a signal, and eventually, through directory inquiries, I got put through to the receptionist of the Hazelwood Castle Hotel, Hazelwood. I explained that my name was Richardson and that we were coming for a big family wedding this weekend, to which she replied, "oh yes, Mr. Richardson, we are so looking forward to having you." So I then very sheepishly asked, "Can you tell me the largest city that you are close to?" She explained that they were just 15 minutes east of Leeds, where we had been 125 miles and two hours ago!

Now, this isn't a story about emotional intelligence, but I was sufficiently emotionally intelligent at the time to realize that I had a choice: I could either get angry or laugh. I decided to laugh, turn the car around, drive 125 miles back north, a 250 mile round trip south of Leeds we hadn't needed to make, and carry on with our weekend. We got to the hotel about two hours late, played hurry up and got into the bar about an hour late, and I promised I wouldn't mention it. Which I didn't—for about 20 minutes!

Now, what went wrong? How come we ended up in completely and utterly the wrong Hazelwood? Think about it. Did we have a plan? Yes. Had we written it down? Yes, my wife had made some notes for herself on the sticker she had put on the map. Had we executed it flawlessly? Yes, we had been on time all day and had arrived right on time at 4 p.m. Had it felt really good while doing so; had we travelled really, really well? Yes.

When did we find out we had gone so horribly wrong? At the very last moment! When did it go wrong? From the very, very beginning! It started going wrong nine months earlier when we first started talking about it. It continued going wrong six months earlier when we booked the flights, three months earlier when we booked all our other hotels and the rental car, three weeks earlier when we did our final detailed planning, Monday when we flew over, Thursday night when we talked about it, 9 a.m. Friday morning when we drove away, and as recently as 2 p.m. Friday afternoon when we drove south out of Leeds.

When I tell this story as I'm facilitating teams, I love to next ask, "Whose fault was it?" That always sparks a fun conversation! Forgive me, ladies, as I don't intend to be sexist, but if we consider the analogy that my wife was the COO of this journey and I was the CEO, then, ultimately, whose fault was it? Mine. Why? Because, it never occurred to me to ask my wife a question, which might cause her to make a decision, to take some kind of action, to verify where Hazelwood was. It never occurred to me.

It was a thought that I never had. It was also a thought that she never had. It was a conversation that we never had.

You see, when you strip things down to their very essence, I suggest to you that strategy is conversation, period! If you don't have much conversation, you probably don't have much strategy! Which means you are taking an awful risk with your business of ending up in the wrong Hazelwood and finding out about it at the last moment!

Linking & accumulating individual thoughts, questions, decisions and actions into a journey

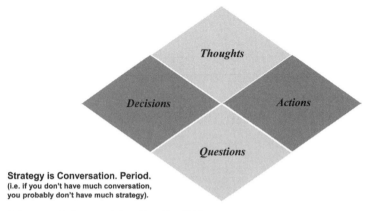

Strategy is Conversation. Period.
(i.e. if you don't have much conversation,
you probably don't have much strategy).

Actions are part of the conversation with reality, which is
talking to you with plenty of feedback, if you are paying
attention and listening with intention and responsibility-for-results.

When I say, "Strategy is conversation," I don't mean it's just a talking shop. Absolutely not! It is as much about walking the talk as talking the talk. To that end, notice that I include "actions" in the broad definition of "conversation." Actions are a conversation with reality, which is talking to us with plenty of feedback, about what's working and what's not working. The only question is, are we listening?!

At a microscopic, granular level, a journey is comprised of how we link and accumulate individual thoughts, questions, decisions, and actions. In planning and implementing our journey to Hazelwood, my wife and I linked and accumulated an awful lot of individual thoughts, questions, decisions, and actions, regarding flights, hotels, rental cars, calendars, dates, kids, friends and relatives, presents, currencies, etc., etc., etc. The trouble is, there were just a few crucial ones missing, and, as a result, we linked and accumulated to the wrong place and found out about it at the last moment!

Now, you might be excused for thinking, "Well, that was pretty stupid, Mike, pretty dumb actually; I am smarter than that, and that would never happen to me!" So consider this. In 2003, here in the United States, 17-year-old Jessica Santillan was having a simultaneous heart and lung transplant operation at Duke University Hospital, Durham, North Carolina, and those involved overlooked having a conversation about cross matching the blood type. She died. Now, I am no expert, but a simultaneous heart and lung transplant operation must be a pretty risky operation in the first place. But we never gave her much of a chance. A whole bunch of really, really smart people—experienced surgeons, professional nurses, and hospital administrators—overlooked having a conversation about something as fundamental as cross matching the blood types. This can be life and death!

Or what about the different conversations we have these days about a piece of foam hitting the space-shuttle wing? Or bridges falling down in Minneapolis? Remember that? Or subprime mortgages and credit default swaps? Or safety recalls with Toyota. Or deep water drilling in the Gulf of Mexico with BP? Why is it that we often have to have a smoking hole in the ground, Eastern Airlines style, before we wake up to the fact that we haven't been talking about the right stuff?

Think back to our Eastern Airlines story. How did the pilots do in that cockpit that day, in linking and accumulating their thoughts, questions, decisions, and actions into their journey? Tragically, not very well.

- They didn't think to monitor their altitude more proactively and consciously as they thought the auto-pilot had it handled.

- They didn't decide more consciously how best to divide their attention span among the three crew members.

- When one of the pilots noticed the altimeter reading 150 feet and posed the question, "We did something to the altitude... we're still at two thousand (feet), right?" they were cognitively disconnected from reality, in a state of confusion. They weren't able to spool back up their cognitive functions quickly enough, think things through, ask key questions, make key decisions, and take key actions. Maybe they could have hit the gas, pulled back on the stick, climbed to safety, and asked more questions later?

- Their conversation of thoughts, questions, decisions, and actions had become so convergently focused on the detail complexity of fixing the bulb that their divergent conversation focused on the dynamic complexity of flying the plane had suffered.

- Tragically, they linked and accumulated to the wrong place and found out about it at the last moment.

We weren't there in the cockpit that day and 20/20 hindsight is a wonderful thing; it isn't my intention to be a Monday morning quarterback. We are just speculating, but the point is that this can be life and death! When our lack of conversation allows our journey to go into an imperceptible descent, in some way, shape, or form, it can be the KISS of death (remember our discussion about this and the simplicity of the KISS principle, Keep It Simple, Stupid, in Chapter 1). In the face of the detail complexity and dynamic complexity of their situation, their conversation had unconsciously become overly simple. Stupid simple! It had lapsed into being about fixing the bulb as an "or" proposition rather than an "and" proposition, together with flying the plane. Their organizational agility had become an "or-deal," not an "and-deal."

When our imperceptible descent becomes perceptible, it is often too late. We suffer some kind of consequence. In the case of our journey to Hazelwood, the consequences were insignificant—a few extra miles and a few extra hours. In the case of the Eastern Airlines story, they paid the ultimate price. We all have stories that span the full spectrum between those two extremes of consequences, in business and in life.

Scary stuff and, yes, I want you to be productively paranoid! I want you to ask yourself if your conversation is allowing your journey to go into an imperceptible descent. Whatever journey that might be, in your business, with your career, or in your life. Maybe it already is, and you just don't know it because it's imperceptible! How do you know? You never can really know for sure, but what you can do is drive different conversations to mitigate the risk as much as possible. And just when you think you have done enough, do some more. Be productively paranoid.

Remember that I am saying "productively" paranoid, not "unproductively" so. Being unproductively paranoid, analysis-paralysis like, will put you into an imperceptible descent for sure! It's all part of mastering the challenge of the "and," not being over planned and not being under planned, dealing in agility as an "and-deal," not an "or-deal."

Of course, we have a recent incident that turned out very differently from our Eastern Airlines story, and that is the story of US Airways Flight 1549 on January 15, 2009, captained by Chesley "Sully" Sullenberger. He became famous for successfully ditching his twin engine Airbus A320 in the Hudson River off Manhattan, New York City, saving the lives of all 155 people on board the aircraft.

Shortly after a mid afternoon takeoff from New York's LaGuardia Airport en route to Charlotte, North Carolina, the plane hit a large flock of birds, disabling both engines, resulting in silence and zero thrust. In the space of only a couple of minutes, Sully was able to link and accumulate his thoughts, questions, decisions, and actions into the journey of successfully executing a smooth ditching into the river, saving all. It could so easily have been a different ending. In the real time unfolding of just a few seconds, tens of seconds and minutes, he had to consider his options, weigh them up, and execute them, working "in" and "on" the journey, divergently and convergently, all at the same time.

Thankfully, with a very different and positive outcome this time. Luckily, Sully was a very experienced pilot and, as it happens, was also a thought-leader looking at error-inducing contexts in aviation and psychology behind keeping an airline crew functioning during a crisis. In a television interview Sully said, "One way of looking at this might be that for 42 years, I've been making small, regular deposits in this bank account of experience, education, and training. And on January 15th, the balance was sufficient that I could make a very large withdrawal."

How is your bank account of experience, education, and training for these kinds of real time journeys? Our purpose in this chapter is to get you thinking about the anatomy of a journey and how it unfolds in real time at a microscopic, granular level. It's about the real time unfolding of our conversation of individual thoughts, questions, decisions, and actions and how we link and accumulate those into our journey. This unfolding conversation is all that we've got. It's everything, with whatever consequences flow from it, good or bad. So what factors influence the colors, shapes, and flavors with which our conversation and journey unfold in real time?

Our individual thoughts, questions, decisions, and actions unfold in the annulus between our inner world/journey and our outer world/journey, simultaneously informing both and being informed by both, through the interfaces of our intention, attention, and responsibility for results.

I came to know the word "annulus" well from my time as a petroleum engineer. I am all too familiar with the journey of drilling deep wells to hit a target zone of oil and gas, and the ever present risks of kicks and blow-outs, as happened with the BP oil spill, and how we mitigate and manage those risks. It's a lot to do with the annulus—

that is the space between the outside edge of the inner component we are running into the hole (the drill bit/drill pipe or casing, for instance) and the inside edge of the hole (and the surrounding geology we are drilling through). Indeed, thinking back to the chain of events from BP's accident investigation report (which we outlined in Chapter 1), "annulus" is the second word they use.

Pretty much all of my work as a petroleum engineer was about the annulus—the drilled material we are removing from it (and analyzing the geology to know where we are at), the liquid mud we are flowing through it to do so (and maintaining the weight, viscosity and other properties of the mud to keep the hole under control), and calculating the volumes involved (not least of all, for when we run casing into the hole and cement it in place). Indeed, if you read the investigative reports about the BP oil spill in the Gulf of Mexico, you will see how predominantly the word "annulus" features.

In his 1990 book, *The Fifth Discipline*, Peter Senge puts it this way:

> "Our organizations work the way they work, ultimately, because of how we think and how we interact. Only by changing how we think can we change deeply embedded policies and practices. Only by changing how we interact can shared visions, shared understandings and new capacities for coordinated action be established.
>
> We have a deep tendency to see the changes we need to make as being in our outer world, not in our inner world. It is challenging to think that while we redesign the manifest structures of our organizations, we must also redesign the internal structures of our 'mental models.' We do not 'have' mental models. We 'are' our mental models."
>
> –Peter Senge, 1990, *The Fifth Discipline*

In other words, our individual thoughts, questions, decisions, and actions unfold in the annulus between our inner world/journey and our outer world/journey, simultaneously informing both and being informed by both. This occurs through the interfaces of our intention, attention, and responsibility for results.

Linking & accumulating individual thoughts, questions, decisions and actions into a journey

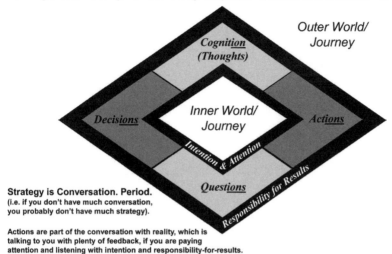

Similarly, pretty much all of our work as CEOs, executives, and managers is about the annulus, between our inner world/journey and our outer world/journey.

Our outer world/journey consists of:

- Our Business Strategies, Organization Structures, Operational Processes
- Our Markets and Customers, Supply Chains and Strategic Alliances
- Our Results
- …and other nuts and bolts kinds of things

Our inner world/journey consists of:

- Our Mental Models and Mindsets, Strengths, and Intelligences
- Our Blind Spots and Hot Spots, Hopes, and Fears
- Our Beliefs, Intuition, and Resilience
- …and other soft and fleshy kinds of things

I started out as a geophysicist, which was my training for the oil and gas industry, studying geophysics as my undergraduate college degree. Geophysics involves the geology, physics, and math of the continuum from the very center of the earth to the very outer edge of the universe (if there is such a thing), from the inner world of our planet to the outer world of space. It's about the quantitative observation of the physical properties of everything in between, how things work, and the fundamental organizing principles, not least of all gravity. My work now is kind of like being a geophysicist of business, helping CEOs, executives, and their teams understand the continuum from the very center of their inner world to the outer edge of their outer world, the properties of everything in between, and the fundamental organizing principles. In particular, I help CEOs, executives, and their teams understand the gravity of our challenge *In the Driving Seat*, from our outermost results, to our innermost beliefs.

Executive Intelligence, Intuition & Resilience

The traction *"ions"* of a Journey
(working simultaneously "in" and "on"
the journey at the same time)   **in   on**
▲
"ion"

Linking & accumulating individual thoughts, questions, decisions and actions into a journey

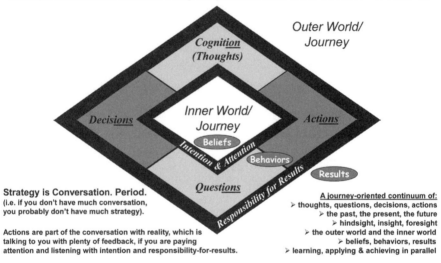

Strategy is Conversation. Period.
(i.e. if you don't have much conversation, you probably don't have much strategy).

Actions are part of the conversation with reality, which is talking to you with plenty of feedback, if you are paying attention and listening with intention and responsibility-for-results.

A journey-oriented continuum of:
➤ thoughts, questions, decisions, actions
➤ the past, the present, the future
➤ hindsight, insight, foresight
➤ the outer world and the inner world
➤ beliefs, behaviors, results
➤ learning, applying & achieving in parallel

In summary, we can think of it as a closed loop of beliefs driving behaviors driving results. Our beliefs are part of our inner world/journey and drive our behaviors of thinking, questioning, decision making, and action taking in the annulus. These behaviors drive our results that are part of our outer world/journey.

The inclusion of actions in our broad definition of conversation now gets a little clearer. As we mentioned earlier, actions are a conversation with reality, which is talking to us with plenty of feedback, if we are paying attention and listening with intention and responsibility for results. That feedback is letting us know loud and clear what's working, what's not working, and what's missing, if only we are listening mindfully enough. Our mindfulness comes from our sense of intention, attention, and responsibility for results, which allows us to listen consciously and perceptibly enough. When our intention, attention, and responsibility for results are fuzzy, that's when things can inadvertently and progressively become unconscious and imperceptible, putting some aspect of reality on mute. It's still there, but we just don't hear it or see it.

Paying attention with intention and responsibility for results is crucial. It closes the loop, with our results reinforcing our beliefs or causing us to evolve our beliefs as part of our inner world/journey. Evolving our beliefs causes us to evolve our behaviors which evolve our results. And so on. If we are awake at the wheel and mindful of this process, it can become a virtuous cycle and upward spiral. If we are asleep at the wheel and unconscious of this process, it can become a vicious cycle and downward spiral.

Think about the vicious cycle and downward spiral in the Eastern Airlines cockpit that day. Their attention to their No. 1 goal (fixing the bulb) on their sequential path of goals undermined their intention and responsibility for results for the subsequent goals in their journey (landing safely and continuing on with a nice life), with disastrous results. Their belief that they were still on autopilot, at 2,000 feet, drove their behaviors, which drove their results.

Think about the vicious cycle and downward spiral with the BP oil spill in the Gulf of Mexico, or with Toyota, or with sub prime mortgages, credit default swaps, and the credit crunch. Think about how easily things can spiral down into an imperceptible descent, followed by a perceptible descent, followed by a nosedive, followed by a tailspin, followed by a smoking hole in the ground.

So now we begin to have a microscopic, granular understanding of the anatomy of a journey and how it unfolds in real time. It is a continuum of how we link and accumulate individual thoughts (or we can substitute the fancier word cognition), questions, decisions, and actions. Noting that each of these words end in "ion," I call these the traction "ions" of a journey. This has several connotations:

- The word "ion" captures the microscopic, granular idea of understanding a journey, which is the purpose of this chapter. An "ion" conveys the idea of a granular, molecular thing, a micro data point.

- The word "ion" itself is an "and" proposition of the words "in" and "on," capturing the idea that we must be working "in" and "on" our business and our journey at the same time. That is today's reality of being *In the Driving Seat* of organizational agility. Just like *In the Driving Seat* of our cars, we are working "in" and "on" our journey all at the same time, being strategic and operational, long-term and short-term oriented, leaders and managers, all at the same time. In these days of satellite navigation, real time traffic updates, and voice activation, we typically don't pull off the road to strategize and work "on" our journey; we work "on" our journey and "in" our journey all at the same time in the unfolding flow of things. Thinking about our Eastern Airlines story, it's about fixing bulbs, working "in" our journey, and flying the plane, working "on" our journey, all at the same time.

• In the field of electronics, "ions" are atoms or molecules in which the total number of electrons is not equal to the total number of protons, giving it a net negative or positive electrical charge, known as "anions" or "cations" respectively. Studying for a geophysics degree at college, I had to know this stuff. Bear with me while I explain a little.

Formed through the process of ionization, ions are essential to life in the cells of living organisms and through practical applications in everyday technologies, such as the widespread use of capacitors in electric circuits. A capacitor consists of a pair of conductors, called a cathode and an anode, separated by a nonconductive insulation material called a dielectric. An electric field applied between the two conductors across the dielectric causes it to ionize and polarize, with anions migrating to the anode and cations migrating to the cathode. This results in a voltage buildup and storage of electrical energy or potential, kind of like a battery. When the voltage buildup reaches a certain maximum, related to the strength of the dielectric material, it breaks down, becoming conductive, with current breaking through and starting to flow across the dielectric and between the two conductors.

This is analogous to the traction "ions" of our journey. Think of this as an invisible, nonfinancial, second balance sheet for our business, which acts kind of like a capacitor, as we have been discussing above. Think of it this way. Every moment of every day, as our conversation of thoughts (cogni*tions*), ques*tions*, deci*sions*, and ac*tions* unfolds, in real time as our journey, we are adding negative "ions" or positive "ions" to the capacitor of this second balance sheet. A good thought adds a positive ion. A not so good thought adds a negative ion. A good thought we needed to have but didn't adds a negative ion by omission. And so on, for questions, decisions, and actions, too.

Invisibly, these ions are accumulating on the capacitor into the balance of a net voltage across the gap. A net positive charge of promise or a net negative charge of peril, up until the point where the net charge builds up to the break down voltage.

At which point it becomes conductive and sparks fly! We get a *breakthrough* in the case of net positive charge of promise. Or we get a *breakdown* in the case of net negative charge of peril. All this happens invisibly and imperceptibly, right up until the last moment, when the sparks fly and it becomes visible and perceptible. Like our journey to Hazelwood. Like in the Eastern Airlines cockpit that day. Like with Toyota. Like with BP. It's the difference between the *breakthrough* of hitting an oil and gas zone successfully and safely transitioning the well into production and the *breakdown* of a kick, a blowout and an oil spill.

So, being *In the Driving Seat* is about linking and accumulating the traction "ions" of our journey, as a continuum:

• **A continuum** of the past (hindsight), the present (insight) and the future (foresight), as we discussed earlier in this chapter. We want to learn as much as we possibly can from foresight and insight, to minimize the pain and expense of learning from hindsight.

• **A continuum** of the outer world and the inner world and our interwoven journeys with each. Just like the double helix of DNA—the DNA of our challenge has changed. Like the double helix of DNA, they are interwoven and inseparable, each simultaneously informing and influencing the other. A very good friend and fellow Vistage chairperson in San Diego, who is very experienced in facilitating deep personal growth work, reinforced this for me. She says that these two worlds often live apart in the minds of the majority and in the world of consulting, training, and coaching. We tend to focus on one or the other. Professional development tends to focus on the outer world of nuts and bolts things like those we listed above. Personal growth tends to focus on the inner world of soft and fleshy things like those we listed above. The reality is that these are inextricably linked and interwoven as a continuum, with the traction "ions" of our journey unfolding in the annulus in between.

• **A continuum** of learning, applying, and achieving in parallel. We have to be ready, willing, and able to figure things out as we go, learning by doing as much as learning by thinking, self-confident in our agility to find a path, navigate it well, and drive traction on our desired trajectory. Just like when we push off from the bank on a whitewater ride. Just like when we set out on a road trip into unfamiliar territory. We must be okay with making mistakes. As the saying goes, "Wisdom comes from judgment, which comes from experience, which comes from mistakes." Hopefully, small mistakes not fatal mistakes! Mistakes build experience, which builds judgment, which builds wisdom, which builds self-belief. We must develop belief in our intelligence, intuition, and resilience as CEOs, executives, and managers. To do that, we must develop our understanding of the anatomy of a journey and how it unfolds in real time, in the annulus between our outer world and our inner world. We must be mindful of how we are linking and accumulating the traction "ions" of our journey, microscopically at a granular level, into promising *breakthroughs* and avoiding perilous *breakdowns*.

This diamond shaped model we have been reviewing is called *Journey-ionics (Ji)* and that's what the journey-oriented, higher-order executive strength of Executive Intelligence, Intuition, and Resilience is all about. It's a multifaceted, journey-oriented continuum, which is integral to our mindful process of integration, alignment and attunement, from gray matter to gray matter. That's what it takes to be *In the Driving Seat* of organizational agility, translating strategy and execution into traction, with nothing getting lost in translation. When something gets lost in translation, we end up with stories like the ones we have been telling so far. Constant whitewater, wrong Hazelwoods, Eastern Airlines, Toyota, and BP! And we all have our own stories, from our own business, professional, and personal journeys.

In particular, we have stories if we have worked in acutely operationally intensive environments like some we have talked about so far and like Karl Weick and Kathleen Sutcliffe studied as mentioned earlier in this chapter. Immersed in these environments, we can't help but become intimately familiar with the detail complexity and dynamic complexity of the unfolding journey in real time and develop an instinct for the longitudinal dimension of journey orientation. Learning from immersion the hard way, experientially in the field, we gradually master the judgment, wisdom, and belief required.

Maybe one of the most acutely operationally intensive and journey-oriented environments that exists is that of a jet fighter pilot and the dynamic complexity of a dogfight. Having already looked at the fighter plane to help us understand agility, now let's look at fighter pilots and what we can learn from them about the anatomy of a journey and how it unfolds in real time, at a microscopic, granular level.

The Jet Fighter Pilot's OODA Loop

Jet fighter pilots implicitly understand the real time anatomy of a journey, as they are trained in something called the OODA Loop, which stands for:

Observe:
Observing what's going on around us, using all the senses, to sustain our situational awareness.

Orient:
Interpreting what we are observing—what just happened, what's happening now, and, most important, what's likely to happen next.

Decide:
In that context, deciding what our options are and what we are going to do.

Act:
Acting on those decisions.

To read more, visit: www.mydrivingseat.com/booklinks booklink #13

And so on, around and around, as a never ending loop. In the dynamic complexity of a dogfight, the OODA Loop persists endlessly. How fighter pilots link and accumulate their Observations, Orientations, Decisions, and Actions, around and around, determines how the fight shapes up, who gets the advantage over the other, who wins and who loses. In a real world situation, with life and death consequences! These Observations, Orientations, Decisions, and Actions are the traction "ions" of a fighter pilot's journey.

The reason that we invest so heavily in the experiential, field training of our fighter pilots, through intensive training and large simulations, is so that they can master the dynamic complexity involved. We can only really learn the skills we need for dynamic complexity the hard way, experientially, in the field. As pilots gain more and more experience, they progressively shrink their OODA Loop. It becomes more intuitive for them, they develop a more instinctive sense of things as experience builds judgment and judgment builds wisdom. They are able to rev up their assessments and reactions, go around their OODA Loop faster, and, as a result, their OODA Loop shrinks.

BONUS

http://bit.ly/qSqeoR

The same thing happens with us *In the Driving Seat* of our cars. While we may not have thought about it this way before, we have an OODA Loop operating when we are driving. Our Observations, Orientations, Decisions, and Actions are the traction "ions" of our journey any time we are behind the wheel. As we gain more experience, it becomes more intuitive and instinctive, as a result of which our OODA Loop shrinks, and we are able to go around it faster, keeping up with the detail complexity and dynamic complexity involved. It wasn't always that way! Remember when you first started learning to drive and how large, slow, and open your OODA Loop was at first. Gradually it became more closed, smaller, and faster.

Not as closed looped, small, and fast as a fighter pilot's, though. A dogfight might last as little as 20 to 40 seconds! Imagine going head to head into a dogfight, with both pilots in similar aircraft, at similar altitude, speed, and fuel remaining, with similar weapons. Neither has the advantage over the other. Who's going to win? Other things being equal, the fighter pilot with the smaller OODA Loop is likely to win. Such pilots can go around their OODA Loops faster, which means they can operate inside their adversaries' OODA Loops. As a result, they are more likely to get on the other pilot's tail first and win the dogfight!

In the rapidly changing circumstances of business these days, the OODA Loop also persists endlessly. In his 2002 article in *Fast Company* magazine, Keith Hammonds puts it well:

"Business is a dogfight. Your job as a leader: outmaneuver the competition, respond decisively to fast changing conditions, and defeat your rivals. Agility is the essence of strategy in war and in business. Connect vibrant OODA Loops that are operating concurrently at several levels. Workers close to the action stick to tactical loops, and their supervisors travel in operational loops, while leaders navigate much broader strategic and political loops. The loops inform each other. If everything is clicking, feedback from the tactical loops will guide decisions at higher loops and vice versa."

–Keith Hammonds, 2002, *Fast Company* magazine,
Issue 59, The Strategy of the Fighter Pilot

To read more, visit: www.mydrivingseat.com/booklinks booklink #13

Agility is the essence of strategy in war and in business. Our agility as an organization depends upon our organizational OODA Loop and connecting vibrant OODA Loops that are operating concurrently at several levels. For instance, we need a strategy process OODA Loop, an operations management OODA Loop, and an infrastructure, of structures, processes, and systems, OODA Loop, among others. These, among others, will feature in our review of our Execution Excellence model in the next chapter.

Our challenge in business these days is the unprecedented and ever increasing uncertainty, turbulence, and volatility of the global economy. This has become our number one adversary as we live in an increasingly revved up world. Things are coming at us thicker and faster. The OODA Loop of the economic environment, the speed of business, and the pace of change is ever shrinking, going around and around, faster and faster. As our number one adversary, we go into a dogfight with it every day. We must keep up, by shrinking our organizational OODA Loop, to keep operating inside the OODA Loop of this, our number one adversary. If we aren't doing that, then we shouldn't be surprised if we aren't winning the daily dogfight!

Our Organizational OODA Loop and Fast-Cycle Teamwork

What have you done lately to massively shrink your organizational OODA Loop, to be operating inside your number one adversary's OODA Loop? I love to ask that question of managers, executives, and CEOs when working with them and their teams. Typically, I am met with blank stares, like a deer in the headlights.

In my experience, most haven't done much to shrink their organizational OODA Loop. They are still operating with the same large, lethargic, and somewhat open-loop OODA Loop, as they always have. Even worse, as things have revved up, many have let their OODA Loops expand and go even more open loop because they "don't have time." For instance, meetings get canceled and become more ad hoc, ill-disciplined and open ended. Wrong answer! We won't win the daily dogfight, and things will go from bad to worse. That's slow-cycle teamwork.

Instead, what we need these days is fast-cycle teamwork. We need to rev up our teamwork from slow-cycle to fast-cycle. We need to massively shrink our organizational OODA Loop, so that we can go around it faster and faster, operating inside the OODA Loop of our number one adversary. That's how we win the daily dogfight!

I always ask teams of managers, executives, and CEOs what their hopes and wants are for a good strategy, execution, and traction process. Invariably, among other things, they will say something like "better communication." That almost always comes up. With some exploration of that, what I suggest they mean is not just communication, but collaboration and coordination as well. That's what fast-cycle teamwork is about. It's about revving up our communication, collaboration, and coordination as a team. It's about collectively linking and accumulating the traction "ions" of our journey, as a much smaller, faster, and closed-loop organizational OODA Loop. That's how we win the daily dogfight!

That's how to be *In the Driving Seat* of our unfolding journey, at a microscopic, granular level. Hopefully, without any deficits of some crucial traction "ions" missing, so that we don't end up in the wrong place and find out about it at the last moment! Avoiding Wrong Hazelwoods and Eastern Airlines scenarios! Let's look more at what causes those deficits.

Attention Deficit and Other Disorders

In my experience, there are three main deficit disorders that afflict businesses. These relate to the interfaces in our *Journey-ionics* model of Executive Intelligence, Intuition, and Resilience above, namely the interfaces of Attention, Intention, and Responsibility for Results. Intention and attention are the interface with our inner world/journey. Responsibility for results is the interface with our outer world/journey. Correspondingly, the three deficit disorders are:

- **Attention Deficit Disorder (ADD).** We are not paying attention to all the right things, in the all the right ways, at all the right times. Consequently, our bandwidth of attention span is somewhat scattered and ad hoc, leaving glaring deficits.

- **Intention Deficit Disorder (IDD).** We have a deficit of intention. We are not clear about where we are going, why we want to go there, and what's in it for all stakeholders. We are not clear about the path we intend to find to get there, and we are not clear about how we intend to deal with the shifting landscape along the way.

- **Responsibility for Results Deficit Disorder (R4RDD).** We are not taking 100% responsibility for the results we are getting in an unqualified way and without excuses. Instead, we tend to deflect and project some share of responsibility onto other things, other people, or other organizations, excusing our results and abdicating our responsibility to some degree.

These disorders can easily become cancerous as a self-fulfilling, self-defeating, vicious cycle and downward spiral. As depicted in our *Journey-ionics* model, our job is to link and accumulate the traction "ions" of our journey with intention, attention, and responsibility for results, without any deficit disorders. Any deficit disorders are likely to cause a few crucial traction "ions" to be missing, and we are at risk of linking and accumulating to the wrong place and finding out about it at the last moment. Wrong Hazelwoods! Eastern Airlines!

Remember what we said from our Eastern Airlines story and the crew in the cockpit that day: their attention to their No.1 goal (of fixing the bulb) on their sequential path of goals undermined their intention of the subsequent goals in their journey (for which they needed also to keep flying the plane), with disastrous results, for which they were held responsible.

Avoiding any risk of these deficits requires us to be driving a different conversation. We have to be simultaneously driving divergent conversations (of flying the plane) and convergent conversations (of fixing bulbs), all at the same time, as part of mastering the challenge of the "and." We have to be able to live in both of these modes simultaneously. In his 2001 book, *Reframing Business: When the Map Changes the Landscape*, Richard Normann puts it well:

"Every true renewal process takes place in stages (not necessarily sequential but often better described as modes of thinking and acting) characterized by the generation of new diversity and information, and then stages of reduction of it and focus on certain types of action. A successful organization must learn to live in both these modes.

Business and other Institutions today have to be very skilled at conceptualizing. Today's free flow of information needs to be transformed into *unique concepts and frameworks* which then focalize action. Action orientation and conceptual thinking are two sides of the same coin."

–Richard Normann, 2001, *Reframing Business: When the Map Changes the Landscape*

A successful organization must learn to live in both of these modes. We must learn some *"unique concepts and frameworks"* which are up to the challenge these days of helping you be in both modes at the same time as an "and" proposition. It's about thinking and acting, conceptualizing and focalizing, as two sides of the same coin. It's about working "in" and "on" your journey at the same time, divergently and convergently, linking and accumulating traction "ions," without any deficit disorders.

It's not surprising that this can be overwhelming for many managers, executives, and CEOs, who can get lost and defocused. As Justin Menkes reminded us in Chapter 2, when we were asking, "Why Executive Intelligence, Intuition and Resilience?", "Many people tend to get lost or defocused when addressing a complex issue... or navigating a complex situation." Our underlying intelligences of EQ and IQ get tested to the limit, insanely so. To stay sane and remain *In the Driving Seat* of things, not letting things be *In the Driving Seat* of us, driving us crazy, around the bend and up the wall, we need unique concepts and frameworks to help us navigate well.

Unique Concepts and Frameworks

That's what we are exploring progressively: unique concepts and frameworks which will help you navigate well. So far in our mindful process of integration, alignment and attunement, from gray matter to gray matter, we have explored the middle level in our new framework of understandings, strengths, and intelligences. Namely, understanding the anatomy of the journey and how it unfolds in real time; the Executive Intelligence, Intuition, and Resilience we need for this as a higher-order executive strength of journey orientation; and the underlying intelligences of EQ and IQ we need as a foundation for that strength.

Higher Order Executive Strengths of Journey-Orientation:

Understanding the Anatomy of Dynamic Complexity:

+ Execution Excellence .... **XQ** .... the anatomy of the **Vehicle** fit for the journey challenge.

+ Executive Intelligence, Intuition & Resilience .... **EQ (IQ)** .... the anatomy of the **Journey** and how it unfolds real-time.

Journey-ionics (Ji)

+ Path-Finding .... **PQ** .... the anatomy of the **Road** and paths of least resistance.

Bottom-line	XQ + EQ (IQ) + PQ = BQ (AQ)

= Organizational Agility .... **BQ (AQ)** .... the anatomy of **Breakthrough Leadership & Architecting Breakthrough Journeys.**

our ability to deal with rapidly changing circumstances, while out-executing our competition and stakeholder expectations (of customers, employees, suppliers and shareholders)

ordinary people achieving extraordinary things, making possible tomorrow, what seems impossible today

You now have a conceptual model for that level (the *Journey-ionics* model), and you can read more at www.mydrivingseat.com/booklinks booklink #14.

As we progress through the rest of the book, we will be exploring a conceptual model for each level in our framework (together with associated links and tools). We will understand how these integrate as a concept suite, model set, and toolbox, which is up to our challenge *In the Driving Seat* of organizational agility and being ready, willing, and able to fill our role fully in that seat.

We intentionally started with this middle level in our framework for reasons you now hopefully have a greater understanding of. This middle level can so easily be an oil slick in our mindful process of integration, alignment and attunement, from gray matter to gray matter, because we don't have a sufficiently microscopic, granular understanding of the anatomy of a journey, and how it unfolds in real time. It can easily cause huge wheel$pin in translating strategy and execution into traction, with a great deal getting lost in translation. The degree to which we have traction or wheel$pin with this middle level is a key determinant of which mode of organizational agility we will be in.

Three Modes of Organizational Agility

There are three modes of Organizational Agility, on a spectrum from postadaptive to preadaptive:

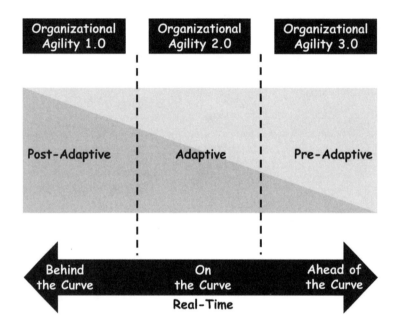

This might be a little counterintuitive. We might think that the words "adaptive" and "agility" are synonymous, as they are often used interchangeably. Therefore, we might easily think that there are only two modalities of organizational agility, "adaptive" and "non-adaptive," which are binary: We are either adaptive, or we aren't. In fact, that's not the point, as we always have to adapt eventually, one way or the other, and it's just a case of how long it takes us begrudgingly to come around to it. BP is adapting. Toyota is adapting. We adapted to get from the Wrong Hazelwood to the right Hazelwood. The aviation industry has adapted with new approaches, processes, and technologies for flight safety. The financial markets are adapting.

More to the point then, there are actually three modes of agility, depending upon whether we are adapting behind the curve, on the curve, or ahead of the curve. Let me explain.

- **Postadaptive**. If we are postadaptive, we are largely reactive. Things happen, and we react to them after the fact, behind the curve. We are constantly running to catch up with what just happened, reacting to it as best we can, postadaptively. We will call this postadaptive mode, "Organizational Agility 1.0." In martial arts, this is called "go no sen": Your opponent strikes, and you strike back with a counterattack.

- **Adaptive**. If we are doing better, we may be adaptive on more of a real time basis, reacting a lot quicker and being more proactive to be on the curve. We are keeping up, and we will call this adaptive mode "Organizational Agility 2.0." In martial arts, this is called "sen no sen": You know what your opponent is going to do from his or her movements in real time, and you strike simultaneously.

- **Preadaptive**. Now it gets a little trickier, as we consider what we mean by "preadaptive." Surely, keeping up with real time is as good as it gets, and we can't do any better than that, can we? How can we go beyond that, getting ahead of the curve and getting ahead of real time? In martial arts, this is called "sen sen no sen": Mysteriously, you sense what your opponent will do even before he or she does, and you prevent it.

When I ask audiences what we mean by "preadaptive," they typically respond with things like: "proactive and preemptive." To which I reply, "Yes, that's part of it, and more than that, what do we mean by preadaptive?" Now they will typically respond with things like: "vision, goal setting, and planning ahead". To which I reply, "Yes, that's also part of it, and *even* more than that, what do we mean by preadaptive?" Now they will typically try things like, "environmental scanning, scenario- thinking, and seeing-around-corners." They may even refer to our discussion of hindsight, insight, and foresight, from earlier in this chapter, calling out the foresight part. To which I reply, "Yes, that's also part of it, and *even* more than that, what do we mean by preadaptive?" Now I typically get blank stares. So what do we mean by preadaptive? Let's return to Charles Darwin's Theory of Evolution by Natural Selection.

> *"It is not the strongest of the species that survives,*
> *nor the most intelligent that survives.*
> *It is the one that is the most adaptable to change."*
>
> **–Charles Darwin**

Darwin became intrigued by the diversity of species he saw all around the world, which were highly suited to their local environment and yet clearly had shared origins. He wondered what process could explain this, and eventually, in 1859, he published his *Theory of Evolution by Natural Selection*, explaining:

> *"If variation be admitted to occur occasionally in some wild*
> *animals, and how can we doubt it when we see thousands of*
> *organisms. If we admit such variations tend to be hereditary,*
> *and how can we doubt it when we remember resemblances*
> *of features and character. If we admit selection is steadily*
> *at work, and who will doubt it when he considers amount*
> *of food on average fixed and reproductive powers act in*
> *geometrical ratio. If we admit that external conditions vary,*
> *as all geology proclaims they have done and are now doing.*
> *Then, if no law of nature be opposed, there must occasionally*
> *be formed races, different from parent races."*
>
> **–Charles Darwin**

"If variation be admitted to occur occasionally in some wild animals" and "there must occasionally be formed races, different from parent races." My translation: In other words, the core of the whole *Theory of Evolution by Natural Selection* is based upon nothing but... luck! Here's how it works. Within the genetic bandwidth of DNA variability, some are born on the lucky side of average, being a little bit stronger, a little bit faster, and a little bit more suited to their particular environment. Some are born on the unlucky side of average, being a little bit weaker, a little bit slower, and a little less suited to their environment. The lucky are more likely to get to the food first. Therefore, they are more likely to survive, reproduce, and spread their lucky DNA. The unlucky are less likely to survive and to reproduce, and their unlucky DNA dies off. And so the process continues, of species branching off into highly evolved variants, acutely aligned and attuned with their local environment, resulting in the diversity of species we see all around the world.

This is the process which we touched upon briefly in Chapter 2, from the book, *The Practice of Adaptive Leadership*, in which Ronald Heifetz, Alexander Grashow, and Marty Linsky talked about preserving, discarding, and creating DNA.

Thus, the whole *Theory of Evolution by Natural Selection* is based upon nothing but luck. So, being preadaptive is about being lucky. Usually, that's still a little uncomfortable for most people, so let's think more about that with some other reminders about luck:

• Supposedly, Napoleon Bonaparte, on being told the virtues of a new general (the man's heroism, bravery, skill in battle, and so on) waved his hand impatiently, saying, "That's all very well, but is he lucky?" Napoleon only wanted generals on his team who had a demonstrated track record of being lucky. He understood that luck is not as accidental as we might think. Did that Eastern Airlines crew have a track record of being lucky in that cockpit that evening? Do you have a track record of being lucky?

• "Luck is where preparation meets opportunity." Being lucky is about always being prepared, recognizing opportunity when it crosses your path, disguised as good luck. Blind luck? Nothing of the sort! We were prepared! If we hadn't been prepared we might not have recognized opportunity at all, or we might perceive a missed opportunity and a problem as bad luck. Did that Eastern Airlines crew experience bad luck in the cockpit that evening? Do you experience bad luck?

• "Chance favors the prepared mind." (Louis Pasteur)

• "Luck is not chance, it is toil." (Emily Dickinson)

• "I am a strong believer in luck and I find the harder I work the more I have of it." (Thomas Jefferson)

• "We have all had those perfect moments, when things come together in an almost unbelievable way, when events could never have been predicted, let alone controlled, remarkably seem to guide us along our path." (Joseph Jaworski, 1996, *Synchronicity: The Inner Path of Leadership*)

• "Many scientists and inventors, like artists and entrepreneurs, live in a paradoxical state of great confidence—knowing that their choices and actions really matter—and profound humility—feeling guided by forces beyond their making. Their work is to 'release the hand from the marble that holds it prisoner,' as Michelangelo put it. They know that their actions are vital to this accomplishment, but they also know that the hand 'wants to be released.'" Jonas Salk, the inventor of the polio vaccine, spoke of tapping into the continually unfolding "dynamism" of the universe and experiencing its evolution as "an active process that... I can guide by the choices I make." (Peter Senge, Joseph Jaworski, Otto Scharmer, Betty Sue Flowers, 2004, *Presence: Human Purpose and the Field of the Future*)

• "Luck exerts a dramatic influence over our lives. A few seconds of bad fortune can unravel years of striving, while a moment of good luck can lead to success and happiness. Luck has the power to transform the improbable into the possible; to make the difference between life and death, reward and ruin, happiness and despair." (Dr. Richard Wiseman, 2004, *The Luck Factor: The Four Essential Principles*). In this 10-year study of the beliefs and experiences of lucky and unlucky people, Dr. Wiseman discovered that good fortune is less about supernatural forces, and more about a positive attitude, and we can learn to be lucky.

So, being preadaptive is about being lucky, through toil, hard work, and preparation, tapping into the synchronicity of things for guidance on our path, the evolution of which we can influence by the choices we make, and learning to be lucky. In other words, luck doesn't happen just by accident. It is not by accident that the preadaptive are lucky, and the lucky are preadaptive. Rather than that old saying , "In business it's always better to be lucky than smart." I want you to be smart about luck.

That's what preadaptive Organizational Agility 3.0 is about, being smart about luck, and making more of our own luck. In his 2007 book, *The Future of Management*, Gary Hamel relates this to business and our organizational agility challenge, putting it this way:

> "Evolution occasionally equips organisms with apparently superfluous, reproductively neutral features that turn out, quite by accident, to be highly useful when conditions change. This is known as pre-adaptation.

> To be resilient, a company needs a lot of lightly scripted pre-adaptation—policies that give associates the chance to pre-adapt rather than react. Too much of what gets done in most companies is in response to some already

pressing issue; there's no slack, no space for improvisation, and no way to defend projects that aren't immediately useful. That's why so many companies end up on the wrong side of the change curve.

Your job as a management innovator is to make sure that the management systems in your company encourage strategic pre-adaptation."

–Gary Hamel, 2007, *The Future of Management*

To read more, visit: www.mydrivingseat.com/booklinks booklink #15

"Your job as a management innovator is to make sure that the management systems in your company encourage strategic pre adaptation." That's our job, to develop the "management systems" we need to achieve this level of Organizational Agility 3.0. In our mindful process of integration, alignment, and attunement, from gray matter to gray matter, it's about a new mindset, a new chassis of business acumen, and a new framework of understandings, strengths, and intelligences. Overall, as those come into integration, alignment, and attunement, it's about future-proofing our business.

Future-Proofing Our Business

Achieving this preadaptive mode of Organizational Agility 3.0 is about future-proofing our business. In business, evolution is about the surviving and thriving of those most ready, willing, and able to adapt, no matter what. No matter what the future brings, we will have the organizational agility to deal with it. No matter how the landscape shifts on us, we will be able to find a pathway through. Being preadaptive means we are lucky in never running out of options. We are lucky in always having some things in motion that allow us to steer our way through. We are lucky with coincidences of timing. Actually, we make our own luck by being preadaptive. It is not by accident that the preadaptive are lucky, and the lucky are preadaptive.

As we have been discussing so far, and will continue discussing throughout this book, developing preadaptive organizational agility is about changing our relationship with luck and some other key attributes of agility (see chart on the next page).

When there is less and less we can count on these days with any certainty, we must be able to count more and more on our agility to cope, no matter what. As we do so, we become more and more future-proofed, success becomes more and more inevitable, no matter what, and we become more and more certain to win, no matter what.

Attribute of Agility	Post-Adaptive	Adaptive	Pre-Adaptive
Changing our relationship with... **OODA Loops**	Large, lethargic, somewhat open-loop OODA Loops	Shrinking our organizational OODA Loop	Vibrant, interconnected OODA Loops
Changing our relationship with... **Change Leadership & Management**	Putting It Right/ Correction/ Intervention After the Fact	Making It Right/ Adjustment/ Intervention During the Fact	Getting It Right/ Assurance/ Intervention Before the Fact
Changing our relationship with... **Risk/Stress/ Hope/Belief**	Human-Doing Hopeless Belief Unbalance		Human-Being Hopeful Belief Balance
Changing our relationship with... **Time**	Not Having Time/ Gridlock/Constant Whitewater/ Just-too-Late	Finding Time at the Expense of Other Things/Just-in-Time some of the time	Making Time/In the Flow/Just in Time, most of the time
Changing our relationship with... **Learning**	Learning From Hindsight (what just happened/in the past?)/Single loop Learning	Learning From Insight (what is happening now/in the present)/ Double Loop Learning	Learning From Foresight (what might happen next/in the future?)/ Triple Loop Learning
Changing our relationship with... **Uncertainty, Volatility & Turbulence**	Problems Focus/ Downside Risks Mitigation/ Contingency Planning/ Pessimism/Fear	Inconvenience	Opportunities Focus/Upside Rewards Maximization/ Fortuity Planning/ Optimism/Hope
Changing our relationship with... **Breakthrough Journeys**	Breaking down/ Between a Rock and a Hard Place/ Catch-22/ Grid-Lock	Breaking-out	Breaking-in/ Breaking-Through/ Architecting Breakthrough Journeys
Changing our relationship with... **Luck**	Unlucky/ Out-of-Luck/ Bad Luck/ Murphy's Law	Serendipity	Lucky/Making Our Own Luck/Trusting Luck as a Real, Predictable Factor
Changing our relationship with... **"The Power Curve"**	Behind the Power Curve/Running to Catch up/Off the Pace	On the Power Curve/ Keeping the Pace	Ahead of the Power Curve/ Setting the Pace
Changing our relationship with... **Focus**	The Parts/Static/ Detail Complexity/ "or" mindset	The Whole/ Dynamic Complexity	The Longitudinal Dimension of Journey Orientation/ 3-D Glasses
The Bottom-Line	**Organizational Agility 1.0**	**Organizational Agility 2.0**	**Organizational Agility 3.0**

Of course, at any moment in time, the reality is that any organization is invariably a mixed bag of the three modes of organizational agility, postadaptive 1.0, adaptive 2., and preadaptive 3.0, in their different facets, processes, departments, or other aspects. The challenge is to overcome traditional approaches and adopt more preadaptive, agile methods, behaviors, and processes. A good example to think about is the process of software development and the evolution to a new, more agile approach called "Agile Software Development."

Think "Agile Software Development"

A great example comes from the field of software development and the emergence of the new paradigm of "Agile Software Development." Let's explore that further:

Agile Software Development is:

• A software development approach based upon the iterative development of requirements and solutions, in a collaborative environment of self-organizing, cross-functional teams.

• A disciplined project management process of frequent inspection and adaptation; teamwork, self-organization and accountability; rapid development and delivery of high-quality software, aligned with customer needs and company goals.

• The evolution of the software product is broken into small incremental iterations ("timeboxes"), typically lasting between one and four weeks.

• Each iteration is worked on by a team, through a full development cycle, to produce an integrated, quality product, available for release (which may or may not be released, depending upon the release strategy), emphasizing working software as the primary measure of progress (as opposed to documentation).

• Teams are cross-functional, self-organizing, and autonomous from existing organizational hierarchies, often co-located in an open-plan, "skunk-works" kind of environment, facilitating real time, on-line-all-the-time, face-to-face communications.

• In addition, teams will use a routine and formal daily face-to-face meeting to stay in sync with one another.

As a result, products are able to be adapted quickly to rapidly changing circumstances, with the agility to sustain relevance, timeliness, and alignment with customer needs and company goals.

Contrast this with the traditional "waterfall" method of software development:

- A strict, pre-planned sequence of: Requirements Capture, Analysis, Design, Coding, and Testing.

- An inflexible division of a project into separate stages, so that commitments are made early on, and it is difficult to react to changes in requirements and iterations are expensive.

- Seen as a heavyweight, bureaucratic, and slow approach, it is inconsistent with the way software developers actually perform effective work.

It's not that the "waterfall" method is wrong. It has its place in circumstances that are more predictable and unchanging. It is unsuitable, however, if requirements are not well understood or are likely to change in the course of the project due to more dynamic circumstances (which have become increasingly prevalent; hence, the emergence of more agile methods).

To read more, visit: www.mydrivingseat.com/booklinks booklink #16

This new paradigm has helped the field of software development shift toward the preadaptive end of the spectrum, by dealing in agility as an "and-deal," not an "or-deal." Agile software development masters the challenge of the "and," as we reviewed in Chapter 3, by navigating a middle road of being not too tight and not too loose, not too structured and not too unstructured, not too ordered and not too chaotic, not too controlled and not too uncontrolled, not overplanned and not underplanned. All at the same time, as a paradoxical blend of both ends of the spectrum. Like a modern jet fighter approach to software development, as an "and-deal," not an "or-deal," and with the shrinking OODA Loop of a fighter pilot.

And yet, can you imagine how vehemently someone could argue against an agile software development approach and for a traditional "waterfall" approach to software development. That person would probably base an argument on not losing control, the need to have a definitive A to Z plan, and the criticality of fully detailing out the specification, budget, and timeline. That person would be exhibiting that his or her relationship with the attributes of agility is stuck in a 1.0 mode or, at best, a 2.0 mode. We must change our relationship with the attributes of agility to get into a 3.0 mode.

In the next chapter, we will help you begin to think "agile software development" for the "software" of organizational agility and the different organizational modules that generate agility. Before that, let's finish this chapter by exploring our changing relationship with another of the key attributes of agility: focus.

The Hocus Pocus of Focus

Not least of all, to develop preadaptive organizational agility, our relationship with focus has to change. In my experience, this can be a very tricky thing for many CEOs, executives, and managers because it is at the heart of the challenge.

I distinctly remember one time, when I was facilitating the management team at one of the businesses I was responsible for. We were exploring the full range of systemic issues, challenges, problems, and opportunities that were confronting us and testing our organizational agility. It was a very complex situation and landscape to navigate, which had proven to be largely intractable. We had been spinning our wheels and were looking to brew a breakthrough to get back into traction.

During lunch, the technical vice president asked me, with what I sensed was a somewhat condescending tone, "Which parts of this problem should we focus on?" I paused, looked him right in the eye, and said, "All of them." He promptly broke out laughing and, in an even more condescending way, explained that I clearly didn't understand the concept of focus!

That's my point exactly. In my experience, most people's relationship with focus is about isolating parts of the problem to work on, at the expense of the whole. The parts they typically choose are the most clear and present dangers:

- **Clear** at a tactical level, not abstract at a more strategic level (i.e., something tactical they can get into action on).

- **Present** right in front of them, in the moment, not something which may or may not be further down the path in the future (i.e., if they fix today's problems, tomorrow will take care of itself).

- **Dangers** such as things that are broken that need to be fixed (i.e., if it isn't broken, don't fix it) or goals that need to be achieved, and they are in danger of not achieving if they don't get super focused.

Exactly! That's the stupid simplicity of "fixing the bulb" and not "flying the plane." Remember our Eastern Airlines story: The malfunctioning bulb was a clear and present danger, and fixing it was the crew's number one goal in their sequence of goals. Fixing the bulb hijacked the crew's focus into too much of an "or" mode and not sufficiently an "and" mode. Organizational agility became an "or-deal," not an "and-deal."

As an "and-deal," our focus must remain inclusive of "fixing bulbs" and "flying the plane." If it becomes too much of an "or-deal," exclusive either way around (too much fixing bulbs and not enough flying the plane or too much flying the plane and not enough fixing bulbs), we can get into trouble. We lapse into a more postadaptive mode of organizational agility, we invite bad luck into the equation, and we are at risk of getting into big trouble. Organizational agility becomes an ordeal.

To stay in a preadaptive mode of organizational agility as an "and-deal," inviting good luck into the equation, our relationship with focus has to change. It has to be about everything we have been exploring in this chapter. That's a challenging equation. It's verging on magical when we experience a person or a team or an organization which is progressively mastering it. They are in the zone, in the flow of things. It's a kind of hocus pocus and we are progressively demystifying it.

The magic wand to demystify it is a shift of mindset to a focus on the journey and the longitudinal dimension of journey orientation. That is the primary, organizing dimension in our mindful process of integration, alignment and attunement, from gray matter to gray matter, tapping into the natural alignment with that of our corpus callosum.

Traction between the rubber and the road is the net result of that end to end process, linking and accumulating individual thoughts, questions, decisions, and actions, divergently and convergently, without any deficit disorders, as the traction "ions" of our journey, in that longitudinal dimension.

Even more than ever before, for organizational agility, focus has become a longitudinal, journey-oriented phenomenon. With wave after wave of dynamic complexity washing over us, being *In the Driving Seat* of organizational agility has evolved into a three dimensional challenge. Our focus must shift from just the static plane of thinking, predominated by detail complexity and the parts, to the dynamic plane of thinking, predominated by dynamic complexity and the whole.

We are progressively exploring these three dimensions, to help you see them as clearly as you need to. In effect, we have been helping you put on 3-D glasses to see the 3-D challenge fully. The emergence of 3-D movies and 3-D TV reminds us to regain a true 3-D perspective for our new leadership and management challenge, *In the Driving Seat* of our businesses, just like we have *In the Driving Seat* of our cars, for which we need to put on our 3 D glasses.

Putting on Our 3-D Glasses

If we watch a 3-D movie without 3-D glasses, we will miss the acuteness of the third dimension. When the dragon swings its head and the whole audience ducks, gasping in unison, we will just see a blurry image on the screen and wonder what all the fuss is about. We will be left wondering what just happened and what did we miss?

In the Driving Seat of organizational agility, the third and longitudinal dimension of journey orientation has emerged, not just as a third dimension, but as the primary dimension around which we must reframe our approach to translating strategy and execution into traction. In other words, we are now participating in a 3-D movie and, if we are watching a 3-D movie without wearing our 3-D glasses, we will miss the acuteness of the third dimension. We must put on our 3-D glasses, to see the three dimensions of our challenge fully.

BONUS

http://bit.ly/oKzo4Z

Leadership and management are a three-dimensional challenge. They always have been and always will be. But many managers, executives, and CEOs are stuck in a two-dimensional mindset. Our education, training, and development systems tend to reduce things into 2-D. Just pick up any business book, and more than likely it will be full of 2-D flow charts, models, and frameworks, majoring in the detail complexity of the static plane of thinking, dominated by our left brain.

How we see is how we think. When we put on our 3-D glasses, we see the three dimensions of the challenge, and we tap into the power of our opposable mind and integrative thinking, with a whole brained approach. Through one lens, we get our left brain in the game, focused on detail complexity. Through the other lens, we get our right brain in the game, focused on dynamic complexity. Right down the middle, in alignment with the longitudinal dimension of journey orientation, our corpus callosum facilitates the process of integrative thinking and taps into the power of our opposable mind and whole brain, for our unfolding journey. To read more, visit: www.mydrivingseat.com/booklinks booklink #17.

In my experience, many CEOs, executives, and managers these days are not wearing their 3-D glasses, for what has become a 3-D movie. As a result, they don't see and understand the third dimension of journey orientation as well as they should, and they don't understand how acutely dynamic complexity is coming at us, thicker and faster, in the longitudinal dimension of the journey, and is *In the Driving Seat* of things. It is driving chaos, frustration, and stress, with all kinds of financial and nonfinancial consequences. Time and again, they are left wondering, what just happened and what did we miss? Part of the problem is that we have always tended to simplify our 3-D world of business, leadership, and management into a 2-D representation and mindset, in the static plane of thinking, dominated by detail complexity. With wave after wave of dynamic complexity washing over us, this has become an oversimplification. Stupid simple. The Keep It Simple, Stupid, KISS of death.

Of course, when we are in a turnaround situation or a startup, this is abundantly clear, as we only have so much financial runway to play with, and we have to get off the ground before we run off the end. We implicitly have our 3-D glasses on, with an acute orientation to the longitudinal dimension of our journey, the amount of runway we have left, the accelerating speed we are developing, and the lift we are beginning to experience. We are also thinking about the big picture whole of our business, not least of all in terms of the brand we are building or protecting and the positioning of our value proposition for the profitability we are building or protecting. We are also thinking about the small picture parts of our business, not least of all the organizational, process, and product components we need to build in the next phase or we will have to figure out how to live without in the next phase. We need our 3-D glasses to see the detail complexity and the dynamic complexity of the challenge.

I am on the board of an aerospace startup called VerTechs, providing paradigm shifting sandwich metal technologies for high temperature applications, in particular as part of the exhaust system for jet engines. In many ways, these technologies are a replacement for titanium, without the temperature, cost, and manufacturing process constraints of that material, while meeting or beating the low weight and high strength requirements. Not surprisingly, we are generating great interest from the big engine and aircraft manufacturers, not least of all GE and Boeing. We have our 3-D glasses on and are working all three dimensions of being *In the Driving Seat* of our journey simultaneously, mastering detail complexity and dynamic complexity, day to day, week to week, month to month, quarter to quarter, and year to year. We are in year three and are shifting up into a next gear of traction, anticipating that we will be moving from static testing to dynamic testing of prototype applications on some big programs.

In a meeting with Boeing only a few weeks ago, we were discussing the progression of a potential program through static testing (of simulated components in an environmentally controlled, simulated system) to dynamic testing (of real components in an uncontrolled, real world environment and system, or as close as we can get to that). It will be the same progression for the journey of the business, being subjected to increasing dynamic testing. As we evolve and grow during the coming months, quarters, and years, dynamic complexity will test our agility in an increasingly uncontrolled, real world environment and business system. We will need our 3-D glasses more and more.

That's what the first four chapters of this book have been about, bringing us to this point—embedding all of the complexity we have been through into the elegant simplicity of putting on our 3 D glasses for the 3-D movie we are now participating in, to see and think differently about the challenge of being *In the Driving Seat.*

That's the hocus pocus of focus and the beginning of our mindful process of integration, alignment and attunement, from gray matter to gray matter. In the next chapter, we continue this process mindful of where we need to be focusing our efforts for organizational agility and for avoiding any deficit disorders.

Chapter 4 Summary

To future proof our business, we must put on our 3-D glasses to see the whole problem of the three-dimensional challenge, adopting a new mindset and changing our relationship with key attributes of our business. Not least of all, we must change our relationship with focus, which has become a longitudinal, journey-oriented phenomenon, understanding how we link and accumulate the traction "ions" of a journey at a microscopic, granular level. Now it has become clear to you why our chapter summaries take the form they take, to help you take the inspiration from the book and add some traction "ions" into your linking and accumulating journey.

Things to Think About

◆ *Think about* your experience of the real time nature of your journey as a business.

◆ *Think about* your organizational OODA Loop, fast-cycle teamwork, and the attention deficit disorders you experience.

◆ *Think about* the mode of organizational agility you are in—post adaptive 1.0, adaptive 2.0, and preadaptive 3.0.

Questions to Ponder

◆ *Ask yourself* what size your organizational OODA Loop is and to what degree it is a somewhat open loop?

◆ *Ask yourself* how can you massively shrink your organizational OODA Loop and rev up your fast cycle teamwork?

◆ *Ask yourself* which of your business processes and management processes can be transitioned to a more agile approach (like Agile Software Development versus Traditional "Waterfall" Software Development)?

Decisions to Make

◆ *Decide* to be productively paranoid.

◆ *Decide* to put on your 3-D glasses.

◆ *Decide* to shift your relationship with key aspects of your business, not least of all focus.

Actions to Take

◆ *Notice* where, when, and how you are suffering deficit disorders and begin pointing them out.

Where Does Organizational Agility Come From?

"The ability to be successful, relaxed, and in control during these fertile but turbulent times demands new ways of thinking and working. There is a great need for new methods, technologies, and work habits to help us get on top of our world. The old models and habits are insufficient."

–David Allen

Can You Trust Your System? That's the question David Allen asks in his 2001 book, *Getting Things Done: The Art of Stress Free Productivity*. He explains that we must have a system that our subconscious mind trusts. If our subconscious mind doesn't trust our system, then we leave our mind no choice but to keep working on loose ends, commitments, and incompletes. As a result, these things remain on our mind, our mind isn't clear, and anxiety, stress, and a sense of losing control start to build up.

This sets in motion a self-fulfilling and self-defeating prophecy, vicious cycle, and downward spiral of declining productivity. This can easily spiral down into a state of being overwhelmed and the postadaptive whitewater of a constant stream of crises. We lurch from one crisis to the next. We are just hanging on tight for dear life, going with the flow, and success is defined as making it to the bottom of the whitewater rapids, with the raft still the right way up and not inadvertently losing anyone off the back!

The trouble is, with wave after wave of dynamic complexity washing over us these days, of increasing turbulence, uncertainty, and volatility, we rarely get much respite of calm water before, right around the next corner, comes the next set of white-water rapids! Things are coming at us so thick and fast these days that life becomes like a constant whitewater ride! We aren't driving things preadaptively; things are driving us postadaptively!

Constant whitewater becomes a way of life. It also becomes the mother of all excuses. We were planning to tackle that strategic initiative we committed to, but then this other crisis happened, so we didn't have time. We also don't have time to attend the meetings we should be attending, or be improving the systems and processes we should be improving, or getting ourselves more organized as we should be doing. It's a catch-22, of being so busy working "in" the business that we don't have time to be working "on" the business. We are so busy fixing bulbs we don't have time to be flying the plane!

We become gridlocked. Between a rock and a hard place. Locked up in jail. Surrounded by brick walls, we can easily end up serving a life sentence, thinking that this is just the way life is. There's no way out. We all know individuals, teams, and organizations stuck in this whitewater, postadaptive mode of organizational agility. With wave after wave of dynamic complexity washing over them these days, they haven't been developing their system to cope and whitewater has taken over.

As we have been exploring, the nature of work has changed, and they haven't been changing with it. David Allen puts it well:

> "A major factor in the mounting stress level is that the actual nature of our jobs has changed much more dramatically and rapidly than have our training for and our ability to deal with work. In the old days, work was self evident. Now, for many of us, there are no edges to most of our projects. The organizations we are involved with seem to be in constant morph mode, with ever changing goals, products, partners, customers, markets, technologies and owners. These all, by necessity, shake up structures, forms, roles and responsibilities.
>
> It is possible for a person to have an overwhelming number of things to do and still function productively with a clear head and a positive sense of relaxed control. That's a great way to live and work, at elevated levels of effectiveness and efficiency. It's also becoming a critical operational style required of successful and high performance professionals. You already know how to do everything necessary to achieve this high performance state. If you are like most people, however, you need to apply these skills in a more timely, complete and systematic way so you can get on top of it all instead of feeling buried."
>
> –David Allen, 2001, *Getting Things Done:*
> *The Art of Stress Free Productivity*

It is possible! "It is possible for a person to have an overwhelming number of things to do and still function productively with a clear head and a positive sense of relaxed control." In my experience, many managers, executives, and CEOs hold the opposite belief, as part of their inner world/journey, that it is *impossible*! With an overwhelming number of things to do, it is *impossible* to function productively with a clear head and a positive sense of relaxed control.

Holding that belief as part of our inner world/journey influences our behaviors of thinking, questioning, decision making, and action taking, and the results we get in our outer world/journey. When we hold the belief that it is impossible, we probably have more thoughts about getting by in this mode than getting out of this mode. We probably ask more questions about surviving in the present than thriving in the future. We probably make more decisions about prioritizing the urgent rather than the important. We probably take more actions about correcting the crisis we are in rather than preventing the next one, which is already taking shape around the next corner. As a result, the next crisis comes. And the next, and the next, and the next!

Then, our belief system gets reinforced in a "see, I told you so" kind of way. Constant whitewater and there's no way out of it! That's just the way it is! When we link and accumulate the traction "ions" of our journey like that, influenced by our belief system, it's a self-fulfilling and self-defeating prophecy, vicious cycle, and downward spiral! We are unaware of the deficit disorders we are suffering. Deficits of intention (things could be different if only I had more intention about things), attention (things could be different if only I paid more attention to some other things), and responsibility for results (things could be different if I took full responsibility for my own reality which I create and sustain). Accumulating more and more "see, I told you so" evidence, we pour cement around our belief system that this is just the way it is, and, over time, it becomes fossilized in place. We end up resigned to our fate, in jail, serving a life sentence.

But, we can launch a jailbreak! We can break out! We need to break the pattern of the vicious cycle and downward spiral, getting onto a virtuous cycle and upward spiral instead. It starts with recognizing that the nature of our work has evolved and we need to evolve with it. As David Allen says above, "A major factor in the mounting stress level is that the actual nature of our jobs has changed much more dramatically and rapidly than have our training for and our ability to deal with work." We need a new system, which our subconscious mind can trust, of new habits of thinking and work, aligned and attuned with the challenge of dynamic complexity. That's what our mindful process of integration, alignment and attunement, from gray matter to gray matter, is all about. We are integrating, aligning and attuning everything with the longitudinal dimension of journey orientation, for the new habits of thinking and work we need these days, from gray matter to gray matter, to have the agility we need to deal with the challenge of dynamic complexity.

As we progress downward toward the gray matter of the asphalt, we experience the benefits progressing back upward toward the gray matter of our brains. Our subconscious mind relaxes with less anxiety and stress. We have a clear head and a positive sense of relaxed control. We begin to experience that elevated level of efficiency, effectiveness, and productivity. Despite the increasingly frenetic speed of business, pace of change, and volatility, uncertainty, and turbulence of our outer world/journey, we experience the increasingly peaceful and calm composure of our inner world/journey.

From our new mindset and our new chassis of business acumen, we are progressing down to the gray matter of the asphalt, via our new framework of strengths, understandings, and intelligences. We are providing new models, methods, and tools as we go. We started by exploring the middle level of our new framework with our new model for the anatomy of a journey and how it unfolds in real time. We explored the journey-oriented, higher-order executive strength of Executive Intelligence, Intuition, and Resilience required, the associated model of *Journey-ionics*, and the underlying intelligences of EQ and IQ, which are the foundation of that strength.

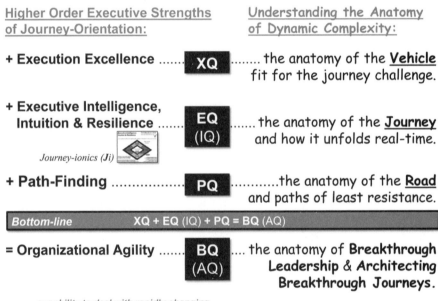

Higher Order Executive Strengths of Journey-Orientation:

Understanding the Anatomy of Dynamic Complexity:

+ Execution Excellence .... **XQ** .... the anatomy of the **Vehicle** fit for the journey challenge.

+ Executive Intelligence, Intuition & Resilience .... **EQ (IQ)** ...... the anatomy of the **Journey** and how it unfolds real-time.

Journey-ionics (Ji)

+ Path-Finding .... **PQ** ....the anatomy of the **Road** and paths of least resistance.

Bottom-line   XQ + EQ (IQ) + PQ = BQ (AQ)

= Organizational Agility .... **BQ (AQ)** .... the anatomy of **Breakthrough Leadership & Architecting Breakthrough Journeys.**

our ability to deal with rapidly changing circumstances, while out-executing our competition and stakeholder expectations (of customers, employees, suppliers and shareholders)

ordinary people achieving extraordinary things, making possible tomorrow, what seems impossible today

We started with this middle level as it is at the core of what David Allen refers to as the changing nature of work and the new habits of thinking and work which we need. The nature of work has evolved, and, if we aren't evolving with it, this middle level can easily become an oil slick in our end-to-end process of integration, alignment and attunement for translating strategy and execution into traction.

Our *Journey-ionics* model helps us think about work in new ways, aligned and attuned with our challenge. Work has become the unfolding flow of a real time journey, at a microscopic, granular level, and this model helps us understand how any deficits of attention, intention, or responsibility for results allow that flow to spiral downward, into a state of constant whitewater. We feel buried, overwhelmed, and things are driving us crazy.

We need a system that can cope with this flow, breaking the pattern of the self-defeating and self-fulfilling prophecy, vicious cycle, and downward spiral, setting in motion a self-fulfilling, virtuous cycle and upward spiral instead. We can get out of whitewater, claw our way back up onto dry land, and climb our way back *In the Driving Seat*, with us driving things, not things driving us. We can get out of a postadaptive mode and into a preadaptive mode of organizational agility.

Where does the organizational agility come from to do that? It comes from a system you can trust to cope with the flow, addressing the whole challenge, the whole problem, and the whole solution of being *In the Driving Seat* of your business. Developing that trusted system allows you to "have an overwhelming number of things to do and still function productively with a clear head and a positive sense of relaxed control," individually as a CEO, executive, or manager, and collectively as team and as an organization. It is possible!

The first few go rounds of a downward spiral and descent can often happen imperceptibly, like in our Eastern Airlines story. Likewise, the first few go rounds of an upward spiral and ascent can be equally imperceptible, like in our discussion of the journey to mastery. We have to plod along, practicing new components of a system, which we progressively implant into our whitewater flow of work, as a new chassis of business acumen for mastering the whole challenge, the whole problem, and the whole solution. We have to plod along on the plateau with no expectations of immediate breakthrough results, but, imperceptibly at first, beneath the surface, we are brewing a breakthrough. If we stick with it, it will surface as an inflection point of an ascent to a next level. And so the process and journey to mastery continues.

The rest of this book is devoted to helping you do that. In this chapter, we will look at the two other levels in our new framework of understandings, strengths, and intelligences, adding an associated model for each level. In Chapter 6, we will look at how to develop all three levels of our framework. In Chapter 7, we will look at how these three levels add up to the bottom line understandings we need. We will understand the anatomy of breakthrough leadership and who we need to be as breakthrough leaders in architecting breakthrough journeys. We will understand the journey-oriented, higher-order executive strength of organizational agility required and the underlying business intelligence and adversity quotient that are the foundation of this strength. First, we will start with the top level of our new framework: Execution Excellence.

Execution Excellence: Missing in Action?

When we asked "Why Execution Excellence?" in Chapter 2, remember what Larry Bossidy and Ram Charran said in their book, *Execution: The Discipline of Getting Things Done*. They said, *"For all the talk about execution, hardly anybody knows what it is. They don't have the foggiest idea of what it means to execute."* That's my experience, too! Many managers, executives, and CEOs don't have the foggiest idea what execution really is, although they might think they do.

In my experience, execution excellence is often missing in action! We are so mired in action that a unifying architecture of execution excellence is missing. It feels good to be busy, but we can so easily be "busy fools" if an architecture for execution excellence is missing in the busyness of that action. Are we doing busyness or business? Here's a recap of what Larry Bossidy and Ram Charran said about execution:

• "Execution is not just tactics—it is a discipline and a system." In my experience, many managers, executives, and CEOs aren't wearing their 3-D glasses, for what has become a 3-D movie in which they are participating. Consequently, they just see execution as tactics—just details to be taken care of—just detail complexity. They don't sufficiently also see it as the dynamic complexity of a discipline and a system. We must be wearing our 3-D glasses, to see and think about execution as an "and" proposition of both—detail complexity and dynamic complexity.

• "Execution hasn't yet been recognized or taught as a discipline, whereas other disciplines have no shortage of accumulated knowledge, tools and techniques." This is the void we reviewed in Chapter 1—a void of knowledge, tools, and techniques, which we are setting out to fill with this book and the associated online resources.

- "The leader who executes assembles an architecture of execution." That's what our model of Execution Excellence will provide, an overall architecture. The word *architecture* itself reinforces our need to be wearing our 3-D glasses, leveraging the science of our left brain and the art of our right brain. We need both for an architecture of execution—art and science.

Our goal here is to understand the whole problem and the whole solution of execution as a discipline and a system. This includes helping you assemble an architecture of execution, addressing the whole challenge of being *In the Driving Seat* of the organizational agility you need these days. As I described in Chapter 1, this is at the heart of the void we are filling with this book, recognizing and teaching execution as a discipline of accumulating knowledge, tools, and techniques.

In my experience, the minority of CEOs, executives, and managers, for whom execution is not missing in action, have an X factor. They are wearing their 3-D glasses, and they get it! They have an X-factor of eXecution. They have an underlying intelligence for execution, which we have called "XQ" in our framework of understandings, strengths, and intelligences. They understand the anatomy of dynamic complexity and the architecture of execution they need as a vehicle that is fit for the journey challenge we face these days. They have developed the journey-oriented, higher order strength of Execution Excellence. This chapter will help you understand how to join that minority.

In our mindful process of integration, alignment, and attunement, from gray matter to gray matter, Execution Excellence is also the master, unifying model, integrating the other models, which will become clear. The Execution Excellence model lives in the dynamic plane of thinking and the longitudinal dimension of journey orientation.

The Execution Excellence model is our journey-oriented window into the whole challenge, the whole problem, and the whole solution of being *In the Driving Seat* of Organizational Agility. Starting with our corpus callosum, this longitudinal alignment engages our left brain and right brain in our Execution Excellence agenda, in a whole-brained way, wearing our 3-D glasses, tapping into the power of our opposable mind and integrative thinking. So let's begin taking a look at our Execution Excellence agenda.

Execution Excellence

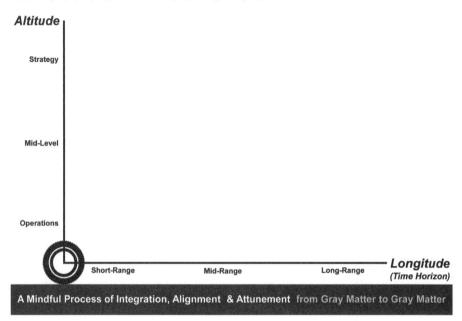

As our journey-oriented window into the whole challenge, the whole problem, and the whole solution of being *In the Driving Seat*, our Execution Excellence agenda is at the intersection of two of the three dimensions of the void which we are filling:

- **Altitude:** from strategy to operations

- **Longitude (Time Horizon):** from short-range to long-range

Our Execution Excellence agenda lives inside these two dimensions, subdivided into three time horizons and three altitudes, which we must attend to simultaneously.

As an example, think about Airbus Industries in Europe and Boeing Commercial Airplanes Group, who are fighting it out right now for market share with the next wide-body airliner, Boeing with its 787 and Airbus with its A380. In December 2009 Boeing finally had its first flight, after repeated delays, and is now heavily into flight qualification testing. Airbus, who also suffered delays, is a few years ahead, having started flight testing after its first flight in 2005 and entering into airline service in 2009. Both are competing aggressively for orders from launch customers, to begin to get a payback on their huge investment in the development of these products. When I got into aerospace in 1990, these aircraft were already on the drawing board, at least conceptually and as advanced research and development programs. So the companies have been working on them for 15–20 years already and have been pumping billions of dollars into product development. That's all they are, just products, which airlines either buy or they don't!

So think about it: How far out do you think they have to look to be able to pencil out a return on investment payback equation on that level of product development investment? What do you think? Probably another 25–30 years. That's 15–20 years already and probably another 25–30 years to go. Let's call it 45 years in total! That is the longitudinal time horizon for these product strategy and investment decisions, on the horizontal axis of our Execution Excellence agenda model.

On the vertical axis of our agenda model, what kind of altitude of strategic issues are Boeing and Airbus having to think up to, across a time horizon of 45 years? What do you think? No doubt, they have to think about things like:

• Global demographics, travel patterns, major city pairs airlines want to be flying between

• Global politics, terrorism, and environmental factors

• Technology trends, oil prices, alternative fuels, and airline economics

• …among many, many others

Inside this Execution Excellence agenda model, at the intersection of these two dimensions, Boeing and Airbus must drive their strategy conversation up to that altitude of strategic issues on the vertical axis and across a longitudinal time horizon of 45 years on the horizontal axis.

Execution Excellence

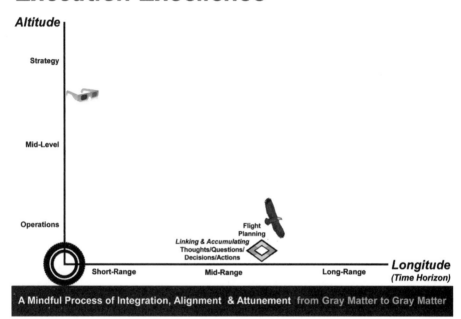

They must be flying around inside this agenda, spending the right time, in the right place, at the right time, linking and accumulating the traction "ions" of their journey (individual thoughts, questions, decisions, and actions). They must be wearing their 3-D glasses to have their whole brain in the game, mastering detail complexity and dynamic complexity, tapping into their opposable mind and integrative thinking. They must be doing all of this without any deficit disorders, to avoid Wrong Hazelwoods and Eastern Airlines scenarios!

Faced with such complexity, uncertainty, and ambiguity, what is the worst thing that can happen? Nothing! Analysis paralysis sets in. It becomes a talking shop. Things get bogged down in thinking and questions, followed by decisions and actions only about things like more research and analysis, followed by more thinking and more questions, followed by more research and analysis. And so on, and so on, and so on.

Faced with such high stakes decisions and consequences, with such little data and information, it would be easy to become paralyzed by such complexity, uncertainty, and ambiguity. We have probably all experienced this in our own businesses, in some way, shape, or form.

BONUS

http://bit.ly/omYhZ4

Suppose that Boeing or Airbus is just 1% better than the other at shaping up their conversation inside this agenda. One percent better at linking and accumulating the traction "ions" of their journey, without deficit disorders, translating strategy and execution into traction. One percent better at having the organizational agility to deal with whatever happens, no matter what.

Just 1% better and they are winning! Remember what Albert Einstein said, from Chapter 1, that *"the most powerful force in the universe is compound interest."* Compounded across a time horizon of 45 years, 1% accumulates into a huge difference! A huge win in terms of a more successful program, higher market share, and increased financial returns. For the other, a huge loss in terms of a less successful program, lower market share, and reduced financial returns. Maybe the difference between an accretive return on investment for one and a dilutive return on investment for the other. So one ends up spiraling upward, and the other is spiraling downward.

As another example, let's return to thinking about our jet fighter pilot and plane. A dogfight might last around 45 seconds. That's the longitudinal time horizon for a jet fighter pilot heading into a dogfight, on the horizontal axis of our Execution Excellence agenda model.

On the vertical axis of our agenda model, across that time horizon of 45 seconds, the altitude of strategic issues for a fighter pilot is things like radar scope, spatial awareness, how much fuel have I got left, and how much longer can I stay in the fight? The operational issues are things like the stick, throttle, weapon selection, and where's my wingman?

Inside this Execution Excellence agenda model, at the intersection of these two dimensions, fighter pilots have to link and accumulate their individual thoughts, questions, decisions, and actions (around and around their OODA Loops) into the traction "ions" of their journey. Suppose one pilot is just 1% better than the other, with a 1% smaller and faster OODA Loop. Compounded across a time horizon of 45 seconds, that accumulates into a huge difference, and the end is in sight for the other. In a real situation, with life and death consequences!

So let's consider these two examples: 45 years and that altitude of strategic issues for Boeing and Airbus, and 45 seconds and that altitude of strategic issues for our fighter pilot. My guess is that your business is somewhere in between those two extremes. Am I right? My point is that the axes of this framework can expand and contract to cope with whatever scaling is right for your business. It's all relative. So think about your business:

- **What are the time horizons of your business?**
    ◦ Long range? (maybe 3–5 years, 5–10 years, or more?)
    ◦ Medium range? (maybe 6–18 months, or more?)
    ◦ Short range? (maybe 1–3 months, or more?)

- **What altitude of strategic things do you need to think up to?**
    ◦ Environmental trends?
    ◦ Competitive forces?
    ◦ Product development, product management, and product strategy?

Whatever are the right scales for these axes of our business, this framework represents our agenda as an executive. We must attend to this whole agenda, without any deficit disorders of attention, intention, and responsibility for results. We must be flight planning our bandwidth inside of this agenda model, flying around and spending the right time, in the right place, at the right time, in the right whole-brained manner, wearing our 3-D glasses.

In other words, whether we are Boeing and Airbus or you and your business, we must be establishing our OODA Loop, strengthening our OODA Loop as more closed loop, and speeding up and shrinking our OODA Loop, just like our fighter pilot.

Execution Excellence

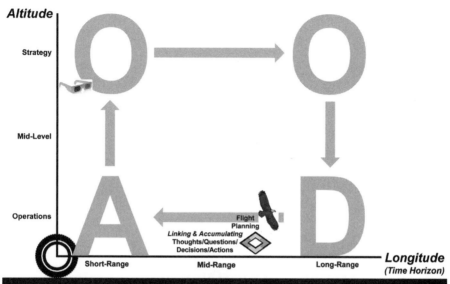

A Mindful Process of Integration, Alignment & Attunement from Gray Matter to Gray Matter

We must link and accumulate the traction "ions" of our journey, all across this agenda, establishing, strengthening, and speeding up our organizational OODA Loop, without any deficit disorders. Any kind of deficit disorder means our organizational OODA Loop is more open loop than it should be and is larger and slower than it should be. Just a 1% difference, relative to our competition, can compound into a huge difference of accretion for them and dilution for us. At the extreme, maybe even with life and death consequences for our business! If we allow any deficit disorders, we risk missing some crucial traction "ions" of our journey and having a Wrong Hazelwood or an Eastern Airlines scenario in our future!

To mitigate that risk, we must strengthen our organizational OODA loop, making sure it is a closed loop and hasn't gone open loop. We must establish and connect component OODA loops, operating vibrantly and concurrently at several levels, informing each other and being informed by each other. In so doing, we strengthen and shrink our organizational OODA Loop, assembling an "architecture of execution." This is the final stage in our mindful process of integration, alignment, and attunement, from gray matter to gray matter, for translating strategy and execution into traction between the rubber and the road. With nothing getting lost in translation!

As we mentioned earlier in this chapter, Execution Excellence is also the master, unifying model that integrates all the other models in our new framework of understandings, strengths, and intelligences. You can see the beginnings of that already with the inclusion of the 3-D glasses and the diamond-shaped *Journey-ionics* model of Executive Intelligence, Intuition, and Resilience, which is integrated by the Flight Planning component of this model. All will become clear as we progress.

Using this Execution Excellence agenda model, we will look at the evolution of a business from Execution Excellence 1.0 (postadaptive) through 2.0 (adaptive) and then to 3.0 (preadaptive). For organizational agility, we must progressively mature from one to the other, in a crawl, walk, run kind of way.

BONUS

http://bit.ly/qTo3EO

In other words, it's kind of like changing the tires at 60 miles per hour! We have to evolve as we go along. With the speed of business and the pace of change these days, we rarely have the luxury of pulling off the road to make changes. We have to be changing things while still driving at high speed, linking and accumulating traction "ions" of our journey, working "in" and "on" our journey, all at the same time. It's really the only way to do it anyway, as we have to learn by doing, not just by thinking, and be learning, applying, and achieving in parallel.

More than just changing the tires at 60 miles per hour, in our mindful process of integration, alignment, and attunement, from gray matter to gray matter, Execution Excellence is about implanting our new chassis of business acumen into our business vehicle. To have the preadaptive organizational agility we need these days, we have to evolve the chassis of our vehicle to be fit for the journey challenge and the anatomy of dynamic complexity involved.

We can think of Execution Excellence 1.0 as being kind of like a rickshaw! It's a three wheeler, not very stable, not much horsepower, all kinds of vibrations, rattles, and bits falling off! It doesn't have much carrying capacity as it's only a three seater.

It's not the kind of vehicle you want to go remotely off-road in, as it doesn't have the tires, chassis, horsepower, and agility for that.

Think of Execution Excellence 2.0 as being more like our SUV. It has the tires, chassis, horsepower, and agility we need for more off-road ability, but still has a limited carrying capacity, which we can easily outgrow.

Think of Execution Excellence 3.0 as being more like the carrying capacity of a bus. Jim Collins speaks about this in his 2001 book, *Good to Great: Why Some Companies Make the Leap... and Others Don't.* He asserts that high performance teamwork requires having the right people on the bus and the right people off the bus, with the right people sitting in the right seats on the bus.

Execution Excellence 3.0 is about building the bus of high performance teamwork, with the right people in the right seats and every seat being a driving seat, from which we are getting traction. It's about making sure that every seat, broadly and deeply throughout our organization, is highly integrated, highly aligned, and highly attuned with the longitudinal dimension of the journey and the challenge of dynamic complexity. It's about every executive, manager, and employee understanding what it takes to be fully filling their seats, translating strategy and execution into traction, *In the Driving Seat* of their roles. In our mindful process of integration, alignment, and attunement, from gray matter to gray matter, it's about building a bigger wheelbase of contact footprint between the rubber and the road.

A few years ago, in the heady days of cheap oil and larger and larger SUVs, I distinctly remember a television ad with a yellow school bus, adorned with bull-bars, roof-rack, flared wheel arches and knobby tires, declared as the "largest SUV on the planet!" That's kind of what we are thinking about for Execution Excellence 3.0!

Let's now begin to look at the progression of Execution Excellence from 1.0 (postadaptive) through 2.0 (adaptive) to 3.0 (preadaptive), evolving the anatomy of the vehicle we need to be fit for the journey challenge.

Execution Excellence 1.0 (Postadaptive)

When we first start a business, we are necessarily in a classic, entrepreneurial, seat-of-the-pants mode. We are making things up as we go along, improvising on the fly, and setting things in motion in a necessarily loose, unstructured, and somewhat chaotic manner.

We are simultaneously creating the flow and going with the flow, all at the same time, dealing with all kinds of unexpected events along the way. It's like pushing off from the bank on a whitewater ride. We know it's going to be a wild ride, underplanned, somewhat out of control and with success being defined as making it to the bottom of the rapids with the raft still the right way up.

Execution Excellence 1.0 *Post-Adaptive*

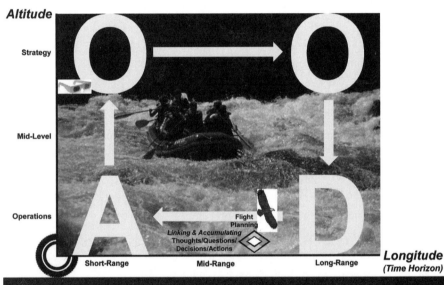

We are simultaneously creating the flow and going with the flow, all at the same time, dealing with all kinds of unexpected events along the way. It's like pushing off from the bank on a whitewater ride. We know it's going to be a wild ride, underplanned, somewhat out of control and with success being defined as making it to the bottom of the rapids with the raft still the right way up.

Our flight envelope is mostly down in the bottom left corner of our agenda model, consumed with short-range, operational issues. We don't have much of an organizational OODA Loop above and beyond that flight envelope, and, consequently, we find ourselves in a very postadaptive mode, with things happening that we don't really see coming. We react to them, after the fact, postadaptively, as best we can. As a result, we tend to get hijacked repeatedly by the tyranny of the urgent, responding to the latest crisis or opportunity. Every time this happens, we get sucked down into the lower left corner of our Execution Excellence agenda model. We are mostly working "in" our business and journey, fixing bulbs, and not "on" our business and journey, flying the plane.

If we aren't careful, this becomes that self-fulfilling and self defeating prophecy, vicious cycle, and downward spiral. We are so busy working "in" our business and journey that we never find the time to be working "on" our business and journey. We get stuck in a postadaptive mode of constant whitewater and crisis management. We have all experienced situations like this, in companies that we have worked for, maybe that we work for presently, or clients, partners, and vendors whom we have some experience with. They seem to be forever stuck in this self inflicted mode, largely because of CEOs, executives, and managers who don't know any different.

This is rooted, cemented, and fossilized in their deep-seated belief system, and they don't know how to break out of it. They are surrounded by brick walls, in jail, and don't know how to launch a jailbreak. They are resigned to serving a life sentence. They are gridlocked and don't know how to unlock the gridlock. It's a catch-22 situation—if only we had more time to work "on" the business, but we are too busy working "in" the business to have the time! It's a doom loop. Because they are so postadaptive, businesses in this mode experience Wrong Hazelwoods and Eastern Airlines scenarios all the time, with all kinds of grave consequences, which they often explain away as bad luck.

This is one way to travel, and necessarily so when we are starting up a business. But if we don't graduate from this mode, it can be crazy making, stress inducing, incredibly painful, and expensive, both financially and nonfinancially. Not least of all, we risk our best talent leaving as soon as they possibly can, maybe going down the street to a competitor that is less chaotic. That would be another go around of the vicious cycle in the downward spiral! It can easily put a business into a nosedive, followed by a tailspin, followed by a smoking hole in the ground! To avoid that, we must graduate to something more.

Execution Excellence 2.0 (Adaptive)

To graduate to the more adaptive architecture of Execution Excellence 2.0, we must start formalizing some new and more robust parts of a chassis for our vehicle, to be fit for the journey challenge:

Execution Excellence 2.0 *Adaptive*
shrinking, connecting & sustaining component OODA loops operating concurrently across our agenda

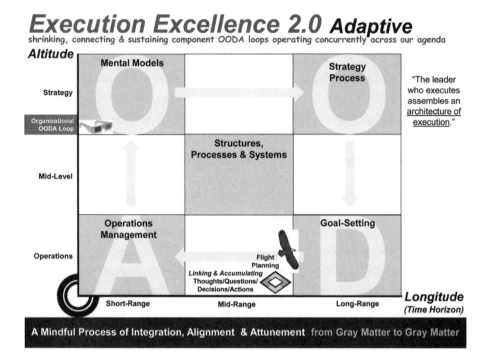

Each of these elements is a component OODA Loop in the bigger organizational OODA Loop of our Execution Excellence agenda model. We strengthen, speed up, and shrink our organizational OODA Loop by connecting component OODA Loops, operating vibrantly and concurrently as several levels. These take shape and mesh like individual gears in the gearbox of our organizational OODA Loop, at the core of our chassis for organizational agility. To graduate to an architecture of Execution Excellence 2.0, we must put each cog in place, get it turning over well, keep it well oiled, and get it meshing well with the other cogs in the gearbox. As we shrink, connect, and sustain these component OODA Loops, operating concurrently across our agenda, we strengthen, speed up, and shrink our organizational OODA Loop, becoming more agile as an organization.

Let's look at each component in turn. In this chapter, we will review each briefly, to understand where organizational agility comes from and to understand the integrated whole. In the next chapter, we will revisit each in more detail, to understand how to develop our organizational agility to the next level. Let's get started.

Operations Management

Paradoxically, our ability to translate more strategy and more execution into more traction starts in the bottom left corner of our agenda model, with Operation Management. This is where the loop closure occurs in the **Action** component of our organizational OODA loop, addressing the short range, operations element of our challenge. This is the first crucial cog in the gearbox of our organizational OODA Loop—if we don't have a good cog in our gearbox here, as a component OODA loop, turning over well and being kept well oiled, then we don't have much spare bandwidth to spend anywhere else in our agenda. We are gridlocked, and the unlocking of the gridlock has to start here.

Often, when I use the term "operations management" with many teams and organizations, they initially think I mean "crisis management" because that is their day-to-day reality. They are lurching from one crisis to the next, barely wiping the sweat off their brow from the last one until they are thrown into the next one. Life is that constant whitewater ride we have been talking about. Their intentions to spend some time working "on" the business, and important improvements that need to be made, constantly get hijacked by the tyranny of the urgent, sucking them down into this lower left corner of working "in" the business: fixing bulbs and not flying the plane!

This is the reality for many CEOs, executives, and managers. So the first thing we have to do is remind them that strengthening our operations management OODA Loop will progressively reduce the torrent of crisis management. It's about becoming that High Reliability Organization (HRO) about which Karl Weick and Kathleen Sutcliffe say: *"HRO environments unfold rapidly, and errors propagate quickly. Understanding is never perfect, and people are under pressure to make wise choices with insufficient information. But whose environment isn't like that?"*

Exactly. Whose environment isn't like that? Whose environment won't benefit from strengthening, shrinking, and closing the loop more with our operations management OODA Loop? In so doing, we will liberate some bandwidth that we can reinvest in the other parts of our agenda, from which we will get a much higher payback of increased agility. Then we have the chance of halting the downward spiral, breaking the pattern, and establishing an upward spiral.

While some degree of agility comes from this operations management cog in our gearbox, most agility does not, instead coming from the other component OODA Loops in our agenda.

Think about our Eastern Airlines story. Their organizational agility problem in the cockpit that day had little to do with better managing the operation of fixing the bulb! Their bulb-fixing, operations management OODA Loop was working fine. Their other, more strategic OODA Loops, for flying the plane, were the problem.

Our challenge in business is the same. Especially during recessionary times, it would be very easy to just hunker down in this bottom-left hand corner of operations management, convincing ourselves that we don't have any spare bandwidth for more strategic OODA Loops. That would be a huge mistake, substantially limiting our agility and maybe setting us up for Wrong Hazelwoods and Eastern Airlines scenarios. We must also sustain a strategy process OODA Loop.

Strategy Process

Notice that I don't use the term "strategic planning." I fundamentally don't believe in traditional "strategic planning and implementation" because that is an old, detail complexity solution for a new, dynamic complexity problem, for the reasons we have explained. In my experience, this subtracts from organizational agility rather than adding to it. In the top-right corner of our agenda model, this is where the loop closure occurs in the <u>Orientation</u> component of our organizational OODA loop, addressing the long-range strategy element of our challenge. We need a more agile and dynamic approach to strategy, with the discipline of an ongoing process and cycle. Our strategy process OODA Loop is the top-right cog in the gearbox of our organizational OODA Loop.

For organizational agility, strategy isn't something you can leave to be ad hoc, every once in a while, when you have time and finally get around to it. Instead, our strategy process cog has to be turning over well and be kept well oiled. It has to be on all the time. Try switching off the strategic part of your brain when you are next driving your car. It won't end well! When we are driving, strategy isn't something we can pull off the road to do every once in a while. Our strategy process is on all the time, in process, while moving, as an integral part of driving. We are working "in" and "on" our journey, all at the same time, linking and accumulating traction "ions."

Think about our Eastern Airlines story. Upon first discovering the problem, they had a strategic review at 2,000 feet, they set a first goal of fixing the bulb, and they got busy with their OODA Loop of managing that operation. At that point, their strategy process OODA Loop went too open loop! What if they had sustained a strategy process OODA Loop? What if, a minute or so later, they had looped back around to reobserve and reorient strategically? Might they have scanned their instruments more thoroughly and noticed they had lost some altitude? Might they have thought about that and questioned what was going on? Almost certainly. At that point, with maybe 1,000 feet of altitude left, they would still have had plenty of options to consider, decide upon, and put into action.

Instead, at 150 feet, they tried to spool back up their strategy process OODA Loop, to reobserve and reorient. But, with only a few seconds left, this was no time for a strategic review. There was no time. Instead, this was the time for a goal setting OODA Loop to kick into high gear. Reobserve, reorient, redecide, react, forget the goal of fixing the bulb, let's switch to a new number one goal, of getting the heck out of here! Hit the gas, pull back on the stick, regain some altitude, and ask questions later! This goal setting OODA Loop is also crucial.

Goal Setting

Goal setting is crucial in translating high level strategy into a trajectory of goals at ground level, grounded in specificity, achievability, and measurability. Goal setting is in the bottom right corner of our agenda model where the loop closure occurs in the **Decision** component of our organizational OODA loop. At the intersection of our strategy process and our operations management, goal setting is about deciding on our path and trajectory of goals. It's about setting out the sequence of hurdles we want to jump, with the performance of our operations management machine, in the direction of our strategic path. Our goal-setting OODA Loop is the bottom right cog in the gearbox of our organizational OODA Loop.

Just like for our strategy process, goal setting can't be left to be ad hoc and once in a while. This is typically once a year for many organizations, resulting in our "annual goals," which are often then cascaded throughout the whole organization as "SMART goals." You know the SMART acronym, of which there are some slightly different variants, but something like: Specific, Measurable, Achievable, Results-oriented, Time-bound.

That approach to goal setting is better than nothing but, in my experience, is woefully inadequate these days. An annual OODA Loop of goal setting just doesn't cut it. Whose business can afford to work with an OODA Loop that is annual anymore? Not many that I know of. Where is it written in stone that "annual" is the periodicity of business? That's just a financial accounting and reporting construct that we use for convenience, comparison, and tax purposes. Our business reality is that we are dealing in a continuum of periodicities of annual, quarterly, monthly, weekly, daily, and even hourly, minute by minute, second by second, moment by moment. We mustn't default into our goal setting being just an annual OODA Loop.

Think about our Eastern Airlines story. After their initial setting of goals at 2,000 feet, their goal-setting OODA Loop went too open loop. They became so focused on their first goal of fixing the bulb that they weren't sufficiently checking in with their trajectory of goals later in the sequence and, in particular, their end goal of landing safely. In particular, they weren't sufficiently rethinking and requestioning their options, keeping them sufficiently open, for finding other paths to the same end goal. Could they have wound the landing gear down manually? Could they have done a fly-by for visual confirmation from the ground? Their systems, processes, and structures OODA Loops also let them down.

Infrastructure of Structures, Processes, and Systems

The infrastructure of structures, processes, and systems OODA Loops is the central cog in our gearbox of organizational agility, which causes all the other cogs to mesh, or not, as the case may be. In the center of our agenda model is the core machinery of our business, which semi-automates our ability to deal with the constant flow of detail complexity and dynamic complexity coming at us, thick and fast. Thicker and faster all the time! It's like our autopilot and leverages the 80/20 rule. If our infrastructure is able to deal with 80% of the routine, recurring, and repetitive stuff coming at us, then we can focus on the 20% of nonroutine, nonrecurring, and novel stuff, which can make 80% of the difference to our performance, profitability, and growth.

This component is in the middle of our agenda model because our structures, processes, and systems primarily deal with mid-range and mid-level planning and execution issues—mid-range on the longitudinal, time horizon axis and mid-level on the altitude axis. These mid-range and mid-level planning and execution issues include such things as capacity planning, materials planning, procurement, master scheduling, sales forecasting, and the like. As the middle cog in our gearbox, this has to be a well-oiled OODA Loop of continual improvement, because the turning over and meshing of all other cogs in the gearbox of our organizational OODA Loop depend upon it.

The problem is that we can so easily outgrow our infrastructure as the flow of detail complexity and dynamic complexity coming at us increases. Not least of all, things go exponential just with the raw math of growth. Think about it. If two of us start a business today, we have one person-to-person conversation to manage. If we add a third person tomorrow, now we have three person to person conversations to manage. A fourth person the day after takes us to six conversations. Then a fifth person takes us to 10 conversations, a sixth person to 15 conversations, and a seventh person to 21 conversations! That last person adds six new conversations to manage, and so on. So the flow of detail complexity and dynamic complexity increases exponentially, just with our simple math of growth. That's before taking into account the increasing diversity of personalities, agendas, clients, products, partners, vendors, markets, geographies, alliances, among many, many other things, as well.

When we start to outgrow our infrastructure, the 80/20 routine/nonroutine balance of our autopilot begins to unravel. Maybe it slips to 70/30, then maybe 60/40, and then maybe 50/50. Now only 50% of the things coming at us are routine, recurring, and repetitive, and can be handled on autopilot, and 50% are nonroutine, nonrecurring, and novel. What if our balance keeps sliding and inverts to 40/60 or 30/70 or even 20/80? That's the 80/20 rule the wrong way round. It's a constant whitewater ride again!

That's how whitewater progressively creeps back into our business. If it creeps back into the middle cog in our gearbox, it won't be long before it seeps back in everywhere else. Our strategy process will go open loop and ad hoc because "we don't have time." Our goal setting will become just about surviving the next clear and present danger that is right in front of us, forgetting about the trajectory of goals in our sequence after that. Our operations management will become crisis management. The self-fulfilling and self-defeating prophecy, vicious cycle, and downward spiral set back in! We spiral right back down to where we started from, at Execution Excellence 1.0 and constant whitewater.

Think about our Eastern Airlines story. Clearly, the autopilot features very prominently in the story. The pilots thought that the autopilot was in an altitude hold mode and was handling 80% of the routine, recurring, and repetitive tasks of flying the plane. They could, therefore, safely devote 80% of their attention to the task of fixing the bulb. Unfortunately, upon accidentally nudging the yoke, the autopilot had slipped out of its altitude-hold mode into a pitch-hold mode, on a slow, imperceptible descent. They didn't realize it, as their infrastructure OODA Loop of structures, processes, and systems, had gone too open loop. They were still operating from the mental model that the autopilot had them covered.

Mental Models

The final cog in the gearbox of our organizational OODA Loop for Execution Excellence 2.0 is in the top left corner, where the loop closure occurs in the **Observation** component of our organizational OODA loop. It relates to the mental models with which we are observing, strategizing, steering, and operating our business.

Our mental models are those paradigms, concepts, theories, blueprints, wiring diagrams, visualizations, metaphors, and stories which we use to conceive our business. Or not, as the case may be! We have all heard of the term "paradigm shift," and that's what this component OODA Loop is about—clarifying, evolving, and shifting the paradigms of our business.

When facilitating teams, I love to ask them, "Why is this mental model's component top left in our agenda model, not top right? It seems very strategic, so why isn't it just rolled into being an implicit part of the Strategy Process cog, top right? Instead, why is it called our explicitly top left?" In his 1990 book, *The Fifth Discipline*, Peter Senge puts it well: *"You don't have mental models, you are your mental models."* Whether we are conscious of them or not, our mental models operate in the present, the here and now, and the very short range. That's why this cog is in the top left corner of our agenda model, not in the top right corner, as the **Observation** component of organizational OODA loop. We are always observing from the present and where we are in our journey.

Mental models are very strategic. Paradigm shifts can be one of the most strategic things we work on, helping us make sense of the world. Mental models are our worldview, our theory of things, and the paradigms we hold about everything—how the economy and our industry work, what our customers want and how we compete, what leadership is and how we best provide it. As we progress, you are evolving a new mental model of organizational agility, and the why, what, when, where, how, and who of it. It's about helping you experience a paradigm shift from traditional "strategic planning and implementation" to an agile approach of translating strategy and execution into traction. Our process of shifting paradigms and evolving new mental models involves:

- **Metaphors** (e.g., *In the Driving Seat*, 3-D glasses, whitewater)

- **Concepts** (e.g., simplicity and complexity; integration, alignment and attunement from gray matter to gray matter; OODA Loops)

- **Models** (e.g., our framework of understandings, strengths, and intelligences; the component models we are progressively reviewing; the master, unifying model of Execution Excellence we are reviewing in this chapter)

- **Stories** (e.g., Eastern Airlines, Wrong Hazelwood)

- **Examples** (e.g., Boeing and Airbus, fighter planes, fighter pilots)

Creating a permanent shift of paradigms and mental models typically requires a combination of all of the above. We have all experienced those epiphanies, when a light bulb comes on in our heads. All of a sudden, we see a different way to look at something, which unlocks our ability to see new possibilities and pathways for progress, in some way, shape, or form. This OODA Loop is about more proactively and adaptively challenging our mental models and exploring new ones, which may unlock paths of least resistance for profitable growth.

If you are in the mobile phone industry, how frequently does that paradigm shift? It goes through a revolutionary shift every 18 to 36 months, for instance when Apple comes out with its latest thing, like the iPhone and the iPad. It goes through an evolutionary shift every 6 to 18 months, as everyone else scurries to catch up, and Blackberry comes out with a clickable screen, for instance. It seems as if it goes through an incremental shift in the news every day, every week, or every month, with the latest announcement from somebody or other. It's a constant flow of a paradigm shift.

In fact, we can't really call these devices phones anymore. They have phone functionality in them, as a part of what they do, but that's far from the whole of what they do now. So what do we call them? Smart phones? PDAs (Portable Digital Assistants)? Palmtops?

What we call something is at the core of our mental models OODA Loop. It's about labeling and naming things, and the words we choose are crucial because, with every choice of word, up comes our mental model for the interpretation of that word. So, in our mental models OODA Loop, the true labeling and naming of the things we observe are critical. They directly affect our orientation through the interpretation of the words we choose, labeling and naming what we see, as truly as we can.

By way of example, what is Starbucks? A coffee shop? A customer experience? Actually, I heard Howard Schultz, the CEO of Starbucks, on the radio once explaining it. He said that, when they were first conceiving Starbucks, their minds turned to the U.K., where, between home and work, there is a third place. It's called the pub! He said that we don't really have that in North America. Yes, we have a few sports bars here and there, but not on every corner. So when they first conceived Starbucks, it was as a "third place" for North America. That's the label they named their mental model with.

When you choose that "third place" label, as opposed to just a "customer experience" or "coffee shop," it changes everything! The strategy for a third place is radically different from the strategy for a coffee shop. As is the infrastructure, not least in the way you design and lay out the stores. As is the way you manage the operation and as are the goals you set. The choice of a third place, not just a coffee shop, changes everything. The true labeling and naming of things is crucial, to avoid mental model confusion and to create paradigm shifts.

Think about our Eastern Airlines story. At 150 feet, with a few seconds to go, the pilot uttered those words that indicate their state of mental model confusion, "We're still at two thousand (feet), right?" Their mental model OODA Loop had gone too open loop. They were cognitively disconnected from reality, and they couldn't get their cognitive functions spooled back up quickly enough. Remember what Richard Normann said in his 2001 book, *Reframing Business: When the Map Changes the Landscape.* He said, *"We must reconfigure or be reconfigured."* Because the crew couldn't reconfigure their cognition quickly enough, the plane became reconfigured through a sudden impact with the ground.

Graduating to Execution Excellence 2.0

So these five component OODA Loops are the cogs in the gearbox of our organizational OODA Loop, for Execution Excellence 2.0, making up our agenda model. We need these in place, turning over well, being kept well oiled, and meshing well to be more adaptive.

We need to be flying around inside this agenda model, spending the right time, in the right place, at the right time, and in the right whole-brained manner with our 3-D glasses on. We need to keep these cogs turning and meshing, in the gearbox of our organizational OODA Loop. It's about connecting vibrant OODA Loops operating concurrently at several levels, not letting any of them go open loop. It's about linking and accumulating the traction "ions" of our journey, all across this agenda model, without any deficit disorders. Unfortunately, that day in that Eastern Airlines cockpit they suffered some deficit disorders of attention, intention, and responsibility for results.

Covering this agenda sufficiently, without any deficit disorders, is where this next level of organizational agility comes from, graduating us from postadaptive Execution Excellence 1.0 to a more adaptive Execution Excellence 2.0. We graduate from a rickshaw to an SUV, as a vehicle which is a better fit for our journey challenge. In so doing, we become an adaptive, learning organization.

Indeed, in *The Fifth Discipline*, Peter Senge outlines the five disciplines of learning organizations, saying, *"Today, I believe, five new 'component technologies' are gradually converging to innovate learning organizations. Systems thinking, mental models, personal mastery, shared vision, and team learning & dialogue are inescapable elements of building learning organizations."* We can map these five components into the Execution Excellence 2.0 model:

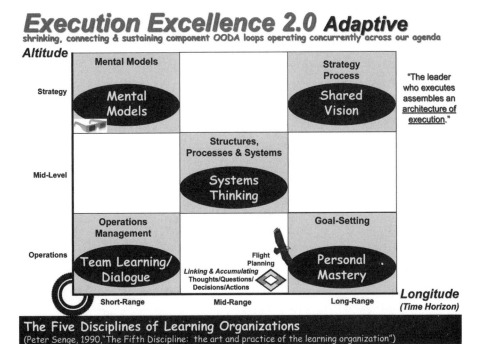

Execution Excellence 2.0 *Adaptive*
shrinking, connecting & sustaining component OODA loops operating concurrently across our agenda

The Five Disciplines of Learning Organizations
(Peter Senge, 1990,"The Fifth Discipline: the art and practice of the learning organization")

These five disciplines, and their related components in our organizational OODA Loop and model of Execution Excellence, are at the core of becoming a learning organization. In particular, they are at the core of learning to be agile and developing the organizational agility we need these days. Peter Senge goes on to say:

> "It is vital that the five disciplines develop as an ensemble. This is challenging because it is much harder to integrate new tools than simply apply them separately. But the payoffs are immense.
>
> That is why systems thinking is the fifth discipline. It is the discipline that integrates the disciplines, fusing them into a coherent body of theory and practice. It keeps them from being separate gimmicks or the latest organization change fads. Without a systemic orientation, there is no motivation to look at how the disciplines interrelate.
>
> By enhancing each of the other disciplines it continually reminds us that the whole can exceed the sum of the parts. Systems thinking also needs the disciplines of building shared vision, mental models, team learning, and personal mastery to realize its potential.
>
> Most of the problems faced by humankind concern our inability to grasp and manage the increasingly complex systems of our world."
>
> –Peter Senge, 1990, *The Fifth Discipline: The Art and Practice of the Learning Organization*
>
> To read more, visit: www.mydrivingseat.com/booklinks booklink #18

Most of the problems we face concern our inability to grasp and manage the increasingly complex systems of our world! That's the never ending flow of detail complexity and dynamic complexity, coming at us thicker and faster. It's no wonder that we are so prone to being overwhelmed, because our system can't cope. We are exploring the system of organizational agility we need, as an ensemble of component parts, to be able to cope. Not just cope, but excel.

Improving and integrating each of the cogs in the gearbox of our organizational OODA Loop and connecting vibrant OODA Loops operating concurrently at several levels allow us to graduate to Execution Excellence 2.0. That's good. It's certainly better than being stuck in a 1.0 mode of constant whitewater! But it is still so 1990s.

Being an adaptive, learning organization is good, but not enough anymore. We need other components in our ensemble to have the organizational agility we need these days. We must graduate to something more preadaptive.

But, "Hang on a minute," I hear you say! "Not so fast!" "Not only do we have these component parts of a learning organization, but we do a whole bunch of other things," such as:

- Business Planning and Budgeting (doing an annual business plan and budget every year!);

- Goals Setting Cascade (doing an annual plan of SMART Goals every year, cascaded throughout the whole organization, with Performance Reviews and Coaching!);

- Forecasting and Operating Plans (doing quarterly reforecasts and adjustments of our operating plans for the remainder of the year);

- Various Total Quality Management (TQM) and Six-Sigma continuous improvement initiatives and the like;

- Lean process improvements and Business Process Re-engineering, for both our manufacturing and nonmanufacturing business processes, and the like;

- Balanced Score-Card, Measures of Performance, and the like.

I am sure there are many more you could add to the list. When I work with client teams, we take all their initiatives, like these and others which they are busy with, and we map them into the Execution Excellence model. Oftentimes, we start the low tech way with a large notice board and pin a printout of the Execution Excellence model in the middle. We then gather up key artifacts from all of the strategic initiatives, processes, and programs (like those listed above and more) and pin them up in an array around the model in the center. If need be, we'll take digital photographs of nondocumentary artifacts (like a project management tracking system on the wall of the operations center that one of my Vistage members has), print those out, and add those into the mix. Then we'll get some ribbon and scissors and pin ribbons to show how each artifact maps into the Execution Excellence model. Any which way we do this, what begins to present itself is where we have missing parts and/or lack of integration, alignment, and attunement. Many of the parts are there, but the whole hasn't emerged and/or isn't working well.

So, you continue, "Surely, with the combination of all these things which we do, we're good, aren't we? Doesn't this add up to execution excellence?" Many teams say this to me when I start this work with them. To which I answer, "No, it's not enough, not anymore." Why?

- Because you can be flying the latest generation technology jet of its time (just like your business), with a highly trained crew in the cockpit (just like you and your team), and still suffer an Eastern Airlines scenario!

- Because, in the busyness of all of this technology and training, the architecture of execution we need these days can still be missing in action!

- Because, we can be doing a great job fixing the one-year bulb and not flying the five-year plane!

Think about General Motors and Chrysler. Did they have any shortage of the latest generation technology of business, or highly trained executives in the cockpit, or access to whatever expertise they wanted? No! Yet they still ended up with an Eastern Airlines scenario—an imperceptible descent, followed by a nosedive, followed by a tailspin, followed by a smoking hole in the ground of bankruptcy.

Think about Toyota. Did they have any shortage of the latest generation technology and highly trained crew? Heck no, they were the originating source of a lot of it, famous for the Toyota Production System. Yet they still ended up with an Eastern Airlines scenario—an imperceptible descent, followed by a nosedive, followed by a tailspin, followed by a smoking hole in the ground. A smoking hole of safety recalls and congressional hearings!

Think about BP. Did they have any shortage of the latest generation technology or highly trained crew? No! Yet they still ended up with an Eastern Airlines scenario—an imperceptible descent, followed by a nosedive, followed by a tailspin, followed by a smoking hole in the ground of the worst environmental disaster ever.

Don't get me wrong! I'm not saying you should necessarily stop doing any of these things or do them radically differently from how you are doing them now. I'm saying that you should continue doing them, but that they aren't enough anymore! If you believe they are, you can easily become busy fools, just like General Motors, Chrysler, Toyota, and BP. They are enough if you are happy getting a C or B grade as a

CEO, executive, or manager, but not if you want to be getting an A. They are enough if you are happy having a 2.0 level of organizational agility in a 3.0 world, risking Wrong Hazelwoods, Eastern Airlines, and constant whitewater in your future.

Old 2.0 solutions will not solve new 3.0 problems. Remember what Peter Senge said: "Conventional forecasting, planning and analysis methods are not equipped to deal with dynamic complexity." Unconventional times require unconventional approaches. Yet, I still see so many organizations applying an old, detail complexity solution, of traditional "strategic planning and implementation," to a new, dynamic complexity problem, and wondering why it isn't working well.

As we were just getting started with a facilitation process with the executive team of a public company client, the human resources VP said to me:

"One of our biggest problems is that we invest so much effort in our annual goal setting process. It's a huge effort every year, cascading it from the very top, of our annual corporate goals agreed on with the board, down through the whole organization, making sure every last person is in alignment with a set of SMART goals. And, in turn, there are all sorts of reward and recognition incentives aligned with the achievement of these goals. The trouble is, if part way through the year the world veers off somewhere else, we are out of luck. We can't turn our ship in that new direction, until the next annual cycle and only then with the same huge effort."

In other words, they are stuck with an annual OODA Loop of goal setting, which is a postadaptive, large, lethargic, and lumbering OODA Loop.

That's not unusual. It's an old, conventional, detail complexity solution of traditional "strategic planning and implementation," applied to a new, unconventional, dynamic complexity problem. It doesn't work very well anymore. It's not that we don't need a goal setting process and OODA Loop. We most certainly do. It's that we need to be massively shrinking our goal setting OODA Loop with a more agile approach. Not too structured and not too unstructured, not too ordered and not too chaotic, not too tight and not too loose, not too hands on and not too hands off, not overplanned and not underplanned. Think modern jet fighter plane: not too stable and not too unstable. An "and" proposition! Too much of an "or" proposition, one way or another, is fragility, not agility.

Indeed, in the case of that public company, their share price had experienced fragility and had gone into a nosedive. They engaged me as part of figuring out why, and it wasn't hard. I said that they had been doing a great job every year of fixing the one-year bulb of their annual business plan, budget, and corporate goals, but not such a good job of flying the five-year plane. Things had gone into an imperceptible descent, which was now becoming perceptible to the analysts on Wall Street, and their buy-hold-sell guidance was shifting, unfavorably, with the resulting share price impact.

The reason is that Execution Excellence 2.0 isn't enough anymore and doesn't fully address our agility agenda yet. There are some missing elements, inviting whitewater to creep back in.

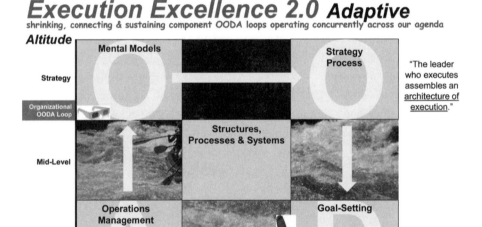

Execution Excellence 2.0 *Adaptive*
shrinking, connecting & sustaining component OODA loops operating concurrently across our agenda

Notice that the missing elements are in the transitions of our organizational OODA Loop (the arrows in the graphic above) between **O**bservation and **O**rientation, then between **O**rientation and **D**ecision, then between **D**ecision and **A**ction and then closing the loop back around between **A**ction and **O**rientation. These are the weak links in the chain of our organizational OODA Loop, where a lot gets lost in translation, and our things easily go open loop. Whitewater can begin to creep back in, and, before you know it, whitewater can start to seep in everywhere, and the downward spiral commences. We can easily end up spiraling right back down to where we started, in the whitewater ride of Execution Excellence 1.0. With Wrong Hazelwoods, Eastern Airlines, and constant whitewater in our future! To future-proof ourselves against these kinds of scenarios, we must graduate beyond being just adaptive, to being preadaptive with Execution Excellence 3.0, by filling in these missing pieces to avoid these weak links in the chain of our organizational OODA Loop.

Execution Excellence 3.0 (Preadaptive)

To graduate to an architecture of Execution Excellence 3.0, we need these crucial additional components, together with some evolutions of existing components and some overall integration:

• Evolving our goal setting with an additional Journey Orientation component;

• Adding three additional components of Productivity, Culture, and Leadership/Communication Skills and Style;

• Evolving the nature of the existing infrastructure component of Structures, Processes, and Systems;

• Integrating all the components, meshing together in agile alignment and attunement, as our overall Enterprise Execution Capability and Capacity;

• Integrating and emphasizing the Flight Planning component, to apportion our bandwidth of time, energy, and attention, spending the right time in the right place at the right time and in the right manner with our 3-D glasses on, to avoid any deficit disorders.

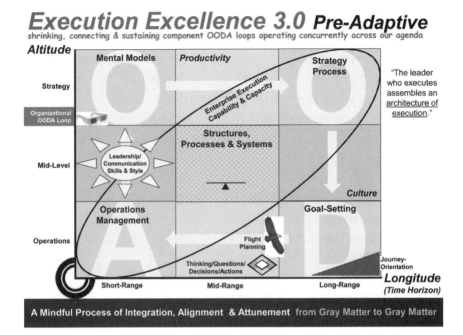

Execution Excellence 3.0 **Pre-Adaptive**
shrinking, connecting & sustaining component OODA loops operating concurrently across our agenda

A Mindful Process of Integration, Alignment & Attunement from Gray Matter to Gray Matter

These become crucial elements in completing, strengthening, speeding up, and shrinking our organizational OODA Loop, as a closed loop that is highly aligned and attuned with our organizational agility challenge. Let's look at each of these new elements in turn.

Journey Orientation

As we discussed earlier in this chapter, for preadaptive execution excellence and organizational agility, the goal setting component on its own is not enough, as it tends to be predominantly annual in nature. If we aren't careful, we go from year to year, doing a great job of fixing the one-year bulb of our annual goals, budget, and business plan, but a miserable job of flying the multi-year plane. Things can easily go into an imperceptible descent.

Jack Welsh was once asked by an analyst, "How do you balance short term versus long term?" To which he answered, "I don't! I need both." It's not an "or" proposition of short term *or* long term, it's an "and" proposition of short term *and* long term. As we discussed in Chapter 4, that "and" proposition is facilitated by a paradigm shift of focus ("the hocus pocus of focus"), to the longitudinal dimension of journey orientation and the trajectory of profitability and growth which we desire.

Like many others, that public company client I mentioned earlier had a declared trajectory of "15/15": 15% revenue growth per year at 15% profitability or better, year in, year out, every year, forever! You don't achieve the longitudinal journey of a profit and growth trajectory like that if you remotely see it as an "or" proposition of short term or long term, rather than an "and" proposition of short term and long term.

We have to be engaged in an agile process of strategy, execution, and traction, forward from the present, backward from the future, and meeting in the middle, so that we are not left reliant upon some kind of miracle happening in the middle of our journey!

Of course, the biggest pressure is the short term-ism of quarterly results, so we can easily toggle into the "or" proposition of short term focus. We might do okay for a few years, but inevitably, we are at risk of things going into an imperceptible decent, versus our desired flight plan for that kind of trajectory.

Indeed, that is what had happened with that public company client. Their share price was being hammered because Wall Street was beginning to perceive that the company's innovation pipeline of new products and services was insufficient to sustain their 15/15 trajectory. They had done well, hitting 15/15 from year to year in recent times. The current year and following year looked okay, and maybe they could even squeak by in a third year. But then things were starting to look shaky because of the long product development lead times involved in their industry and cavitations in their pipeline. The imperceptible descent was starting to become perceptible, and they were losing their shine as a growth stock warranting their price/earnings ratio. Their share price got hammered, as did the personal net worth of many of the executives with stock and options. They were experiencing the ordeal of organizational agility, which had become an "or-deal," not an "and-deal."

The elegant simplicity of the wedge shape, of this journey orientation element, embeds these complexities, and more, as we will explore later in this chapter. It provides a journey-oriented framework, intuition, and instinct, which is crucial to graduating our goal setting from a 2.0 mode of execution excellence and organizational agility to a preadaptive, 3.0 mode. It's kind of analogous to share price.

While I am not making the case for perfect stock markets, especially given the turmoil of recent years, I find it helpful to encourage private companies to imagine that they had a publicly quoted share price, imagining that they were actively followed by analysts giving buy-hold-sell guidance. For a public company, like the client I have been mentioning, share price and market capitalization reflect an aggregate perception of how a company is doing with its profit and growth journey. Underlying this perception, to some degree, is a journey-oriented, longitudinal, discounted cash flow analysis of the future, as far out to time horizons deemed relevant and appropriate to the type of business and the type of industry.

Share price movements on a day-to-day basis represent an aggregate perception of how a company is linking and accumulating the traction "ions" of its journey, translating strategy and execution into traction, and what the market makes of all of that. As we discussed in Chapter 4, does the market believe that the company is adding positive "ions" or negative "ions" to the capacitor of its invisible, second balance sheet, and what is happening to the net stored charge of promise or peril? Is the voltage difference approaching the breakdown point, which will produce a positive *breakthrough* or a negative *breakdown*? From all of which, in some way, shape or form, is derived some perception of the Discounted Net Present Value and, therefore, market capitalization and, therefore, share price. This is more intuitive and instinctive for a public company, as it is the day to day reality it lives with and the question it is always asking: What will the market make of this?

I like to push this a little further. If aggregate market perception was listening into our conversation, real time, all the time, of how we are translating strategy and execution into the traction "ions" of our journey, what would likely happen to our share price and market capitalization today? Would we be creating or destroying shareholder value? Imagine getting an e-mail alert at the end of every meeting, letting you know how your share price had moved according to what analysts made of the conversation that occurred in that meeting. Even if you are a private company, imagine if you had a share price. This is implicitly a longitudinal, journey-oriented instinct— imagining we had a share price, and what the hour-to-hour, day-to-day, and week-to-week movements might be. This can help private companies develop their longitudinal sense of journey orientation.

Think about our Eastern Airlines story. A number of pilots have said to me that "in aviation, it's all about altitude." In our story, altitude is kind of like the equivalent of share price. With altitude we have options. Without it, we don't. Clearly, this story is about an imperceptible loss of altitude and, therefore, options. When it became perceptible, it was pretty much too late already. They were out of options. Their organizational agility had become an "or-deal," not an "and-deal," as they lost focus on the longitudinal dimension of journey orientation and the flight plan trajectory they desired.

Scary stuff! So, using this story, I explained to the management team of the public company client that their extensive goal setting process was good, but not good enough. I pushed them to understand that organizational agility requires more these days. What do you think they did? You guessed it, they pushed right back! This was a pretty large and very smart team, with quite a few M.B.A.s and Ph.D.s around the table. Even in the face of such compelling arguments, and stock options that are underwater, why do teams like this push back so strongly? Because what they hear is more work, when their productivity bandwidth is already being stretched thin. Productivity is another element we have to bring into focus, to graduate to Execution Excellence 3.0.

Productivity

For preadaptive execution excellence and organizational agility, we need to bring a productivity component into focus, which runs down the middle vertical of our agenda model. As a mid-range component, running from top to bottom, it creates continuity between the short range and the long range at all three levels, from operations to strategy, as a go-between in the continuum of present forward and future backward. Any discontinuity in that continuum, to whatever degree, is like gridlock in our mindful process of integration, alignment and attunement, from gray matter to gray matter. If the productivity of our management system is not able to process the short-range, present forward demands upon us, our long-range, future backward strategic initiatives don't have any chance of making it into our day-to-day bandwidth.

This productivity component runs from top to bottom in our agenda model because we must think about our productivity at each of three different levels:

- **Operational Level Productivity**. In the continuum between our operations management and goal setting, this relates to the productivity of our day-to-day operations management, in pursuit of our desired trajectory of goals, sequentially on our path, as an "and" proposition. This is a crucial component in closing the loop of our organizational OODA Loop in the transition between **Decision** and **Action**. A weak link in the chain of our organizational OODA Loop here is very costly to our organizational agility and we pay a price with wheel$pin.

- **Mid-Level Productivity**. This relates to the productivity of our infrastructure of structures, processes, and systems, as the central cog in the gearbox of our organizational OODA Loop (as we discussed earlier in this chapter). Not least of all, as a core part of this central cog, this also relates to the productivity of our meetings, in two senses: first, the productivity of the individual meetings that we run and second, the productivity of our overall portfolio of meetings. As we will discuss further in the next chapter, like it or not, meetings are at the core of our productivity as a business.

• **Strategic Level Productivity**. In the continuum between our mental models and strategy process, this relates to the productivity of our strategy process and the work product it evolves, as helped or hindered by the mental models we are working in, individually and collectively, consciously and unconsciously. This is a crucial component in closing the loop of our organizational OODA Loop in the transition between **O**bservation and **O**rientation. A weak link in the chain of our organizational OODA Loop here is very costly to our organizational agility and we pay a price with wheel$pin.

This productivity component of our agenda model interfaces with every other component and is, therefore, crucial to graduating every other component from a 2.0 mode of organizational agility to a preadaptive 3.0 mode.

Not least of all, as CEOs, executives, and managers, we have to think about the productivity of our management system in dealing with the accelerating workflow of detail complexity and dynamic complexity, coming at us thicker and faster all the time. We must think about it collectively and individually. Not least of all, individually, we must think about our personal productivity process, for managing our own work flow and workload, and, in particular, to be able to handle the increasing challenge of dynamic complexity.

In my experience, most CEOs, executives, and managers don't spend enough time thinking about that. If they do, they tend to think about it in conventional ways of time management and priority management. Yet managing our attention span with traditional approaches to time management and priority management doesn't work well with increasingly dynamic complexity. It has become much more like an ongoing dynamic process of triage.

In his 2002 book, *Getting Things Done: The Art of Stress Free Productivity*, David Allen puts it well:

> "The ability to be successful, relaxed, and in control during these fertile but turbulent times demands new ways of thinking and working. There is a great need for new methods, technologies, and work habits to help us get on top of our world. The old models and habits are insufficient.

Neither our standard education, nor traditional time-management models, nor the plethora of organizing tools available, such as personal notebook planners, Microsoft Outlook, or Palm personal digital assistants (PDAs), [have] given us a viable means of meeting the new demands placed upon us. If you've tried to use any of these processes or tools, you've probably found them unable to accommodate the speed, complexity, and changing priority factors in what you are doing.

What you've probably discovered, at least at some level, is that a calendar, though important, can really effectively manage only a small portion of what you need to organize. And daily to-do lists and simplified priority coding have proven inadequate to deal with the volume and variable nature of the average professional's workload."

–David Allen, 2002, *Getting Things Done: The Art of Stress Free Productivity*

The old models and habits are insufficient! Yet, how many managers, executives, and CEOs do you know who are still trying to survive with the simplicity of a calendar and a daily to-do list? In the face of the increasing dynamic complexity, which David Allen describes, that just doesn't cut it anymore! That's stupid simplicity that ignores complexity, not elegant simplicity that embeds complexity. No wonder many managers, executives, and CEOs feel overwhelmed and in a constant state of whitewater. Our personal productivity processes and collective productivity system need to embed these complexities in new, elegantly simple ways of thinking and working.

Think about our Eastern Airlines story. Tragedies like this, and others since, stimulated new approaches to such things as Crew or Cockpit Resource Management (CRM) and the associated situational awareness and human factors issues involved. All of these initiatives are focused on the productivity of leadership, communication, and teamwork in the cockpit and their unfolding flow of thinking, questions, decisions, and actions. As a result, air safety statistics have improved enormously and have kept well ahead of traffic growth statistics. Had that not been the case, the explosive growth of passenger miles flown during the last few decades would have resulted in accidents being headline news every week! With foresight of that trend, the aviation industry responded preadaptively, with a range of technologies, processes, and approaches to achieve a succession of breakthroughs in airline safety.

The aerospace division I used to run was a leader in one of these approaches, in the field of Flight Operations Quality Assurance (FOQA). Over and above having a cockpit voice recorder (CVR) and a flight data recorder (FDR) onboard a modern airliner, both of which are crash protected, airlines started flying with a non crash protected device known as a Quick Access Recorder (QAR). The FDR and CVR are constantly overwriting their recorded data and only freeze the data after an accident (or sometimes an incident). In contrast, a QAR routinely records many channels of flight data on high capacity removable media (initially magnetic tape cassettes, then optical compact disks, then solid state memory cards) which the airline can get quick access to after every flight or cycle of flights. They remove the recorded media and replace it with a blank.

These removed data are then analyzed and added to a growing database, which allows the airline to look for trends across its fleet of different aircraft, routes, and airport hubs. They look for "events," where a single "event" is a deviation outside the normal safe flight envelope defined by the airline. This enables an airline to spot trends in its events data, well before they are at risk of incidents and accidents. They can diagnose the issue, set corrective actions, and track the trend back into the safe flight envelope, preadaptively. FOQA is a great example of a technology, process, and approach which provides a preadaptive 3.0 mode of execution excellence and organizational agility. It's an information system at the heart of an airline's productivity process for preadaptive incident and accident prevention, as an organizational OODA Loop for flight safety. That's integration, alignment, and attunement from the OODA Loop in the cockpit to the OODA Loop at the head office.

At the heart of this approach is one of the most influential underlying theories and models of what causes accidents and the associated risk analysis and risk management of human systems, called the Reason Model, pioneered by James Reason—what a very fitting last name. My FOQA related business unit was at the leading edge of understanding and applying this theory and model to aviation safety during the 1980s, 1990s, and 2000s. It is also affectionately called the "Swiss cheese" model of accident causation as "holes," just like in Swiss cheese, are at core of the theory. Normally, accidents don't happen because of a series of barriers between us and the hazards of particular industries, forming layers insulating us from harm. Each of these layers has holes in it, reflecting individual weaknesses in parts of the system, continually varying in size and position. The system as a whole fails if and when these holes line up, permitting a "trajectory of accident opportunity" to propagate through the insulating barrier layers, from the hazards toward harm.

Lo and behold, "the National Commission report into the BP oil spill builds its case around the theme that "complex systems almost always fail in complex ways" and page 181 of BP's internal Accident Investigation Report into the Deepwater Horizon drilling rig disaster refers explicitly to the Reason Model. It identifies the eight barrier layers that were breached and the critical factors allowing a "trajectory of accident opportunity" to propagate from the hazard (the reservoir hydrocarbons) to the harm (the fire and the spill). The barriers and critical factors identified are:

Barriers	Critical Factors
Annulus Cement	Well Integrity Was Not
Mechanical Barriers	Established or Failed
Pressure Integrity Testing	Hydrocarbons Entered
Well Monitoring	the Well Undetected, and
Well Control Response	Well Control Was Lost
Hydrocarbon Surface Containment	Hydrocarbons Ignited on
Fire and Gas System	Deepwater Horizon
Blowout Preventer (BOP)	Blowout Preventer Did Not
Emergency Operation	Seal the Well

In his 2008 book, *The Human Contribution: Unsafe Acts, Accidents and Heroic Recoveries*, James Reason says: *"The purpose of this book is to explore the human contribution to both the reliability and resilience of complex well-defended systems. The predominant mode of treating this topic is to consider the human as a hazard, a system component whose unsafe acts are implicated in the majority of catastrophic breakdowns. But there is another perspective, one that has been relatively little studied in its own right, and that is the human as hero, a system element whose adaptations and compensations have brought troubled systems back from the brink of disaster on a significant number of occasions."*

Think Eastern Airlines versus US Airways Flight 1549 captained by Chesley "Sully" Sullenberger. Human as hazard or human as hero? Think GM and Chrysler. Human as hazard or human as hero? Think Toyota. Think BP. Human as hazard or human as hero?

So the question for you is: Will you be a hazard or a hero? As they relate to your business system, are your human contributions in the category of unsafe acts or adaptations and compensations? How well defended is your complex business system, for preadaptive reliability and resilience? Or is it a postadaptive, troubled system on the brink of catastrophic breakdown and disaster? And what will you do about your productivity to move the needle from the latter toward the former?

Preadaptive execution excellence and organizational agility require new approaches to productivity at all three levels, down the middle vertical of our agenda model. Some of the approaches to productivity enhancement, which we will review in the next chapter, are so elegantly simple, they are almost embarrassingly so, which is why most people don't do them. I urge you to get over it! It's about changing culture, which is another crucial component in graduating to Execution Excellence 3.0.

Culture

For preadaptive execution excellence and organizational agility, we need to bring the culture component into focus, which runs along the middle horizontal of our framework. As a mid-level component from left to right, it creates continuity between strategy and operations at all three time horizons, from short range to long range, as a go-between in the continuum of top down and bottom up. Any discontinuity in that continuum, to whatever degree, is like an oil slick in our mindful process of integration, alignment and attunement, from gray matter to gray matter. It results in our top down strategy and bottom-up operations being out of alignment and attunement with a "them and us" discontinuity.

The culture component runs from left to right in our agenda model because we must think about our culture at each of three different time horizons:

• **Short-Range Culture**. In the continuum between our operations management and mental models, this relates to our culture with regard to the short-range pressures and performance expectations upon us and our mindsets regarding those. This is a crucial component in closing the loop of our organizational OODA Loop in the transition between **Action** and **Observation**. A weak link in the chain of our organizational OODA Loop here is very costly to our organizational agility, and we pay a price with wheel$pin.

• **Mid-Range Culture**. This relates to the culture of our infrastructure of structures, processes, and systems, as the central cog in the gearbox of our organizational OODA Loop (as we discussed earlier in this chapter). Not least of all, as a core part of this central cog, this also relates to the culture and teamwork which occurs through our meetings, before, during, and after. As we will discuss further in the next chapter, like it or not, meetings are at the core of our culture and teamwork as a business.

• **Long-Range Culture**. In the continuum between goal setting and strategy process, this relates to our culture regarding long-range thinking and commitment to advance strategic initiatives. This is a crucial component in closing the loop of our organizational OODA Loop in the transition between <u>O</u>rientation and <u>D</u>ecision. A weak link in the chain of our organizational OODA Loop here is very costly to our organizational agility, and we pay a price with wheel$pin.

This culture component of our agenda model interfaces with every other component and is, therefore, crucial to graduating every other component from a 2.0 mode of organizational agility to a preadaptive 3.0 mode.

Not least of all, as CEOs, executives, and managers, we have to think about our culture in dealing with the accelerating demands of detail complexity and dynamic complexity, coming at us thicker and faster all the time. We must think about it collectively and individually. In my experience, culture is something which most CEOs, executives, and managers don't spend enough time thinking about and working on, at all three time horizons. Patrick Lencioni speaks to culture at each of these time horizons in his series of books:

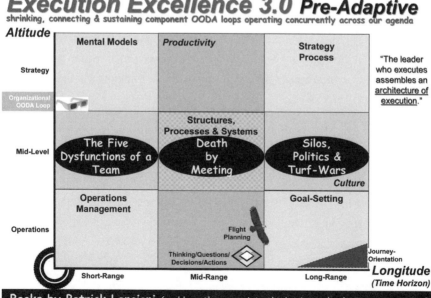

Execution Excellence 3.0 *Pre-Adaptive*
shrinking, connecting & sustaining component OODA loops operating concurrently across our agenda

Books by Patrick Lencioni (and how they map into the horizontal culture component of our Execution Excellence model)

In his 2002 book, *The Five Dysfunctions of a Team*, Lencioni says:

"Two critical truths have become clear to me. First, genuine teamwork in most organizations remains as elusive as it has ever been. Second, organizations fail to achieve teamwork because they unknowingly fall prey to five natural but dangerous pitfalls, which I call the five dysfunctions of a team:

- Inattention to Results
- Avoidance of Accountability
- Lack of Commitment
- Fear of Conflict
- Absence of Trust

The true measure of a team is that it accomplishes the results that it sets out to achieve. To do that on a consistent ongoing basis, a team must overcome the five dysfunctions, embodying the behaviors described for each one.

If this sounds simple, it's because it is simple, at least in theory. In practice, however, it is extremely difficult because it requires levels of discipline and persistence that few teams can muster."

–Patrick Lencioni, 2002, *The Five Dysfunctions of a Team*

"It requires levels of discipline and persistence that few teams can muster." This model of five dysfunctions is an elegantly simple distillation of the challenge most teams have with their culture regarding their short-range pressures and performance expectations, in the moment, day-to-day, week-to-week, and month-to-month.

Beyond this short-range time horizon, we must think about the influence which our portfolio of regular meetings has on our culture. In his 2004 book, *Death by Meeting*, Lencioni says:

"For those of us who lead and manage organizations, meetings are pretty much what we do. Whether we like it or not, meetings are the closest thing to an operating room, a playing field, or a stage that we have. How pathetic is it that we have come to accept that the activity most central to the running of our organizations in inherently painful and un-productive. There is simply no substitute for a good meeting—a dynamic, passionate, and focused engagement—when it comes to extracting the collective wisdom of a team.

Our problem is not that we are having too many meetings. Our problem is that we're having too few of them. I'm not saying we need to be spending more time in meetings, necessarily. But we definitely need to be having more than one type of meeting. By taking a contrarian, nontraditional view of meetings… we can transform what is now painful and tedious into something productive, compelling and even energizing. In the process, we can also differentiate ourselves from our competitors who continue to waste time, energy, and enthusiasm lamenting the drudgery of meetings.

When properly utilized, meetings are time savers. Good meetings provide opportunities to improve execution by accelerating decision making and eliminating the need to revisit issues again and again. But they also produce a subtle but enormous benefit by reducing unnecessarily repetitive motion and communication in the organization - "sneaker-time". I have no doubt that sneaker time is the most subtle, dangerous, and under-estimated black-hole in corporate America… because it is mixed in with everything else we do, we fail to see it as a single category of wasted time."

–Patrick Lencioni, 2004, *Death by Meeting*

Meetings are pretty much what we do, we are having too few of them, not too many, and they are time savers, not time consumers! In my experience, too, that's a change of culture for most organizations and many of the managers, executives, and CEOs who run them. For preadaptive organizational agility, meetings should be part of our management process for processing mid level and mid-range issues of detail complexity and dynamic complexity. When they aren't, we create a counterculture of what Patrick Lencioni calls "sneaker-time," which is worth dwelling on some more:

Sneaker-Time

"Most executives I know spend hours sending e-mail, leaving voice-mail, and roaming the halls to clarify issues that should have been made clear during a meeting in the first place. But no one accounts for this the way they do when they add up the time they spent in meetings.

Consider that an executive team with just seven people has twenty-one combinations of one-to-one relationships that have to be maintained in order to keep people on the same page. That alone is next to impossible for a human being to track. But when you consider the dozens of employees down throughout the organization who report to those seven and who need to be on the same page with one another, the communication challenge increases dramatically, as does the potential for wasting time and energy. And so, when we fail to get clarity and alignment during meetings, we set in motion a colossal wave of human activity as executives and their direct reports scramble to figure out what everyone else is doing and why.

It never ceases to amaze me when I see executives checking their watches at the end of a meeting and lobbying the CEO for it to end so they can go do some real work. In so many cases, the real work they're referring to is going back to their offices to respond to e-mail and voice-mail that they've received only because so many people are confused about what needs to be done. It's as if executives are saying, can we wrap this up so I can run around and explain to people what I never explained to them after the last meeting?

It is at once shocking and understandable that intelligent people cannot see the correlation between failing to take the time to get clarity, closure, and buy-in during a meeting, and the time required to clean up after themselves as a result."

–Patrick Lencioni, 2004, *Death by Meeting*

In other words, what doesn't get handled preadaptively in meetings gets handled postadaptively as sneaker-time! Beyond this mid-range time horizon, sneaker-time becomes something even more insidious when we consider the long-range time horizon. In his 2006 book, *Silos, Politics and Turf-Wars*, Lencioni says:

"Even when leadership teams become behaviorally cohesive, they face another challenge, a more structural one, that often thwarts their efforts and creates unnecessary politics within an organization. What I'm referring to are silos. Silos are nothing more than the barriers that exist between departments within an organization causing people who are supposed to be on the same team to work against one another.

And whether we call this phenomenon departmental politics, divisional rivalry, or turf warfare, it is one of the most frustrating aspects of life in any sizable organization. In most situations, silos rise up not because of what executives are doing purposefully but rather because of what they are failing to do: provide themselves and their employees with a compelling context for working together.

If there is a place where the blame for silos and politics belongs, it is at the top of an organization. Every departmental silo in any company can ultimately be traced back to the leaders of those departments, who have failed to understand the interdependencies that must exist among the executive team, or who have failed to make those interdependencies clear to the people deeper in their own departments."

(Patrick Lencioni, 2006, Silos, *Politics and Turf Wars*)

Silos rise up because of what many managers, executives, and CEOs are failing to do, providing themselves and their employees with a compelling context for working together. That's why this third Patrick Lencioni book maps into the long range time horizon of the culture component, in the continuum between our strategy process and goal setting components. These two components must deliver the outcomes of common goals aligned with collective strategy, which must then be reinforced with accountability for progressing strategic, long-range initiatives. Together, these create that compelling context which Patrick Lencioni speaks to. Any missing piece of that equation, of collective strategy, common goals, or accountability for strategic, long-range initiatives, and we allow silos, politics, and turf-wars to creep into our culture, from the long-range end.

As Patrick Lencioni says, "even when leadership teams become behaviorally cohesive, they face another challenge." In other words, it's not enough for them just to master The Five Dysfunctions of a Team, as that can relate only to their short-range culture regarding short-range pressures and performance expectations. When there is the clear and present danger of a fire to fight, most teams come together well in an "all hands to the pumps" kind of way. They readily work across silos, not least of all because the manager, executive, or CEO is watching closely, and/or is involved in a roll-our-sleeves-up kind of way.

The bigger challenge is what happens when that crisis has passed, in particular when nobody is watching that closely. That's why the middle component of meetings is so crucial, in the mid-range component of culture. As Patrick Lencioni says, "There is simply no substitute for a good meeting—a dynamic, passionate, and focused engagement—when it comes to extracting the collective wisdom of a team." It is in meetings that so much of our culture plays out before our very eyes and ears. It is in meetings that we drive dialogue to create and resolve conflict and context. It is in meetings that we close the loop on accountability and commitment, tapping into the power of peer pressure. It is in meetings that we get to see and hear trust in action.

Meetings let us put our finger on the pulse of culture and reinforce the context we want and the context we don't want. They are the place in which we master the challenge of the "and," navigating a middle road. The whole and the parts, long range and short range, strategy and operations, working "in" and "on" our journey! Besides working "in" our culture, meetings are a place to also work "on" our culture. They are a training ground and a rehearsal for what happens outside the room when we all leave.

In my experience, many managers, executives, and CEOs don't spend enough time working on culture, in particular across these the three time horizons. While we may have identified some core values as an organization, we haven't invested in detailing those out, into observable operating norms that we can create accountability around, along the lines of The Five Dysfunctions of a Team. Our meetings aren't working very well, inviting a general sense of "meetings overload." We suffer silo mentality as soon as no one is watching closely. How many managers, executives, and CEOs do you know who are struggling with these issues, especially in the face of the increasing flow of dynamic complexity, coming at us thicker and faster all the time?

Think about our Eastern Airlines story. For all kinds of reasons in that cockpit that day they became a crew of high performance individuals coming together in a culture of low performance teamwork. Their agility got tested, and they should have passed with flying colors. Instead they failed the test.

Achieving a preadaptive, 3.0 mode of organizational agility requires new approaches to culture, at all three time horizons along the middle horizontal of our agenda model. As already started to become evident in our discussion above, the culture and productivity components of our agenda model intersect at the infrastructure component of structures, processes, and systems. As the central cog in the gearbox of our Organizational OODA Loop, this infrastructure component has to evolve in nature for us to graduate to Execution Excellence 3.0.

Structures, Processes, and Systems Evolving in Nature

As depicted by its speckled nature in the Execution Excellence 3.0 agenda model, the central component of structures, processes, and systems needs to evolve in nature, to better facilitate the intersection between productivity and culture for preadaptive organizational agility 3.0.

As we discussed in Chapter 3, our infrastructure needs to find the balance point between not too loose and not too tight, not too structured and not too unstructured, not too ordered and not too chaotic. In other words, not too bureaucratic and not too seat-of-the-pants!

Too bureaucratic and we will still get things done, because someone is cracking the whip, but we aren't having much fun doing it, and our best talent will leave as soon as they possibly can, going down the street to a competitor that is less bureaucratic. Too seat of the pants and we still get things done because someone is cracking the whip, but we aren't having much fun doing it, and our best talent will leave as soon as they possibly can, going down the street to a competitor that is less chaotic.

When we have the right balance, we can get an awful lot done and have a lot of fun doing it. Loose and tight, structured and unstructured, hands-on and hands-off, all at the same time! To achieve that, we must leverage the power of systems thinking. As Peter Senge reminded us earlier in this chapter, *"Most of the problems faced by humankind concern our inability to grasp and manage the increasingly complex systems of our world."* Systems, processes, and structures influence our thinking, questioning, decision making, and action taking, in the continuum of our beliefs, behaviors, and results.

Every system is perfectly designed to produce the results we are getting. If we want more agile results, we need to change to more agile behaviors, which means we need to change to more agile systems, processes, and structures, which influence those behaviors. Changing to more agile behaviors, systems, processes, and structures mean we also need to change our belief system about agility and the need to find the balance point of the "and." Hardwired beliefs about running a very tight ship or keeping things loose and organic are not easily rewired, but must be for preadaptive organizational agility and Execution Excellence 3.0.

We must also address our full spectrum of structures, processes, and systems, from the most tangible, like our physical layout, our organizational chart, and our enterprise software system, to the most intangible, like our core values, culture, and teamwork environment. We must be thinking agile across that full spectrum.

Think about our Eastern Airlines story. Clearly, the crew's structures, processes, and systems let them down that day. Checks and balances for crew resource management, situational awareness, and flight operations quality assurance, which are institutionalized into cockpit structures, processes, and systems today, were not in place back then.

The agile intersection of culture and productivity, facilitated by an infrastructure of agile structures, processes, and systems, places new demands upon our leadership and communication skills and style as CEOs, executives, and managers.

Leadership/Communication Skills and Style

If we are responsible for an organization or team and don't have the agile intersection of culture and productivity we need, there is only one place to look. In the mirror! As leaders, we are simultaneously the solution and the problem. How are we the problem? We get what we invite, we become what we tolerate, and we encourage what we allow. We are the source of what we have.

Our leadership and communication skills and style set the tone for the intersection of culture and productivity that we have. If our culture and productivity are intersecting in a preadaptive 3.0 mode of organizational agility, well done! Great job! If we are in an adaptive 2.0 mode, not bad, but we have a lot more to do. If we are in a postadaptive 1.0 mode, watch out! We are simultaneously the problem and the solution and we have a lot of work to do, and fast. We may have a Wrong Hazelwood or Eastern Airlines scenario in our very near future.

A great deal has been written about leadership and communication skills and style, and it isn't my intention to do a deep dive on that here. My purpose is to position the criticality of this component in our agenda model. It all comes home to roost with us as the leader. As we will review in Chapter 7, it's all about who we need to be as breakthrough leaders *In the Driving Seat* of organizational agility, which will test us, sometimes mildly and sometimes brutally. As we will review in Chapter 8, it's all about how ready, willing, and able we are to pass that test.

Our leadership and communication skills and style set the tone for the intersection of culture and productivity which we have. In their 2002 book, *Primal Leadership*, Daniel Goleman, Richard Boyartis, and Annie McKee put it this way:

> "The fundamental task of leaders, we argue, is to prime good feeling in those they lead. That occurs when a leader creates resonance—a reservoir of positivity that frees the best in people. At its roots, then, the primal job of leadership is emotional. We believe this primal dimension of leadership,

though often invisible or ignored entirely, determines whether everything else a leader does will work as well as it could. Our basic argument, in a nutshell, is that primal leadership operates at its best through emotionally intelligent leaders who create resonance. The leader's mood can energize or deflate an entire organization.

Typically, the best, most effective leaders act according to one or more of six distinct approaches to leadership and skillfully switch between the various styles depending upon the situation:

1. Visionary
2. Coaching
3. Affiliative
4. Democratic
5. Pace-Setting
6. Commanding

Leaders with the best results didn't practice just one particular style. Rather, on any given day of the week, they used many of the six distinct styles, seamlessly and in different measures, depending upon the business situation. Imagine the styles, then, as an array of clubs in the golf pro's bag. Over the course of a match, the pro picks and chooses from his bag based upon the demands of the shot. Sometimes he has to ponder selection, but usually it is automatic. The pro 'senses' the challenge ahead, swiftly pulls out the right tool, and elegantly puts it to work. That's how high-impact leaders operate too. Although these styles of leadership have all been identified previously by different names, what's new about our model of leadership is an understanding of the underlying emotional intelligence capabilities that each approach requires, and—most compelling—each style's causal link with outcomes. For executives engaged in the daily battle of getting results, such a connection adds a much-needed dose of science to the critical art of leadership."

–Daniel Goleman, Richard Boyartis, Annie McKee, 2002,
Primal Leadership: Realizing the Power of Emotional Intelligence

Of course, golf is also another great analogy for a journey that, by definition, is about linking and accumulating the individual shots of our journey, into our score for the round, above par or below par.

Also, whether the leader's mood is above par or below par can energize or deflate an entire organization. As leaders, our emotional intelligence lives in our inner world/journey, at the core of the diamond-shaped *Journey-ionics* model of Executive Intelligence, Intuition, and Resilience, which we reviewed in Chapter 4. Our emotional intelligence influences our leadership and communication skills and style. It influences the golf clubs we have in our bag, our range of skill with the different clubs, and the club we default to when we are under pressure.

That sets the tone for the culture of our team and organization and the mood that pervades throughout it. In turn, that influences the emotional intelligence of our team members and employees, which in turn influences their leadership and communication skills and style. And so on and so on, as part of our self-defeating downward spiral or our self-fulfilling upward spiral. I call this our organizational MOODA Loop (as opposed to OODA Loop).

Think about our Eastern Airlines story. Something happened with the mood loop in that cockpit that day. The mood shifted to one of frustration and inconvenience, which influenced the way the crew's conversation of thinking, deciding, questioning, and acting unfolded in real time.

As CEOs, executives, and managers, it all comes home to roost with us and our leadership and communication. For preadaptive organizational agility and execution excellence 3.0, we have to take the lead in getting all the component parts in our agenda model in place, getting them turning over well, and keeping them well oiled. They are the cogs in the gearbox of our organizational OODA Loop, and we have to get them to mesh well together, enterprise wide and enterprise deep, as an integrated capability and capacity to execute.

Enterprise Execution Capability and Capacity

Now that we have reviewed most of the component parts required for organizational agility and execution excellence 3.0, as the gearbox of our organizational OODA Loop, a final piece of the puzzle is to get them all to work well together. All of the cogs in our gearbox need to mesh together in an agile alignment, attunement, and integration, as our overall execution capability and capacity as an enterprise. How hard can that be?

This is the hardest part of all! This really tests our agility as leaders and communicators. Creating and sustaining an agile alignment, attunement, and integration of the system comprising all of these component parts is not to be underestimated, especially when we are trying to do it enterprise wide and enterprise deep, to build a bigger wheelbase of contact footprint between the rubber and the road. Especially when we are trying to build the bus of high performance teamwork, with the right people in the right seats and every seat being a driving seat, from which we are getting traction.

This final ellipse-shaped component in our agenda model is like the transmission system in your car, from gray matter to gray matter:

- From our hands on the steering wheel, our feet on the pedals, with our whole brain in gear (i.e., the "strategy process" component in the top right corner of our agenda model) and wearing our 3-D glasses

- Down through the gearbox of our business (i.e., the central component of "structures/processes/systems")

- Down through the running gear of our business (i.e., the "operations management" component in the bottom left), down to creating traction between the rubber and the road.

Any degree of disconnect anywhere in this system and we get less traction than we should have, more wheel$pin than we should have, and, by definition, we are on a lower road than we otherwise could be on. As we discussed in Chapter 1, with Premise No. 2, that wheel$pin is costing us a fortune, in avoidable costs and opportunity costs!

Building this unifying architecture of execution, fully integrated, aligned, and attuned, doesn't happen by accident! It happens by design. Oftentimes, many of the parts are there, but the whole hasn't emerged and/or isn't working well. We are losing something in translation.

Think of our Eastern Airlines story. The crew lost something in translation that day. They had all of the parts for execution excellence (a latest technology jet, highly trained crew, and communication with an air traffic controller), yet the whole didn't emerge and or wasn't working well. It wasn't sufficiently integrated, aligned, and attuned to their challenge.

Unfortunately, during those few minutes, they didn't do a great job dividing their time, energy, and attention across their full execution excellence agenda, wearing their 3-D glasses (for the whole challenge of detail complexity and dynamic complexity), and, in particular, paying attention to the longitudinal dimension of their journey orientation to their sequence of goals, not just the first one of fixing the bulb. While they clearly had a macroscopic flight plan for their overall flight into Miami International Airport that day, their microscopic flight planning in those few minutes failed the test.

Flight Planning

Now that we have reviewed all the other component parts of our organizational OODA Loop and Execution Excellence model, we are able to further understand the critical importance of the Flight Planning component. This is the final component of our agenda model for Execution Excellence 3.0 and integrates the diamond shaped *Journey-ionics* model of Executive Intelligence, Intuition, and Resilience from Chapter 4. We need to be flying around our agenda model for execution excellence, spending the right time in the right place at the right time and in the right manner wearing our 3-D glasses, linking and accumulating the traction "ions" of our journey.

When we get this right, we avoid any deficit disorders. When we don't, we suffer deficits of intention, attention, and responsibility for results. When we suffer deficit disorders, bad things can happen:

- Our OODA Loops expand to large, lethargic, and somewhat open-loop OODA Loops. We don't have all the component OODA Loop cogs we need in the gearbox of our Organizational OODA Loop, and they aren't being kept well oiled, turning over well, and meshing well. Our need for connecting vibrant OODA Loops operating simultaneously at several levels breaks down.

- Discontinuities begin to creep into our journey-oriented continuum at a microscopic, granular level. As we have been exploring, a journey comprises a continuum of thoughts, questions, decisions, and actions; of the past, the present, and the future; of the outer world and the inner world; of beliefs, behaviors, and results; of learning, applying, and achieving in parallel.

- We invite the self-fulfilling and self-defeating prophecy, vicious cycle, and downward spiral back into our equation, risk it taking hold and spiraling downward, imperceptibly at first. When the descent becomes perceptible, it's often too late, and it can quickly become a nosedive, followed by a tailspin, followed by a smoking hole in the ground. Eastern Airlines. Wrong Hazelwoods. GM, Chrysler, Toyota, BP!

Our agility gets audited, sometimes mildly and sometimes brutally, and mild audits can often turn brutal. When we allow our organizational OODA Loop to expand, becoming a large, lethargic, and somewhat open loop, with discontinuities creeping in and inviting the downward spiral back into the equation, imperceptibly at first, very bad things can happen.

Every journey starts with a single thought, or the lack of a single thought, and it all unfolds from there. Flight planning is about being productively paranoid, doing everything we can to make sure there aren't thoughts we should be having but we aren't or thoughts we are having which we shouldn't, all across the map of our execution excellence agenda. I want you to be productively paranoid, not unproductively so! That's what it takes to be getting an A these days as a great manager, executive, or CEO.

Getting an A

These are the 13 component parts for an architecture of Execution Excellence 3.0 and preadaptive organizational agility.

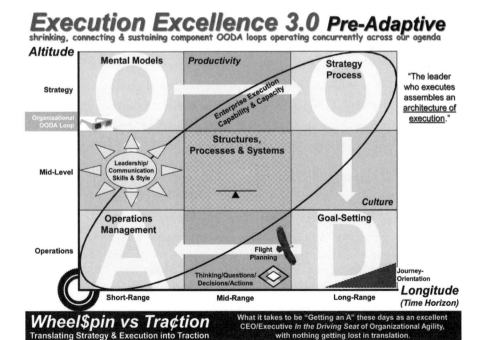

This is what it takes to get an A these days as an excellent CEO, executive, or manager *In the Driving Seat* of organizational agility, with nothing getting lost in translation. Remember, that's where we started back in Chapter 2, asking why so much gets lost in translation.

We also call this our *Journey-judgment (Jj)* model, as it is about judging where we are in our journey and judging where we can best spend our time, to best reduce wheel$pin and create traction for the next phase of our journey. It's about diagnosing wheel$pin and treating it with traction, judging the next phase of traction "ions" to link and accumulate, in service of our journey.

It is complicated. But no more complicated than it needs to be. Remember what we quoted from Einstein in Chapter 1, that *"Everything should be made as simple as possible, but no simpler."* Mind you, it should be no surprise that it is complicated. If it was easy, anybody could do it, everybody would already be doing it, nobody would be struggling with it, and somebody would have taken the lead in your organization. Talking about anybody, everybody, nobody, and somebody, you've probably seen that poem about responsibility from Charles Osgood:

"A Poem About Responsibility"
by Charles Osgood

There was a most important job that needed to be done,
And no reason not to do it, there was absolutely none.
But in vital matters such as this, the thing you have to ask
Is who exactly will it be who'll carry out the task?

Anybody could have told you that everybody knew
That this was something somebody would surely have to do.
Nobody was unwilling; anybody had the ability.
But nobody believed that it was their responsibility.

It seemed to be a job that anybody could have done,
If anybody thought he was supposed to be the one.
But since everybody recognized that anybody could,
Everybody took for granted that somebody would.

> But nobody told anybody that we are aware of,
> That he would be in charge of seeing it was taken care of.
> And nobody took it on himself to follow through,
> And do what everybody thought that somebody would do.
>
> When what everybody needed so did not get done at all,
> Everybody was complaining that somebody dropped the ball.
> Anybody then could see it was an awful crying shame,
> And everybody looked around for somebody to blame.
>
> Somebody should have done the job
> And Everybody should have,
> But in the end Nobody did
> What Anybody could have.

"Somebody should have done the job and everybody should have, but in the end nobody did what anybody could have!" In my experience, in many businesses, that sounds like, "If only we could just execute better around here." That is something I often hear reverberating around a business, or some other similar venting. Like, "People just need to hold themselves more accountable around here," or "We just need to communicate better." That's the essence of the problem: There is no "just" about it! It's complicated.

In the face of that, many CEOs, executives, and managers bounce off that complexity, adopting the stupid simplicity of something like, "We'll just focus on achieving this year's budget and annual plan," or "If we just focus on customer service, everything else will take care of itself." Or they reach for the familiarity and comfort of the conventional tools and approaches of traditional "strategic planning and implementation."

Wrong answer! That is, if we want to be getting an A as a great CEO, executive, or manager, driving things to be preadaptive and experiencing more good luck and less bad luck. That is, if we want to translate more strategy and more execution into more traction. If we are happy being a B or C player, then we don't worry about it. If we are happy with things driving us to be postadaptive and experiencing more bad luck and less good luck, then we don't worry about it. If we are happy experiencing more wheel$pin, and Wrong Hazelwoods, Eastern Airlines, and constant whitewater, then we don't worry about it.

It's our choice. It's about how ready, willing, and able we are. To be ready, willing, and able, we have to master all these component parts, as vibrant and connected OODA Loops and cogs in the gearbox of our organizational OODA Loop. They need to be present, kept well oiled and turning over well, and mesh together, with alignment, attunement, and integration.

They need to be attuned to the anatomy of dynamic complexity by being aligned with the longitudinal dimension of journey orientation, from gray matter to gray matter. From the gray matter of our brains, and the longitudinal alignment of our corpus callosum, facilitating the power of our opposable mind and integrative thinking. To the gray matter of the asphalt, between the rubber and the road, longitudinally aligned with our traction and forward momentum on the evolutionary path we are finding with our business.

In that mindful process of integration, alignment, and attunement, from gray matter to gray matter, and the new framework of strengths, understandings, and intelligences we have been exploring, we have now accumulated a model for each of the first two levels:

Higher Order Executive Strengths of Journey-Orientation:	Understanding the Anatomy of Dynamic Complexity:
+ Execution Excellence ...... **XQ**	.... the anatomy of the **Vehicle** fit for the journey challenge.
Journey-judgment (Jj)	
+ Executive Intelligence, Intuition & Resilience ...... **EQ (IQ)**	.... the anatomy of the **Journey** and how it unfolds real-time.
Journey-ionics (Ji)	
+ Path-Finding .... **PQ**	...........the anatomy of the **Road** and paths of least resistance.

Bottom-line   XQ + EQ (IQ) + PQ = BQ (AQ)

= Organizational Agility ...... **BQ (AQ)**	.... the anatomy of **Breakthrough Leadership & Architecting Breakthrough Journeys.**

our ability to deal with rapidly changing circumstances, while out-executing our competition and stakeholder expectations (of customers, employees, suppliers and shareholders)

ordinary people achieving extraordinary things, making possible tomorrow, what seems impossible today

As we mentioned earlier in this chapter, the *Journey-judgment* model of Execution Excellence is also the master, unifying model that integrates the other models, capturing the whole challenge, the whole problem, and the whole solution of being *In the Driving Seat* of organizational agility. We can now see the other models in the *Journey-judgment* model of Execution Excellence.

First, the Flight Planning component integrates the diamond-shaped *Journey-ionics* model of Executive Intelligence, Intuition, and Resilience from Chapter 4 and the second level in our new framework of understandings, strengths, and intelligences. To be getting an A, we need to be getting our flight planning right, dividing our bandwidth so that we don't suffer any deficit disorders. We need to be spending the right time, in the right place, at the right time, and in the right manner, wearing our 3-D glasses, linking and accumulating the traction "ions" (our individual thoughts, questions, decisions, and actions) of our journey.

To help facilitate this, we need tools to stake out our Execution Excellence agenda and drive our conversation. Driving different conversations requires unconventional tools for unconventional times. Among others, here are some of the key tools which map into our agenda framework:

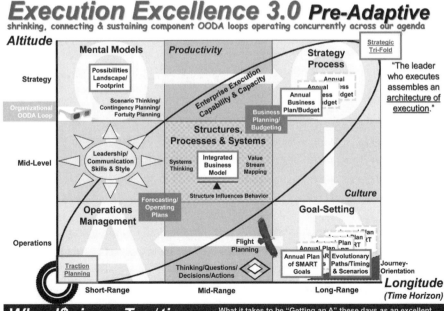

We will begin referring to some of these tools as we progress from here.

Second, the Journey Orientation component integrates a wedge shaped model of pathfinding, which is the third level in our new framework of strengths, understandings, and intelligences. The tools which are mapped into our Execution Excellence 3.0 agenda model on the secondary diagonal, of top left to bottom right, relate to this pathfinding strength, namely:

- Possibilities Landscape/Footprint
- Integrated Business Model
- Evolutionary Path/Scenarios and Timing

It is this pathfinding strength which we explore next.

Pathfinding: The Art of Possibility and Probability

Pathfinding is about finding an evolutionary path through, no matter what. No matter how the landscape is shifting upon us. No matter what kind of plate tectonics are occurring beneath the surface, threatening to turn our world upside down. No matter what kind of complicated topography we face, of tangled issues, complex circumstances, and seemingly intractable situations. No matter how acutely and rapidly our environment is changing and we are evolving and adapting, in the Darwinian manner we have discussed. Pathfinding is about finding an evolutionary path through, no matter what!

As we develop the self-confidence in our organizational agility to do that, we are future-proofing our business. No matter what the future brings, we will be able to deal with it, prevailing by surviving and thriving. Success becomes increasingly inevitable, and we are more and more certain to win. It's about an unfolding journey of possibilities and probabilities and finding an evolutionary path through, so that we are choosing our future and not letting our future choose us. If our future chooses us, it's likely to be ugly, rife with Wrong Hazelwoods, Eastern Airlines, and constant whitewater!

This journey-oriented, higher-order executive strength of Pathfinding requires an understanding of the anatomy of the road, finding paths of least resistance and the underlying intelligence we call PQ. This intelligence is about developing an instinct and intuitive sense for Pathfinding. The anatomy of the road is about understanding the typical evolutionary phases of the journey of a business and the dynamic complexities and transitions involved. Finding paths of least resistance is about being creative enough to avoid harder paths when there are easier ones. More resistance means more inertia to overcome, which means a greater tendency to encounter wheel$pin and more difficulty getting into traction. Less resistance means it's easier to get into traction, build momentum, and brew up breakthroughs.

From Road Mapping to Pathfinding

A road map! This is most often the answer I get when facilitating teams and asking them, "what are your hopes and wants for the process we are embarking upon, which will make it a valuable investment of your time, energy, and attention?" They want to know where we are going, where we are starting from, and how we will map out a road to get from here to there. As we have discussed, that's the macroscopic understanding of a journey.

These days, though, a road map is no longer enough. Because life has become like a dynamic journey on a shifting landscape of increasing uncertainty, turbulence, and volatility. As the ink is drying on a road map, it is already becoming out of date, progressively redundant, and increasingly irrelevant. It rapidly becomes part of our problem. It's the HR VP talking about how rigidly overengineered they are with their annual goals, unable to make course corrections mid-year. It's the waterfall model of software development. It's the CEO we mentioned who had become very jaded about a previous strategy process as being overplanned and, as a result of his fear of that happening again, had flip-flopped into a mode of being underplanned.

To be part of the solution and not part of the problem, instead of road-mapping we need the more agile approach of pathfinding. No matter how the landscape is shifting, we keep finding an evolutionary path through. A path of least resistance, forwards, onwards, and upward. It's about the art of possibility and the art of probability coming together. As you will recall from Chapter 2, Rosamund Stone Zander and Benjamin Zander say, in *The Art of Possibility: Transforming Professional and Personal Life,* *"Draw a different frame around the same set of circumstances and new pathways come into view. Find the right framework and extraordinary accomplishment becomes an everyday experience... bringing possibility to life."*

I tend to think of the art of possibility as being about a divergent, creative process of how we *could* reframe things and the art of probability as being a convergent, rational process of how we *should. Could* is about generating creative options for ways in which we might reframe things. *Should* is about assessing the feasibility, risks, and rewards of our options, weighing them up and sensing the best path of parallel and/or sequential options, combinations, and hybrids.

As Richard Normann reminds in his 2001 book, *Reframing Business: When the Map Changes the Landscape*, changing the map can change the landscape. We have to leverage the art of possibility and probability to find an evolutionary path through, because, as Richard Normann also says, *"Today's market game is much more about who can creatively design frame breaking systemic solutions—reconfiguration of value creating systems—we must reconfigure or be reconfigured."*

We must reconfigure or be reconfigured! That's the difference between preadaptive and postadaptive organizational agility. Do we want to be postadaptively reacting to others' reconfiguring of our landscape or be preadaptively doing the reconfiguring? Having the self-confidence to be out in front requires the art of possibility and probability. As we explored, Richard Normann explains that this occurs as the interplay between two realms of thought: the business realm and the mental realm. The tools we mentioned earlier, on the secondary diagonal of our Execution Excellence agenda model, facilitate the combination of these two realms into the art of possibility and probability.

In particular, the "Evolutionary Path/Scenarios and Timing" tool takes us back to the discussion of Darwin's *Theory of Evolution by Natural Selection*. It's about the preadaptive path of the evolution of a species, becoming and remaining acutely suited to its changing environment and, as a result, being future-proofed against extinction. Of course, part of our pathfinding challenge is that we live life forward but understand it backward; we understand life backward with hindsight about the singular path we ended up coming along to arrive at where we are. But we live life forward, needing to have foresight about the multiple paths we *could* take and which we *should* take. Foresight is a lot harder and involves a constant process of what ifs. We have to link and accumulate a great deal of traction "ions" of our journey (our individual thoughts, questions, decisions, and actions) to process all of these what ifs.

In the military's Special Forces they call this analysis "branches and sequels." When we hit the beach, what if we discover a different scenario from the one we expected? Let's preadaptively process our options (the "branches" in our path) and play out each pathway through the phases of what might unfold sequentially thereafter (the "sequels"). Of course, each sequel will involve other branches and vice versa, kind of like an agile version of a decision tree. We are looking for the path of least resistance, in the form of the shortest, fasted route, with the least risk, and the best damage limitation and contingency plan options in case of trouble.

Finding that path of least resistance through that array of branches and sequels takes some critical path analysis, kind of like we do for project management. When we are analyzing the cost time resource loading and criticalities of a project plan, we do two passes, a forward pass analysis, from the present forward, and a backward pass analysis, from the future backward. In combination, these allow us to identify the critical path running through the project plan. It's a longitudinal study of branches and sequels, of cost-time-resources, forward and backward, to get a line of sight on a pathway through. It's about sniffing it out, getting on the scent, and staying on the scent, of a path which is prone to success, not failure.

All of this takes a lot of mental effort and work. A seemingly overwhelming amount if we have not been developing our pathfinding strength and the underlying intelligence, instinct, and intuition for it. Consequently, we are less likely to do it. Consequently, we are more likely to find ourselves in a postadaptive mode of organizational agility. Consequently, we are more likely to encounter scenarios we haven't preprocessed, we lack a repertoire of branches and sequels that we have already thought through, and we lack an understanding of the critical paths involved. In the heat of the moment, we are more at risk of choosing wrong, or choosing too slowly, or not choosing at all, paralyzed like a deer in the headlights! Unlucky? No, not really, more like unprepared. As we have explored, if "luck is where preparation meets opportunity," being lucky is about being prepared. Being unlucky is about being unprepared. If we don't do the work of preadaptively preparing a repertoire of branches and sequels, we are more likely to be unlucky.

Being lucky is about being prepared. Being prepared is about developing our pathfinding strength so we can do the work involved without it seeming like an overwhelming mental effort. It's about being able to think about it efficiently and effectively, so as not to feel overwhelmed. That way, we can iterate our "what if" thinking to find the evolutionary path of least resistance and improvise a way through.

It's about finding a way to get liftoff before we run out of runway and developing the rest of the flight plan from there. It's about hitting the lead pin in the bowling alley, which will cause the other pins to fall. It's about picking the beachheads to land our forces on, from which we can launch an invasion. Whichever analogy you prefer, it's about the longitudinal study of critical paths, branches, and sequels, for the parts and the whole of the business at the same time. We call this *Journey-holonics*.

From *Journey-ionics* to *Journey-holonics*

In Chapter 4, we reviewed a different understanding of a journey and how it unfolds in real time, at a microscopic level, which we call *Journey-ionics*. Here we return to a different understanding of a journey at the macroscopic level, which we call *Journey-holonics*.

The word *holonic* means simultaneously seeing the part in the whole and the whole in the part, like a hologram. If you shatter a hologram and pick up any piece, you see the whole picture in that part. It's fractal. Any fractured fragment embodies the whole. The *Journey-judgment* model of Execution Excellence is fractal in nature. We can apply it to the whole of our business and to any part of our business, any which way we choose to unbundle our business into its component parts, fragments, or fractals.

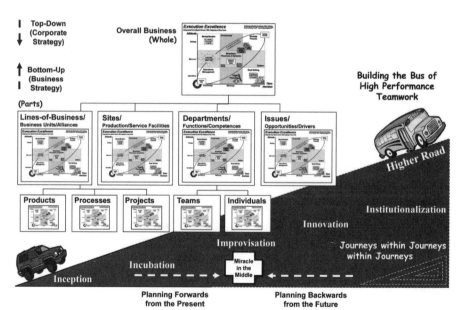

Path-Finding

"Holonic": simultaneously seeing the part in the whole and the whole in the part.

Not only can we apply the *Journey-judgment* model of Execution Excellence to any part of our business, any way we choose to unbundle it, but we must. It is the last piece of our mindful process of integration, alignment, and attunement, from gray matter to gray matter. This is how we build the bus of high performance teamwork, broadly and deeply across an organization, with every seat being a driving seat, from which we need traction.

Whether people are responsible for a department, product, process, project, facility, business unit, key account, strategic alliance, issue, or whatever, we need them *In the Driving Seat* of their roles, translating strategy and execution into traction, with the organizational agility required these days to prevail. We need traction from every seat, integrated, aligned, and attuned, from gray matter to gray matter, enterprise wide and enterprise deep. That's how we build out the wheelbase of our bus and get more contact footprint between the rubber and the road.

Our *Journey-ionics* model helps us understand a journey at a microscopic level and how we link and accumulate the traction "ions" of our journey (individual thoughts, questions, decisions, and actions). That diamond-shaped model is integrated into the *Journey-judgment* model of Execution Excellence via the Flight Planning component. Here we are looking at the *Journey-holonics* model, understanding a journey at a macroscopic level and how we link and accumulate the traction "holons" of our journey (individual departments, products, processes, facilities, etc.). That wedge shaped model is integrated into the *Journey-judgment* model of Execution Excellence via the journey orientation component. Why a wedge shape? Let's explore.

Wedge-Shaped Journeys

Throughout this book and in the various graphics contained in it, including on the previous page, you will have noticed my use of a wedge shape to signify a journey. I have always used a wedge shape as an elegantly simple icon embedding the complexities of a breakthrough journey.

The thick end of the wedge represents the big ending we want our journey to have, and the thin end of the wedge represents the small beginnings our journey will necessarily have. Every journey begins with a single step—a single thought, question, decision, or action, and the traction "ions" of our journey we link and accumulate, divergently and convergently, from there.

The diagonal of the wedge represents the desired trajectory we want to gain traction upon, in whatever measure we decide. Maybe revenue and profit measures like that public company I mentioned with a desired trajectory of 15/15 (15% revenue growth per year at 15% profitability or better, year in, year out, every year, forever). For a private business, and in particular an owner managed one, revenue and profit growth may not necessarily be the trajectory you desire. It might be that you are happy to stay the size you are, but you want to achieve that in a more sustainable way, in less time and with less stress, and with more distributable cash flow. Or your trajectory might be more about value creation, wealth management, transition planning, and migration. The point is, if you have some constructive dissatisfaction with things, you have some kind of trajectory in mind.

Whatever your trajectory happens to be, achieving it involves planning forward from the present and backward from the future, as an "and" proposition, as we discussed earlier in this chapter. Only then can we avoid being dependent upon some kind of miracle happening in the middle of our journey, to sustain our desired trajectory. You know what I mean, as you have probably seen that cartoon with the complex milestone chart for a major project in the middle of which it says, "miracle happens here!"

The body of the wedge is made up of nested journeys. In systems theory, there is the concept of nested systems, being systems within systems within systems. The human body is a good example of nested systems, comprising the following:

- Circulatory system/Cardiovascular system (heart, blood, vessels)
- Respiratory system (nose, trachea, lungs)
- Immune system (many types of protein, cells, organs, tissues)
- Lymphatic system
- Skeletal system (bones)
- Excretory system (lungs, large intestine, kidneys)
- Urinary system (bladder, kidneys)
- Muscular system (muscles)
- Endocrine system (glands)
- Digestive system (mouth, esophagus, stomach, intestines)
- Nervous system (brain, spinal cord, nerves)
- Reproductive system (male and female reproductive organs)

Nested journeys are about journeys within journeys within journeys. Each nested journey is a complex journey to mastery in its own right, with a series of s-curves and plateaus. Consequently, every journey becomes messy in the middle. To understand that messiness, let's look at the five phases of a breakthrough journey.

The Five Phases of a Breakthrough Journey

In my experience, the wedge shape of a breakthrough journey unfolds in five macroscopic phases:

- **Inception**: We launch the inception of a journey by identifying a need and fostering some attention and intention around it. Things can easily get trodden on in this phase, maybe inadvertently, and get killed off before the journey ever had a chance.

- **Incubation**: We incubate the fledgling beginnings of the journey, keeping it on a life support system. Things can easily get trampled on in this phase as we run into resistance, inertia, and FUD (fear, uncertainty, and doubt).

- **Improvisation**: As we begin to encounter bigger tangible and intangible barriers, obstacles, and hurdles, we have to improvise a way through. Things can easily get wrestled to the ground in this phase by competing priorities, leaving us with woefully inadequate time, information, and other resources.

- **Innovation**: Our persistence eventually pays off and we have won enough support and resource allocations to really start innovating and building momentum. We can easily stub our toe in this phase if we suffer a failure, which can easily set us back one, two, or even three phases.

- **Institutionalization**: We have made it this far and are now focused on embodying the innovations into our business as permanent shifts that then become self-sustaining. We can easily stop short in this phase because of pressures to declare victory and redeploy resources too soon.

These are the five macroscopic phases of a breakthrough journey, within which we are linking and accumulating the traction "ions" and the traction "holons" of our journey (for which our *Journey-ionics* and *Journey-holonics* models apply, respectively). As we have been explaining in this section, the elegant simplicity of the wedge shaped icon, which we use to signify a breakthrough journey, embeds a lot of complexity, which we have been progressively exploring. As we mentioned above, the journey with our business and organization is actually comprised of a nested journey, of journeys within journeys, and no two journeys are exactly alike. That's why architecting breakthrough journeys is so difficult and overwhelming for many CEOs, executives, and managers. It is the anatomy of dynamic complexity relating to the road and finding paths of least resistance, which is mentally very taxing. It calls up a pathfinding intelligence we call PQ, which underpins this higher-order executive strength, and developing it doesn't happen by accident.

Our new framework of understandings, strengths, and intelligences, and accumulating models, now looks like this:

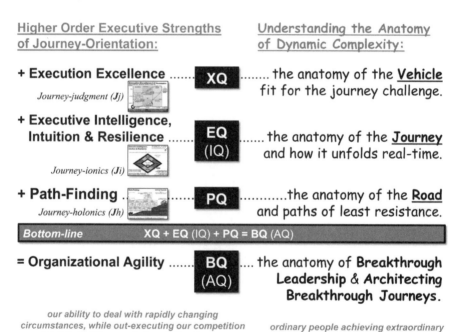

Higher Order Executive Strengths of Journey-Orientation:

Understanding the Anatomy of Dynamic Complexity:

+ Execution Excellence ...... **XQ** .... the anatomy of the **Vehicle** fit for the journey challenge.
Journey-judgment (Jj)

+ Executive Intelligence, Intuition & Resilience .... **EQ (IQ)** .... the anatomy of the **Journey** and how it unfolds real-time.
Journey-ionics (Ji)

+ Path-Finding .... **PQ** ....the anatomy of the **Road** and paths of least resistance.
Journey-holonics (Jh)

Bottom-line   XQ + EQ (IQ) + PQ = BQ (AQ)

= Organizational Agility .... **BQ (AQ)** .... the anatomy of **Breakthrough Leadership & Architecting Breakthrough Journeys.**

our ability to deal with rapidly changing circumstances, while out-executing our competition and stakeholder expectations (of customers, employees, suppliers and shareholders)

ordinary people achieving extraordinary things, making possible tomorrow, what seems impossible today

While our *Journey-judgment* model of Execution Excellence relates to the top level in this framework, we now understand how it is also the master, unifying model, integrating the others. It is our journey-oriented window looking through the dynamic plane of thinking into the whole challenge, the whole problem, and the whole solution of being *In the Driving Seat* of organizational agility.

As we conclude this chapter, we now have a greater understanding of where organizational agility comes from. It comes from all the moving parts we have reviewed in the *Journey-judgment* model of Execution Excellence, as component OODA Loop cogs in the gearbox of our organizational OODA Loop and agility. It comes from each of these cogs being present, well oiled, turning over well, and being well integrated, aligned and attuned, meshing together well. It comes from us simultaneously linking and accumulating the traction "ions" and the traction "holons" of our journey, enterprise wide and enterprise deep. It comes from our mindful process of integration, alignment, and attunement, from gray matter to gray matter, building our wheelbase and contact footprint, between the rubber and the road, with every seat being a driving seat from which we are getting traction. Translating strategy and execution into traction, with nothing getting lost in translation.

Now that we understand where it comes from, in the next chapter we will understand how we can develop our organizational agility.

Chapter 5 Summary

For organizational agility, you must have a system of execution excellence that you can trust. Most managers, executives, and CEOs don't. Worse than that, they don't have the foggiest idea what execution excellence is and the disciplined system of knowledge, tools, and techniques it needs to be. They are not getting an A and are, at best, getting a B or a C. Don't let that be you. Here are some more ideas for traction "ions" you can link and accumulate as part of your journey.

Things to Think About

◆ *Think about* the degree to which you can trust your system and discipline of execution excellence, enterprise wide and enterprise deep, linking and accumulating the traction "holons" and traction "ions" of your journey.

◆ *Think about* the mode of execution excellence you are in—postadaptive 1.0, adaptive 2.0, or preadaptive 3.0.

◆ *Think about* your flight planning to cover fully the map of your execution excellence agenda and avoid deficit disorders and the grade you are getting—A, B, or C.

Questions to Ponder

◆ *Ask yourself* how strong is the pull of the downward spiral into the constant whitewater of postadaptive 1.0?

◆ *Ask yourself* what else you need to do to break the pattern of the self-fulfilling and self-defeating vicious cycle?

◆ *Ask yourself* how that needs to start with your own personal productivity process and system to catch up and get ahead of the changing nature of work?

Decisions to Make

◆ *Decide* that Execution Excellence will no longer be missing in action, in any way, in your business.

◆ *Decide* to change your flight planning, to cover the map of your execution excellence agenda, no matter what.

Actions to Take

◆ *Start* keeping a record of where you are spending your time and how it is distributed across the execution excellence agenda.

How Do We Develop Organizational Agility?

"Any competent person is capable of bearing problems in mind until they yield their secrets; what not everybody possesses is the requisite will, passion, or insane obsession that will let them hold the problem long enough or fiercely enough."

–**Ken Wilber**

It takes will, passion, and insane obsession to develop organizational agility. In my experience, many CEOs, executives, and managers are not holding the problems in mind long enough or fiercely enough, with the requisite will, passion, or insane obsession. As we progress, I am trying to change that for you.

I am trying to inspire you to stay on the journey to mastery of organizational agility, by holding the problem in mind until it yields its secrets. I want you to be holding the problem in mind long enough and fiercely, with the requisite will, passion, and insane obsession! I want you to be insanely obsessed with the whole challenge, the whole problem, and the whole solution of being *In the Driving Seat* of organizational agility. If you are ready, willing, and able to do so, it will yield.

So far, we have yielded the secrets of *Journey-judgment (Jj)*, *Journey-ionics (Ji)*, and *Journey-holonics (Jh)*, mapped into our new framework of strengths, understandings, and intelligences. In the remaining chapters, we will yield the secrets of how to put it all together *(Jhij)* into the equation of:

$$Jhij = Jh + Ji + Jj$$

We have progressed through our mindful process of integration, alignment, and attunement, from gray matter to gray matter, in phases of reviewing the new mindset, the new chassis of business acumen, and the new framework of strengths, understandings, and intelligences. We have arrived at an understanding of the *Journey-judgment* model of Execution Excellence as the master, unifying model, integrating the other models. It is our journey-oriented window, looking through the dynamic plane of thinking, into the whole challenge, the whole problem, and the whole solution of being *In the Driving Seat* of organizational agility and evolving from a postadaptive 1.0 mode through 2.0 to a 3.0 preadaptive mode.

BONUS

http://bit.ly/oZ7iRg

We tackle the whole equation of $Jhij = Jh + Ji + Jj$ through the *Journey-judgment* (*Jj*) window and the 13 component parts of the Execution Excellence 3.0 agenda model. You can find a summary these in a two-page downloadable pdf adobe acrobat file at www.mydrivingseat.com/booklinks booklink #19, comprising a Journey-Judgment Opportunity Assessment and a 90 Day Plan. It is worth taking a moment to download this handout as all the links on it are live and will take you to various references we are about to review.

The Journey-Judgment Opportunity Assessment translates the 13 moving parts of the *Journey-judgment* model of Execution Excellence into 13 driving disciplines for reducing wheel$pin, increasing traction, and brewing up a **BREAKTHROUGH!** with your organizational agility:

- Bringing Journey Orientation into Focus
- Reinforcing a Mindset of Operations Management
- Enhancing Strategic Productivity
- Accentuating Short-Range Culture
- Keeping our Flight Planning envelope expanded to our full Execution Excellence agenda
- Tackling Operational Productivity
- Holding a Recurring, Rigorous & Rallying Strategy Process
- Re-engineering Structures, Processes & Systems
- Orchestrating a Goal-Setting Cascade & Review Process
- Unlocking & Challenging Mental Models
- Guiding Leadership/Communication Skills & Style
- Handling Accountability for Long-Range Culture
- !ntegrating our Enterprise Execution Capability & Capacity

The Journey-judgment Opportunity Assesment provides a template with which to judge where you are in your journey, evolving from a 1.0 postadaptive mode through 2.0 to a 3.0, preadaptive mode, for each of the 13 driving disciplines and associated component parts of *Journey-judgment* model of Execution Excellence. It helps you assess your opportunities for improvement and architecting a **BREAKTHROUGH!**

The 90-Day Plan gives you tips, tricks, and tools you can use during the next 90 days to shift up a gear with traction and building momentum. If you hired me as a general manager for your business (which clearly you won't), these are the kinds of things I would be doing in the first 90 days, to move the needle on our execution excellence and organizational agility, regardless of your particular situation. Upon learning about your precise situation, on the fly, I might do more of some and less of another and do some sooner and some later, but, by and large, I would do some mix of all of these things. Let's review each of the 13 driving disciplines of **BREAKTHROUGH!**

Bringing Journey Orientation into Focus

It isn't by accident that this is the first of our 13 driving disciplines. This whole book is about a paradigm shift, of helping you get oriented to the longitudinal dimension of journey orientation. Business has become like a dynamic journey on a shifting landscape, of increasing uncertainty, volatility, and turbulence. With wave after wave of dynamic complexity washing over us, our agility gets audited every day, sometimes mildly and sometimes brutally. Mild audits often turn brutal!

Passing these audits depends upon our mindful process of integration, alignment, and attunement, from gray matter to gray matter, enterprise wide and enterprise deep. It's about attunement with the anatomy of dynamic complexity and alignment with the longitudinal dimension of journey orientation, to master the challenge.

For preadaptive organizational agility, we need to bring journey orientation into focus, broadly and deeply throughout our organization, as part of our process of integration, alignment, and attunement. This is a paradigm shift of focus for many CEOs, executives, and managers, as we reviewed in Chapter 4 with our discussion of "the hocus pocus of focus." In my experience, this is out of focus for the majority of CEOs, executives, and managers.

Bringing the longitudinal dimension of journey orientation into focus is both unsettling and settling, all at the same time. On the one hand, it is unsettling because it is complicated, necessarily so, as we have been progressively exploring. On the other hand, it is settling because it changes our definition to one of focus on the journey, how it is unfolding in real time, and the agility we are developing to cope, no matter what. It is settling because we are progressively future-proofing our business, with success becoming increasingly inevitable, and we are more and more certain to win. It is settling because we stop fighting the flow of detail complexity and dynamic complexity, coming at us thicker and faster. We stop trying to control the flow and overly predicting, planning, and stabilizing the flow. We stop getting frustrated by the flow and our wishful thinking that we could somehow stop the flow for long enough to catch our breath and chart our course. Instead, we accept the flow as situation normal, and we start going with the flow, steering the flow, and creating new flow. That helps us settle into the composure of a calm and courageous confidence.

As my 16-year-old son, who has a black belt in karate, reminds me, it's kind of like martial arts. We don't try to fight the momentum of our opponents. Instead we go with the flow of that momentum and use it against them. When my son was breaking his first wooden block, he told me that the secret is not to focus on the block, but to focus beyond the block, to where his fist would end up in breaking through it. That's the longitudinal dimension of journey orientation.

This paradigm shift is also unsettling because it fights the conventional wisdom that focus is about a part of a thing and not the whole of a thing. Which part should we focus on? As we now know, for organizational agility not to be an ordeal in your business, it has to be an "and-deal," of the parts and the whole. For preadaptive organizational agility, focus can no longer be about this or that part at the exclusion of other parts. Focus has to be about keeping the whole and all of the parts in mind at the same time, as an ongoing dynamic process of triage, without any deficit disorders, of intention, attention, and responsibility for results.

It is the longitudinal dimension of journey orientation that facilitates this new paradigm shift of focus, tapping into the power of our opposable mind and integrative thinking, in natural alignment with our corpus callosum. This facilitates our left brain, which is good at the parts, and our right brain, which is good at the whole, getting into the flow in a whole-brained way.

This is the first of our 13 driving disciplines for preadaptive organizational agility 3.0.

Bringing Journey Orientation into Focus:
• Change has changed, becoming much more like a dynamic journey on a shifting landscape. The longitudinal dimension of journey orientation has emerged as a third and primary dimension around which we must reframe our approach to translating strategy and execution into traction. This requires higher-order executive strengths, to master a new mindset/ chassis of business acumen for organizational agility.

Common Source of Wheel$pin:
- Applying conventional forecasting, planning, and analysis methods, in unconventional times.

90-Day Plan:
- Hold a workshop to educate your team about Execution Excellence/ Organizational Agility.

Resources:
- Read more about the related concepts, models, tools, and other resources at: www.mydrivingseat.com/booklinks booklink #20.

Bringing journey orientation into focus is about creating a paradigm shift, from a traditional mode of "strategic planning and implementation," to a more agile, journey-oriented mode, around which we are reframing our approach to translating strategy and execution into traction. Unconventional times demand unconventional approaches! A shift to the longitudinal dimension of journey orientation is both timely and timeless, like the discovery of DNA. It is timeless in that it has always been there. It is timely in that its discovery makes all kinds of new things possible, just in time, when it seems we are most in need of them. As we have been progressively exploring, journey orientation is part of the DNA of organizational agility.

The most common source of wheel$pin I see is CEOs, executives, and managers continuing to apply conventional forecasting, planning, and analysis methods in unconventional times. Remember the quote from Peter Senge in Chapter 1: *"Conventional forecasting, planning and analysis methods are not equipped to deal with dynamic complexity,"* and that's *"the reason that sophisticated tools of forecasting and business analysis, as well as elegant strategic plans, usually fail to produce dramatic breakthroughs in managing a business."* That's why this is the first driving discipline of **BREAKTHROUGH!**

If we aren't bringing journey orientation into focus, we are unwittingly stuck on a static plane of thinking, trying to stop the flow, to take a static snapshot of things, so that we can chart a course. This static plane of thinking is dominated by detail complexity, and, as a result, we typically get sucked into trying to overcome detail complexity with the detail complexity. We end up with long-winded plans with lots of spreadsheets, action lists, and due dates, wondering why it's not working. In an effort to fix it, we typically add more spreadsheets, action lists, and due dates! As the landscape shifts, all of these rapidly lose their relevance, become increasingly obsolete, and the process loses its credibility and becomes part of our problem, not our solution.

We are applying an old, detail-complexity solution to a new, dynamic complexity problem! No wonder it's not working! Or worse, we adopt the stupid simplicity of giving up, with echoes of "we tried strategic planning and it didn't work" (and other such things, which we covered in previous chapters). Stuck in the paradigm of organizational agility being an "or-deal," we flip-flop from being overplanned to being underplanned, as we discussed with our spectrum in Chapter 3. We default into not doing anything at all, believing that "our business is too fast moving for strategic planning," and "we don't have time."

That's right! We won't have time, as a self-fulfilling, self defeating prophecy, vicious cycle, and downward spiral. We will spiral down into being so consumed by the constant whitewater of postadaptive organizational agility 1.0, that we are right, we don't have time. In particular, your people will follow your lead and believe that they don't have time, either. As a result no one will find the time or make the time. But, when we have a Wrong Hazelwood or Eastern Airlines scenario in our future, we will have to make the time to recover from it.

Just like GM and Chrysler! They had to make the time to go into bankruptcy, go through bankruptcy, and emerge from bankruptcy. Ford made the time not to go into bankruptcy. Which would you rather make time for? This brings up the old adage from the days of Total Quality Management (TQM): If you can find the time to put it right, then you can make the time to get it right in the first place. Just ask GM and Chrysler! Just ask Toyota and BP!

Or in other words, more haste, less speed. Less haste, more speed. Don't be so hasty working "in" your business, to assume that you can't make more time to be working "on" your business, in a more agile way, translating more strategy and more execution into more traction. Bringing journey orientation into focus will help us do that, enterprise wide and enterprise deep, working "in" and "on" our businesses at the same time, accumulating the traction "ions" of our journey. It will help us evolve from postadaptive organizational agility 1.0 through 2.0 to preadaptive organizational agility 3.0.

Among other things we can do to develop this driving discipline (read more at www.mydrivingseat.com/booklinks booklink #20), the number one thing I recommend as part of a 90 day plan, is to hold a workshop with your team to educate them about execution excellence and organizational agility. Go to the book link above, and/or click on the links in the Opportunity Assessment and 90 Day Plan you downloaded, to find resources to help you with this. Not least of all, you will find several presentation files you can use to hold a briefing session with your team, together with other articles, blogs and videos.

It's amazing what can happen when you take this step. The president of the $100 million wholesale distribution business I mentioned in Chapter 3 set about educating her whole executive team and management structure across their whole system nationally. In her own words: *"This is the most powerful approach to working 'in' and 'on' the business we've ever used. People resonate with the simplicity of the core ideas and we've had the widest acceptance, company-wide, of key concepts than any others we'd tried in the past. It's really helping us gain traction in the right areas and enabling us to truly leverage all the personnel talent we have on our team."*

"If you think education is expensive, try ignorance."

–Derek Bok

In my experience, most people have not had much, if any, exposure to these ideas and concepts. Using yourself as a benchmark example, have you? My guess is, probably not. As a result, your people haven't compounded much interest on the journey to mastery and, at best, are stuck just dabbling with them. Worse still, they are stuck in detail complexity, untrained in dynamic complexity, and fighting detail complexity with detail complexity, applying an old detail complexity solution to a new dynamic complexity problem. Even worse, they have reversed out of complexity to stupid simplicity, of not doing much at all and, quite possibly, doing nothing! As a bumper sticker I saw once said, *"If you think education is expensive, try ignorance."*

What is that ignorance costing? Not knowing any better, your people are self-imposing constant whitewater into their everyday existence, as a self-fulfilling, self-defeating prophecy, vicious cycle, and downward spiral. They are stuck in a postadaptive mode of organizational agility 1.0, not knowing any better. They are in jail, serving a life sentence, not knowing any better. Help them know better. Give them and yourself more options for a better future, breaking the pattern and getting onto a self-fulfilling prophecy, virtuous cycle, and upward spiral. Your organizational agility depends upon it!

Reinforcing a Mindset of Operations Management

This is the second of our 13 driving disciplines. As we have discussed, good strategy often starts with good operations. If our operations management is not working well, then everything else gets harder. We keep getting sucked back into the tyranny of the operationally urgent and managing the next operational crisis! This propagates the self-fulfilling and self-defeating prophecy, vicious cycle, and downward spiral into the constant whitewater of postadaptive organizational agility and execution excellence 1.0.

For more preadaptive execution excellence and organizational agility, we must understand the nature of operations management and reinforce the necessary mindset. We must intervene in the downward spiral to break the pattern and establish a self-fulfilling prophecy, virtuous cycle, and upward spiral of well-managed operations.

Reinforcing a Mindset of Operations Management
- In continuous process businesses, errors unfold rapidly and propagate quickly, often with disastrous consequences. High reliability operations management prevents crises management, and all businesses are continuous process businesses to some degree.

Common Source of Wheel$pin:
- Systemic crisis management and poor communication, collaboration, and coordination, cross-functionally.

90-Day Plan:
- Instigate a Morning Meeting (or Daily Huddle) and Situation/War Room.

Resources:
- Read more about the related concepts, models, tool, and other resources at: www.mydrivingseat.com/booklinks booklink #21.

All businesses are operationally intensive, continuous process businesses, to some degree! Whether we are a product, service, or knowledge intensive business, all businesses have an assembly line of some description, whether it is visible or invisible. Clearly, a car manufacturing plant has a very visible, continuous-process assembly line. The product, process-steps, tooling, and equipment are very tangible and visible. While a law practice has a much less visible and tangible assembly line and continuous process, it is present nevertheless. The product, process-steps, tooling, and equipment are intangible and invisible, but are equally present.

Regardless, for preadaptive execution excellence and organizational agility, we need to establish a clear mindset of high reliability operations management, which is about expecting and managing the unexpected. In their 2007 book, *Managing the Unexpected: Resilient Performance in an Age of Uncertainty*, Karl Weick and Kathleen Sutcliffe identify five principles of HROs (High Reliability Organizations) that help them anticipate and contain the unexpected:

Capacity to Anticipate Unexpected Problems:
- HRO Principle 1: Preoccupation with Failure
- HRO Principle 2: Reluctance to Simplify
- HRO Principle 3: Sensitivity to Operations

Capacity to Contain Unexpected Problems:
- HRO Principle 4: Commitment to Resilience
- HRO Principle 5: Deference to Expertise

–Karl Weick and Kathleen Sutcliffe, 2007, *Managing the Unexpected: Resilient Performance in an Age of Uncertainty*

Read more at www.mydrivingseat.com/booklinks booklink #22.

To reinforce a mindset of operations management, we must routinely expect the unexpected and be ready, willing, and able to manage these events as part of our operations management routine. We must, preadaptively, institutionalize routines in our business to increase our capacity to anticipate and contain the unexpected, becoming an increasingly high reliability organization.

One of my Vistage member CEOs runs a business called MyOffice Facility Solutions, with a one-stop-shop brand promise of "Back to Business. No Headaches. Guaranteed." As managers, executives, and CEOs, we aren't in the business of moving, we are in the business of business. If we are in building A at 5 p.m. on a Friday and want to be in building B at 8 a.m. on Monday, we want peace of mind that we will be back in business on time, with no headaches. All the technology will be working (phones, computers, printers, network, Internet, e-mail, etc.), all the office partitions, cubes, and furniture will be in the right place, and the environment will be damage free and spotlessly clean and tidy. Ready to get back to business. Clearly, to be able to pull that off, we must be an increasingly high reliability organization, in the field and in the office. They must be intimately familiar with and masters of detail complexity and dynamic complexity. They must be reinforcing operations management by expecting, anticipating, and containing the unexpected. That's the business they are in.

In my experience, this is counter to the mindset which many CEOs, executives, and managers have regarding operations management. They are typically focused only on managing the expected, not managing the unexpected. Their operations management mindset is about building their capacity to anticipate, contain, and manage expected problems, as an extension of their infrastructure of structures, processes, and systems (the middle component in our *Journey-judgment* model of Execution Excellence model). That's what structures, processes, and systems are meant to do. They are the embodiment of expected events and our capacity to anticipate, contain, and manage them, preferably achieving the autopilot 80/20 balance we have discussed. In my experience, many CEOs, executives, and managers see operations management as just an extension of this. Build an infrastructure of structures, processes, and systems, to anticipate, contain, and manage expected events and operate it accordingly.

Wrong! Whereas our mindset for our infrastructure of structures, processes, and systems is about *expected* events, our mindset for operations management should also be about *unexpected* events and how we anticipate, contain, and manage them. If we don't do this, we will continually be surprised and consumed by unexpected events, and, as a result, we will be at constant risk of rapidly spiraling downward, as a vicious cycle and self-defeating, self fulfilling prophecy of constant whitewater, Wrong Hazelwoods and Eastern Airlines—overly reliant on autopilot, with a dangerous dose of complacency, resulting in poor communication, collaboration, and coordination! Think Eastern Airlines.

Indeed, this is one of the most common sources of wheel$pin I see, which is systemic crisis management with poor communication, collaboration, and coordination, cross functionally. People have become resigned to a constant state of crisis management as a cross-functional, systemic problem. They believe that this is just the way it is and has to be, as they don't know any different and feel powerless to change it. Under the stress and strain of it, they have hunkered down into their own silos, looking after number one, as we heard from Patrick Lencioni in his 2006 book, *Silos, Politics and Turf-Wars*. As a result, cross-functional communication, collaboration, and coordination have been reduced.

"Crises management" has typically become a chronic, cross functional, systemic problem, for which we need the cross functional systemic solution of "operations management." The challenge is that systemic solutions to systemic problems don't happen by accident! They happen by design and a collective breakthrough effort of communication, collaboration, and coordination as a team. Not ready, unwilling, or unable to tackle that breakthrough, teams are often unconsciously colluding in the status quo. They end up lurching from one crisis to another, barely recovering from the last one before the next one is already taking shape.

Among other things you can do to develop this driving discipline (read more at www.mydrivingseat.com/booklinks booklink #21), the number one thing I recommend as part of a 90-Day Plan, is to instigate a morning meeting or a daily huddle at some other time of day, if shift patterns, time zones or something else dictates that. Put aside a situation room or war room if you can. Yes, I do mean you and your top executive team, same time, same place, every day, rain or shine! I ran a morning meeting at 8:30 a.m. every day, for 30 minutes maximum, in every business I ever ran, regardless of our situation—turnaround, organic growth, or breakthrough growth.

Why? To break the pattern of the downward spiral and to establish an upward spiral of communication, collaboration, and coordination as a cross-functional team. It's about revving up our fast-cycle teamwork and massively shrinking our organizational OODA Loop, to be a daily OODA Loop for winning the daily dogfight. It is an opportunity for a rapid-fire debrief of yesterday's mission and a prebrief of today's mission, not just of expected events but, even more important, of unexpected events. It is a pivotal part of building our capacity to anticipate, contain, and manage unexpected events, both postadaptively and, most crucially, as preadaptively as we can.

In the field of agile software development, they call it the "daily scrum" meeting. A scrum is that part of the game of rugby where both teams are hunkered down, head to head, shoulder to shoulder, pushing and shoving, until someone comes up with the ball and runs with it, beginning the next phase of play. A scrum is a short and intense embodiment of detail complexity and dynamic complexity, as part of the bigger, flowing game. Like similar games of closely matched teams, it's about which team is able to master the flow of dynamic complexity and detail complexity better than the other, with the difference between victory and defeat often coming down to just inches—in the flow of dynamic complexity and detail complexity, were we able to get that final pass inch perfect?

Various other authors recommend daily meetings of different descriptions. For more inspiration and tips, tricks, and techniques on how to implement it, read more at www.mydrivingseat.com/booklinks booklink #21. As you will read, choosing whether or not to do these is not a function of company size. When I speak to audiences of CEOs, I often see them getting a little prickly when I push this point, which I normally tee-up as the most provocative thing I am going to say during the session. Often, one of them says something like, "but I run a big company. I can readily understand how this works well for small companies, but not big ones like mine, right?" Wrong! It's not a function of company size. It's only a function of the mode of organizational agility you want to be in. Postadaptive or preadaptive, it's your choice! Visit the booklink above to read more.

A morning meeting has always been, and will continue to be, the first thing I do when entering a new business, starting on day two and continuing forever, or at least as long as I am there. Why? Because I know I cannot fail to benefit from a quantum shift in our organizational agility, revving up our fast-cycle teamwork of communication, coordination, and collaboration as a team. It's our daily OODA Loop for winning the daily dogfight, often by just inches. It also sends a clear message that things are going to be different around here, with a much greater sense of urgency for both the expected and the unexpected, and a revved up culture as a team working together better both postadaptively (invariably there are lots of lingering problems to work through and skeletons to get out of the closet) and increasingly preadaptively.

Indeed, when I first became a president, walking into a turnaround situation, I announced a two-week amnesty for getting skeletons out of the closet—anybody could bring out anything without consequence, for two weeks; two weeks and one day would be a different matter! It was amazing what came out and how quickly and how fully. I realize now it was part of my instinctive strategy of quickly getting things out and visible, preadaptively, at least compared to them coming out slowly, invisibly, and having to deal with them more postadaptively. It worked great, and the morning meeting was my daily opportunity to move the needle of our culture and our executive strengths in the right direction.

Running a morning meeting (or a daily huddle or a daily scrum) can be a small, easy, and pivotal first step in a systemic breakthrough. It will help you rev up your fast-cycle teamwork of communication, collaboration, and coordination cross functionally. It will help you break through, from a norm of the constant whitewater of crises management to a new norm of high reliability operations management, expecting and managing the unexpected.

A common misconception is that a morning meeting is somehow meant to be a replacement for other meetings, resulting in confusion, therefore, about how we are going to find enough time in a daily meeting of only 30 minutes to discuss everything we need to discuss. Absolutely not! A daily meeting is a supplement to the portfolio of other meetings, which we need to be running with other frequencies (weekly, monthly, quarterly, annually) and for other purposes. I call this a "Meetings Matrix and Annual Calendar," which we will discuss more later in this chapter; you can read more about it at www.mydrivingseat.com/booklinks booklink #21.

In my experience, when they finally take the leap of faith and get started with a morning meeting, most CEOs, executives, and managers are surprised at how impactful it can be and how quickly. As described further at the booklink above, they experience two interwoven benefits. First, the morning meeting is a very effective and efficient way to stay on top of all the details and dynamics coming at us every day. Second, the morning meeting helps each of the other meetings in our portfolio to be so much more effective and efficient, as they become unburdened of many of the details and dynamics, so we can get more focused on the bigger and more strategic issues. Your organizational agility depends upon it!

Enhancing Strategic Productivity

This is the third of our 13 driving disciplines. Improvement of our operations management liberates more bandwidth of time, energy, and attention, to invest in strategy and execution. Therefore, we had better improve the return on investment we get from our strategy process by enhancing our strategic productivity.

Enhancing Strategic Productivity:

• We need an integrated concept suite, model set, and tool box, aligned and attuned to the dynamic complexity of our challenge, formulating a progressive work product. The acid test of good strategic tools is how quickly we can pick up the conversation next time from where we left off last time.

Common Source of Wheel$pin:

• Strategy conversations which veer off track/get stuck in a rut of more "talk" than "walk."

90-Day Plan:

• Hold a **BREAKTHROUGH!** session on your single most intractable/ wheel$pin issue.

Resources:

• Read more about the related concepts, models, tools, and other resources at: www.mydrivingseat.com/booklinks booklink #23.

Our productivity at a strategic level depends upon using an integrated framework of concepts, models and tools, which are aligned and attuned to the challenge of dynamic complexity that we face. Unconventional times demand unconventional approaches, to formulate a progressive work product that creates traction, not wheel$pin. For the reasons we have explored, conventional approaches don't work well anymore. In fact, they subtract from our strategic productivity rather than adding to it.

In these times of more uncertainty, more volatility, and more turbulence, we need to translate more strategy and more execution into more traction. Therefore, our strategic productivity is as crucial as our operational productivity. When we distill it down to its very essence, strategy is conversation, period. If we don't have much conversation, we probably don't have much strategy. The acid test of good strategic tools is how quickly we can pick up the conversation next time, from where we left off last time, keeping it on track and in traction. The most common source of wheel$pin I see is strategy conversations which veer off track and get stuck in a rut of more "talk" than "walk." It becomes a "talking shop" of wheel$pin, not traction.

As a reminder, when I say that "strategy is conversation," actions are a part of our definition of conversation, which is as much about the "walk" as the "talk," and we need both as an "and" proposition. It is so easy for strategy conversations to get stuck in a rut, spinning our wheels in the mud of important strategic issues that just seem to remain intractable. It is so easy for our strategy conversations to veer off track down the wrong path, which we blindly follow, and often becomes a dead end street. As a result, our strategic productivity declines, our attempts lose credibility, and we are prone to not continuing in a disciplined manner. The self-fulfilling and self-defeating prophecy, vicious cycle, and downward spiral begin to set in.

Instead, we must find ways to break through these tendencies, to be strategically productive in finding our path, navigating our journey, and creating traction on our desired trajectory, linking and accumulating the traction "ions" of our journey through conversation, talk, and walk. Among other things you can do to develop this driving discipline (read more at www.mydrivingseat.com/booklinks booklink #23), the number one thing I recommend as part of a 90-Day Plan, is to hold a **BREAKTHROUGH!** session on your single most intractable, wheel$pin issue.

Choose the issue (or problem, opportunity, or challenge) which has been stuck in a rut the longest, or the deepest, or has been subject to the most repeated attempts, but is still in wheel$pin. It just seems intractable. It just seems impossible. And yet, if we could make it possible, it would radically transform our future. If we could just get into traction on this issue, everything else would get easier. I call these "wheel$pin issues," and we all have them, in business and in life. It's a question of which one is at the top of our list as our most wheel$pin issue. Maybe:

- Our product innovation and development pipeline has slowed down and isn't delivering enough new product launches (as in the public company I mentioned)

- Our sales and marketing process isn't delivering enough leads, conversion rates, and wins

- Our quality, customer service, and reputation are suffering

- ...or many, many other systemic, wheel$pin issues

Now hold a **BREAKTHROUGH!** session (or, more likely, a series of sessions) focused solely on that wheel$pin issue, and yes, inevitably, the systemic interrelationship with other issues in the business. Remember the quote from Peter Senge, that *"Most of the problems faced by humankind concern our inability to grasp and manage the increasingly complex systems of our world."* Most wheel$pin issues are such because they are a tangled web of interrelated, complex systems, and we haven't yet mustered enough multidisciplinary interest and a journey-oriented focus on this issue to compound our interest in a systemic solution to a systemic problem. We have been "tickling" this problem, not "tackling" it.

It is time to tackle it with a series of focused **BREAKTHROUGH!** sessions. For tips, techniques, and templates on how to hold that session, read more at www. mydrivingseat.com/booklinks booklink #23. Among other things, you will find a tool to break the ice and begin a conversation in the framework of our *Journey-judgment* model of Execution Excellence, called an *Ice-Breaker & Conversation Starter*. Often times, wheel$pin issues persist because we aren't considering all of the component parts of the issue, and we end up focused on some of the parts but not the whole. When we are reminded to focus on the whole Execution Excellence agenda for that issue, we will begin unlocking, uplifting, and unfolding the conversation on that issue, linking and accumulating the traction "ions" of a **BREAKTHROUGH!** journey with it.

One of my Vistage members has stuck with this process across the years. CPS/ Cordius is a commercial printer who, several years before the 2008/9 recession hit, had the foresight to invest heavily in new digital printing technologies, with all of the new paradigm shifting possibilities that brings. Thank goodness, because the recession brought carnage in the traditional offset printing space, or "scorched earth" as the CEO calls it. They got scorched too, testing their organizational agility to the limit, but their preadaptive strategy paid off in helping them survive. Only with repeated breakthrough thinking sessions, though. Like any new technology, creating traction with early uptake of new paradigm technologies can be an intractable, uphill struggle, which tests our organizational agility. They are passing the test and are beginning to thrive again.

If you stick with it, you too will begin to make tractable the intractable. Not only will you gain the benefits of traction on that wheel$pin issue, but you will have created a case study example of what is possible when you put your minds to it. Relating this to our Eastern Airlines story, you will be fixing a strategic bulb, which had stubbornly withstood repeated attempts to be fixed. This will be an early win which the team needs to build its confidence and gain a sense that, if we can fix one bulb, we can fix them all!

In my experience, in most businesses, it feels as if we have an overwhelming array of bulbs to fix and, in trying to fix them all, we end up fixing none, at least not properly. We end up "tickling" all of them rather than truly "tackling" any of them, because we don't have the strategic productivity we need. Things seem intractable with a wide array of wheel$pin issues. The next time your team is discussing a seemingly intractable situation, you will be able to remind them that they know how to make tractable the intractable. They just need to truly tackle it with the strategic productivity of a **BREAKTHROUGH!** approach.

As they begin gaining traction on more and more parts (fixing bulbs) of a seemingly overwhelming situation, they will gain traction on the whole (flying the plane), with the strategic productivity they need. Your organizational agility depends upon it!

Accentuating Short-Range Culture

This is the fourth of our 13 driving disciplines. With improving strategic productivity, we must also be evolving our culture to guard against the short-termism we can easily default into.

Because of the increasing dynamic complexity of the short-range pressures we are under, we can easily spiral downward into that postadaptive mode of constant whitewater and a culture of crisis management, as a vicious cycle and self-fulfilling, self-defeating prophecy. To break the pattern and guard against that, we must accentuate certain short-range aspects of our culture.

Accentuating Short-Range Culture:
- [Accentuating: to stress or emphasize; intensify; single out as important; mark with an accent]. More than ever before, the culture we need to cope with short-range pressures and performance expectations must be loud and clear to all, with leaders turning up the volume.

Common Source of Wheel$pin:
- Falling prey to a "we become what we tolerate/we encourage what we allow" downward spiral.

90-Day Plan:
- Single out one aspect of your culture (which is causing wheel$pin) to accentuate.

Resources:
- Read more about the related concepts, models, and tools and other resources at: www.mydrivingseat.com/booklinks booklink #24.

Our culture with regard to the short-range pressures and performance expectations we are under depends upon us making loud and clear the standards of behavior we need and want. These are our behaviors of thinking, questions, decisions, and actions, to help us to continue linking and accumulating the traction "ions" of our journey. These are standards of behavior we must sustain to keep working "in" and "on" our journey, all at the same time, to keep it from veering off track. Under assault from the short range pressures of dynamic complexity, crises management, and whitewater, it is easy for us to lower our standards and let undesirable behaviors creep in.

Before long, we fall prey to the downward spiral of "we become what we tolerate, and we encourage what we allow." As we allow and tolerate degrading standards of behavior, we encourage more, and the situation becomes worse. This is the most common form of wheel$pin I see and is part of the self-fulfilling and self defeating prophecy, vicious cycle, and downward spiral into constant whitewater. Instead of us defining our culture, our culture is defining us! In many organizations what we find is:

- We haven't defined a list of core values (maybe five or seven or ten) that are at the core of our culture, such as honesty, accountability, and teamwork.

- Even if we have done that, we haven't defined an interpretation of what each these means for us in our organization, in one paragraph.

- Even if we have done that, we haven't translated each of these paragraphs into observable operating norms of what we always want to see and hear and what we never want to see and hear. If we can't translate our core values into observable norms, it's very difficult to create real accountability around them.

- Even if we have that, we haven't institutionalized our core values in many places around the business, except seeing them on the walls in a few places. I challenge my clients and Vistage members with institutionalizing their core values in 100 places in their business. Yes, 100! And putting up a dozen, poster size, framed versions on the walls around the place only counts as one. Ninety-nine to go! Giving each employee a plasticized card or a desk paperweight is two. Ninety-eight to go! Integrating them into our performance appraisal system is three. Ninety-seven to go!

- Even if we have done all that, in my experience, those core values definitions and observable operating norms tend to come out of an organizational agility 1.0 or, at best, 2.0 mindset. They haven't been extended and revved up for a

3.0 mindset for a 3.0 world. Consequently, our core values, operating norms, and culture are not up to the challenge of the increasing dynamic complexity and short-range pressures and performance expectations we are under.

For organizational agility 3.0, we must extend and rev up our core values, operating norms, and culture. We need a 3.0 culture for a 3.0 world. In Chapter 4, we talked about the example of Agile Software Development. Extending and revving up your core values, operating norms, and culture is about developing the "software" of organizational agility 3.0. As we have been reviewing, this entails:

- Revving up our collaboration, coordination, and communication for Fast-Cycle Teamwork;

- Overcoming the Five Dysfunctions of a Team by building trust, mastering conflict, achieving commitment, embracing accountability, and focusing on results;

- Expecting and managing the unexpected;

- Driving constant improvisation, innovation, and breakthrough thinking;

- Being preadaptive by mastering the higher order strengths of journey orientation.

Culture is a small word for a very complex system, which is integral to the infrastructure of our businesses. It's the intangible, inner universe, operating "software" of our organization, the soft, fleshy part of our inner world/journey as an organization. It is no less integral to our infrastructure than the tangible, outer universe, operating "hardware" of our organization, the nuts and bolts of our business processes, systems and structures, among others, of our outer world/journey as an organization. Yet, how much time, energy, and attention do we typically invest in the design, engineering, and communication of this operating "software" of our organization, compared to that which we invest in the operating "hardware?" Probably not much. And yet our organizational agility for a 3.0 world depends upon it!

Among other things you can do to develop this driving discipline (read more at www.mydrivingseat.com/booklinks booklink #24), the number one thing I recommend as part of a 90-Day Plan, is to single out one aspect of your culture that is causing wheel$pin to accentuate. Choose that aspect of your team's or organization's day-to-day, short-range cultural behavior, which is most continually frustrating, distracting, or worrying to you, that you would like to change. Maybe something like:

- People arriving late to meetings

- Inattention to detail

- Lack of a can-do attitude

- People over-promising and under-delivering

- Lack of closed loop accountability for commitment

- ...the list goes on!

Choose just one. Yes, just one. Now start thinking of ideas for how you might accentuate that one aspect of your culture to influence behaviors away from those that you don't want and toward those that you do want. Here are a few I have done through the years, just as examples:

- **Morning Meetings**. When I first became a president, I took on a turn-around situation. On day one, I discovered that our most strategic client, by an order of magnitude, was at risk of canceling because of a systemic tangle of issues.

  While we have discussed my experience with morning meetings earlier in this chapter (refer back to Reinforcing a Mindset of Operations Management), this was before that and before I had read any of the authors who reinforce the same. I wondered what was best to do.

  As I dug in, I was bemused that the culture seemed to be one of finger pointing and back stabbing around the issues rather than jumping into the middle and digging ourselves out. I'm not sure exactly how, but I had the idea to hold a morning meeting every morning with all my key players, who needed to unravel that tangle. I hesitated, as it seemed a little draconian, almost embarrassing, and I knew it would raise a lot of eyebrows. But I realized it would accentuate the new culture I wanted to establish of better teamwork on the short-range issues we faced. So I thought, what the heck, and did it anyway, starting on day two.

  Six months later, we had dug ourselves out of the hole. I realized it worked so well that I took the idea up a level and continued doing it at the level of the business as a whole. I wanted to accentuate our sense of urgency, attention to detail, and operations management mindset, for the unexpected, as an executive team. From that point forward, I ran morning meetings in every business I ever ran, from day two, regardless of the situation of the business. I knew it would always accentuate our short-range culture.

• **No. 6 and No. 8**. As part of the above turnaround, I merged the business with another just across the street, one with a street address of No. 6 and one with No. 8. I had stood my ground with my parent company bosses, who were naturally expecting there to be some layoffs as a result of this merger, asserting that we weren't doing it for that—instead, I asserted, we were doing it to liberate more bandwidth of resources for growth. In so doing, I had put myself under the microscope, and I better deliver, and fast.

I knew one of the biggest challenges would be a cultural integration, which would be held back if I allowed people to keep referring to each other and the two facilities by the old company names (one was called "Avionics" and one was called "Recorders.")

So I announced that I never wanted to hear those words again and, from this moment forth, we would only refer to the two buildings as "No. 6" and "No. 8." It worked. "Avionics" and "Recorders" quickly evaporated from the vocabulary around the place, and this helped to accentuate the short-range cultural integration we needed.

• **P&G**. As part of that integration, the business was actually called "P&G" for short (no, not Procter & Gamble). Not only did we want to achieve a cultural integration, but I also needed a cultural inspiration, to break the pattern of the self-fulfilling and self defeating prophecy, vicious cycle, and downward spiral we were in, which had sucked the business down into a turnaround situation.

After undertaking a breakthrough program with the executive team, we held an all-employee conference. To their surprise, I asked for two screens and overhead projectors (that was the technology back in those days) to be set up. I told a story of two companies called "P&G" who were head to head competitors—one was called "**Profit & Growth**" and the other was called "**Problems & Gripes**." With one projector and screen for each, I played out a parallel story of the two companies starting out with equal market share, revenues, profitability, and cash flow, but different cultures. That was the only difference.

One, "Problems & Gripes," had a culture stuck in the self-fulfilling and self-defeating prophecy, vicious cycle, and downward spiral of the constant whitewater of problems and gripes. The other, "Profit & Growth," figured out how to break the pattern and begin to get on the self-fulfilling, virtuous cycle, and upward spiral of profitability and growth, investment and rewards, productivity and fun.

I played this out progressively during the course of 30 minutes and, of course, you know the ending. One ended up with 20% market share, lots of layoffs, and no investment. The other ended up with 80% market share, lots of investment in facilities, training, and development, and rewards and recognition. When I was done, I explained that those were the two possible futures for us. Which P&G did they want? I explained that they would choose, via the "problems and gripes" or "profit and growth" mindset, behaviors, and culture they exhibited, moment by moment, hour by hour, day by day, starting tomorrow. This accentuated the short-range cultural inspiration we needed.

• **Wedge**. As I have explained, I use a wedge shape to signify a journey and engage people in the dialogue about the inner workings and complexities of architecting a breakthrough journey. Not least of all, of course, detail complexity and dynamic complexity. I have used this for years. I have used it with my executive team, employees, vendors, partners, and clients. I became known for this. So much so that, one time, one of my clients had pre-drawn it for me on his whiteboard when I walked into a meeting!

Before I had even arrived, I had accentuated the short-range culture of the meeting we were about to have. Internally, in the businesses I have run, it became increasingly clear to me that people struggle with the complexities of architecting a breakthrough journey. My experience is that they tend to get focused on the big-fix solution at the thick end of the wedge in an "if only we had this…" kind of way. They start to hatch plans for quantum shift changes and, no doubt, the expensive investments which go hand-in-hand with them. Very often, the investment of money and management bandwidth is out of proportion to what we can afford at that stage in our journey—our cash flow journey and our journey of triaging our management bandwidth. So it becomes an exercise in futility.

Instead, the wedge allows us to do three things simultaneously. First, to acknowledge and honor the big-fix solution and whole vision at the thick end of the wedge, from which we can plan backwards. Second, it accentuates the need to ask which parts of this whole vision future can we pull forward into the present at the thin end of the wedge, to improvise ways to make tomorrow a little bit better than today. And the next day, and the next day, and the next day. So that next week is a little bit better than this week, and next month is a little bit better than this month, and so on. Third, in gradually unlocking the gridlock, we create the wiggle room we need in our management bandwidth and cash flow journeys to make bigger investments, in an increasingly self-funding way, earning our way to ultimately making the investment in the big-fix solution and whole vision future we wanted in the first place. The wedge accentuates our short-range culture of starting small and finishing big.

• **Cats and Dogs**. As a Vistage chairman, facilitating my groups can be a bit like herding cats, in particular with my group of CEO members and the A-type personalities. They are prone to coming back late from the break, doing the Blackberry thing beneath the table, and falling asleep after lunch.

So we created a set of core values and operating norms like we have been discussing in this driving discipline, but I knew I would need to accentuate certain aspects of that to herd the cats! So I found an image of a whole bunch of dogs herding a whole bunch of cats, set our core values and operating norms on top of that as a backdrop, and printed posters to have in our meeting room.

But I knew that would not be enough. I had to accentuate it even more. So I bought a beanie baby toy cat and a beanie baby toy dog, which we refer to as the "head-cat" and the "lead-dog." These get lobbed around in the meeting, not by me, but from the members to the members, peer to peer. The lead-dog is a good thing and gets lobbed to the person who brought leadership to the equation, over and above my role to do that as the chairman, by maybe calling a time out, asking a great clarifying question, or making a very impactful recommendation. The head-cat is a bad thing and gets lobbed at the person who is being the head cat we have to herd the most right now. If that person comes back late from the break, he or she will likely find it in the chair. If that person is doing the Blackberry thing beneath the table, he or she will likely find it lobbed into the lap. If that person is falling asleep after lunch, he or she will likely find it propped on a shoulder.

The point? In the fun and productive process of a three second trajectory, of the head-cat being lobbed in someone's direction, we send a private message and a public message accentuating our culture: It says, "Hey, we have important work to do here, and we need you fully present." If I don't bring the symbolic "structure" of these toys into the room, I can't influence behaviors as easily and tap into the power of a peer process and peer pressure; the only other option is for me to call a halt to proceedings, climb up on my soap box, and deliver a lecturette! It puts the emphasis back on me, takes lot more time, is ugly, and we don't want to do it. Which means we probably won't. Which means we will let it go, and we are on the downward spiral of "We become what we tolerate, we encourage what we allow." A self-fulfilling and self-defeating prophecy, vicious cycle, and downward spiral. You should see my CEO members: They are rarely late back from the break!

As we discussed in Chapter 5, structure influences behavior. As illustrated by the examples above, some structures which influence our behavior are so elegantly simple that they are almost embarrassingly so, which is why most people don't do them. Get over it! Along the lines of the examples above, I got over that a long time ago and I urge you to do the same. Think cats and dogs! These elegantly simple approaches can be instrumental in accentuating your short-range culture and turning cultural weaknesses into cultural strengths. By progressively accentuating key aspects of your core-values, operating norms and culture, you can turn more weaknesses into more strengths, revving up your fast-cycle teamwork of collaboration, coordination, and communication and becoming more preadaptive. Your organizational agility depends upon it.

Keeping Our Flight Planning Envelope Expanded to Our Full Execution Excellence Agenda

This is the fifth of our 13 driving disciplines. As we discussed in Chapter 5, a most important aspect of our culture is that we must keep addressing the full agenda of what it takes to be "getting an A" with Execution Excellence 3.0. For preadaptive organizational agility, we mustn't allow any deficit disorders. No attention, intention, or responsibility for results deficit disorders.

To prevent those deficit disorders, we must fly around inside our Execution Excellence agenda, spending the right time in the right place at the right time, in the right manner with our 3-D glasses on, linking and accumulating the traction "ions" of our journey (individual thoughts, questions, decisions, and actions). To stay in a preadaptive mode of organizational agility, we must constantly be "flight planning" our time, energy, and attention, to divide our bandwidth accordingly across this agenda. It's about judging where we are in our journey and, in the face of dynamic complexity coming at us thicker and faster, triaging our time in the most wheel$pin reducing and traction creating way possible, in the best service of our journey.

Any deficit disorder of any kind invites whitewater to creep back into the equation, beginning the vicious cycle and downward spiral of a self-defeating and self-fulfilling prophecy. Things begin to spiral down into the postadaptive mode of organizational agility of constant whitewater, Wrong Hazelwoods, and Eastern Airlines. Any kind of deficit disorder across our Execution Excellence agenda leaves us flying blind to some degree and prone to the imperceptible descent of an Eastern Airlines scenario. It can often be subtle and insidious. Just ask Toyota! Just ask BP! These days, any weakness in our ability to cover our full Execution Excellence agenda can get exposed very quickly, very fully, and very finally!

Keeping our Flight Planning Envelope Expanded to Our Full Execution Excellence Agenda:
• Our flight envelope is prone to collapsing back to the bottom left hand corner of our Execution Excellence agenda because of conspiring forces, including (i) the tyranny of the urgent and (ii) our unconscious resistance to the more ambiguous and abstract work of strategy and the long range. That leaves us flying blind.

Common Source of Wheel$pin:
• Being "too busy"/ "busy fools," insufficiently tackling systemic problems with systemic solutions.

90-Day Plan:
• Insist that your direct reports define their Meetings Matrix and Annual Calendar, including cycle of one-to-ones.

Resources:
• Read more about the related concepts, models, tools, and other resources at: www.mydrivingseat.com/booklinks booklink #25.

When trying to keep our flight planning envelope expanded, we are fighting at least two conspiring forces that tend to suck us down into the bottom left hand corner of our Execution Excellence agenda. These two forces are trying to consign us into a 2.0 mode of organizational agility, at best, and a 1.0 mode of constant whitewater, at worst. These two forces are "The Tyranny of the Urgent" and "Subconscious Resistance." They are always conspiring against us, plotting our downward spiral into the chaos of constant whitewater. In his book, *Getting Things Done*, David Allen puts it this way:

> "A huge number of business books, models, seminars, and gurus have championed the "bigger view" as the solution to dealing with our complex world. Clarifying major goals and values, so the thinking goes, gives order, meaning and direction to our work. In practice, however, the well intentioned exercise of values thinking often does not achieve its desired results:
>
> • There is too much distraction at the day-to-day, hour-to-hour level of commitments to allow appropriate focus on the higher levels. [The Tyranny of the Urgent]
>
> • Ineffective personal organization systems create huge Sub-conscious Resistance to undertaking even bigger projects and goals that will likely not be managed well, that will in turn cause even more distraction and stress.
>
> When loftier levels and values actually are clarified, it raises the bar of our standards, making us notice that much more needs changing. We already have a serious negative reaction to the overwhelming number of things we need to do."
>
> –David Allen, 2001, *Getting Things Done:*
> *The Art of Stress Free Productivity*

In the face of these two conspiring forces, our flight planning envelope can easily collapse down into the bottom left hand corner of our Execution Excellence agenda, resulting in glaring deficit disorders across the rest of our agenda and leaving us flying blind.

This is the most common source of wheel$pin I see. CEOs, executives, managers, and their teams can easily become "too busy" to strategize because "we don't have time," and "we already have too much to do." They consign themselves to being busy fools. Also, any efforts we make to tackle intractable, wheel$pin issues, and brew up bigger breakthroughs, are typically prone to failure because we insufficiently tackle systemic problems with systemic solutions. We are too busy and don't have time.

Instead of "tackling" an issue systemically, all across the map of our Execution Excellence agenda (refer to our Enhancing Strategic Productivity driving discipline earlier in this chapter), we are "tickling" it, a little here and a little there, wondering why nothing is really changing. Oftentimes, after half-heartedly launching, leading, and managing a change initiative, we end up with another problem on our hands (a time, energy, and attention consuming change initiative that is breaking down) rather than a solution (the breakthrough we were trying to brew up). So things got worse, not better, in an increasingly self-fulfilling and self defeating kind of way! It is hard enough for us to sustain our flight planning envelope. Times 10 for our direct reports! And their flight planning envelope will directly affect ours. If theirs has spiraled down into postadaptive whitewater and crises management, they keep dragging us into the next crisis. So we have to start there, with them.

Among other things you can do to develop this driving discipline (read more at www.mydrivingseat.com/booklinks booklink #25), the number one thing I recommend as part of a 90-Day Plan, is to insist that your direct reports define their matrix and calendar of meetings, including one-to-one coaching sessions with their direct reports. We mentioned the Meetings Matrix and Annual Calendar earlier in this chapter (refer to Reinforcing a Mindset of Operations Management). Later, in another driving discipline, we will talk about defining your matrix and calendar of meetings, including one-to-one coaching sessions, with your direct reports. But, for now, the breakthrough starts with them. In Chapter 5, we reviewed the mission critical importance of meetings, as the central cog in the gearbox of our Execution Excellence and organizational agility.

In my experience, if meetings are haphazard at our level, they are 10 times more so at the level of our direct reports, and we are paying a huge price with our organizational agility. Here's what I did, time and again. I instigated a renewed process, cycle, and discipline of one-to-one meetings with my direct reports. Top of the agenda for those sessions was the topic of our meetings matrix and annual calendar. I shared how my thinking and matrix were shaping up at my level, including these one-to-ones and a morning meeting, which we had already got rolling. I would help each direct report think through the portfolio of meetings that person needed to be running at his or her level, including one-to-ones with direct reports. I didn't insist that that person run a morning meeting or daily huddle with the team at their level, unless we mutually sensed it was very appropriate.

However, I did insist that those people run a weekly huddle in a similar agile mode as a morning meeting. So much so that, in one turnaround situation, I had a big whiteboard put up in each department, on a wall that would allow a huddle around it in some way. I insisted that each department head subdivide the whiteboard into different agenda categories to capture open items, as a working agenda of what was on the plate as a department. Then I insisted the department head hold a weekly huddle around the whiteboard for 30 minutes. Standing, sitting, whatever worked! The department head needed to facilitate everyone actively participating and reporting out, in the same agile mode as a morning meeting, revving up their collaboration, communication, and coordination as a team.

And I let the department head know that I would sit in as often as I could, which I did, rotating through the different departments. It was great and served multiple purposes. I got to put my finger on the pulse of that department, what department members had on their plate, the sense of urgency they had, and how full their plate was. Not least of all, I got a sense of how preadaptive they were being, looking and thinking ahead, anticipating and managing the unexpected, not just the expected. I would mostly be passive, like a fly on the wall, maybe offering a little input on particular items and during the round-robin at the end. Invariably, my input would be to help them be more preadaptive, challenging them to look and think ahead more and on more of a what-if scenario basis, to be on their toes for the unexpected, not just the expected.

I also got to put my finger on the pulse of the department heads and how they were doing in leading and managing for execution excellence in their departments. Relatively quickly, during the course of a few weeks and months, I could see how they responded to my coaching feedback in these meetings and in our one-to-ones. I was able to get a good read on who had the potential to be "getting an A" and who didn't.

Expanding our flight planning to our full execution agenda, at our level and that of our direct reports, is crucial to avoid any deficit disorders. Your organizational agility depends upon it!

Tackling Operational Productivity

This is the sixth of our 13 driving disciplines. With our improving flight planning for coverage of our full execution excellence agenda, we will be generating more workload. Good workload, mind you! Flying-the-plane workload, not just fixing-bulbs workload. So we had better take a harder look at the productivity of our operations management and other operational level aspects of our business to liberate additional bandwidth for this additional workload.

The nature of work has changed and, oftentimes, our approach to our operational level productivity hasn't. It hasn't kept up. David Allen puts it well in his book, *Getting Things Done: The Art of Stress Free Productivity*:

> "A major factor in the mounting stress level is that the actual nature of our jobs has changed much more dramatically and rapidly than have our training for and our ability to deal with work. In the old days, work was self evident. Now, for many of us, there are no edges to most of our projects. The organizations we are involved with seem to be in constant morph mode, with ever changing goals, products, partners, customers, markets, technologies and owners. These all, by necessity, shake up structures, forms, roles and responsibilities.
>
> Executives at the top are looking to instill 'ruthless execution' in themselves and their people as a basic standard. They know, and I know, that behind closed doors, after hours, there remain unanswered calls, tasks to be delegated, unprocessed issues from meetings and conversations, personal responsibilities unmanaged and dozens of e mails still not dealt with."
>
> –David Allen, 2001, *Getting Things Done:*
> *The Art of Stress Free Productivity*

Do you wonder about that, too? How many unanswered calls, tasks to be delegated, unprocessed issues, unmanaged personal responsibilities, and e-mails not dealt with are behind closed doors when you and your team leave for the day? The nature of work has changed, and, often, our approach to productivity hasn't. In particular, the increasing dynamic complexity of things these days means that our operational productivity is increasingly about how well we are triaging our time. As we discussed in Chapter 1, traditional approaches to time management and priority management for operational productivity don't work well anymore and are like applying an old, detail complexity solution to a new, dynamic complexity problem. It doesn't work very well.

Tackling Operational Productivity:

• Our productivity at an operational level is about handling day-to-day work flow and crisis management, among shifting priorities, problems, and opportunities. It's about our time management, priority management, project management, and many other related concepts, as a team.

Common Source of Wheel$pin:

• Applying detail complexity solutions to dynamic complexity problems/ not triaging our time well.

90-Day Plan:

• Single out one operational productivity bottleneck (which is causing wheel$pin) to tackle.

Resources:

• Read more about the related concepts, models, tools, and other resources at: www.mydrivingseat.com/booklinks booklink #26.

We need operational productivity systems, processes, and disciplines that are up to the challenges of managing the changing nature of work, the day-to-day workflow, and crisis management, among shifting priorities, problems, and opportunities.

Our team-based, time management, priority management, project management, and many other related concepts, have to be up to the challenge of dynamic complexity. If our approach to productivity has fallen behind the curve, we are in trouble. With wave after wave of dynamic complexity washing over us in recent times, we are always at risk of spiraling downward into a postadaptive mode of constant whitewater. To counterbalance that tendency, we must spiral upward with our operational productivity process.

Often, it can be as simple as the personal productivity process of the CEO, executives, managers, and their teams of direct reports. In my experience, many CEOs, executives, and managers like to think they are highly productive and that their personal systems, processes, and disciplines of time management and priority management are up to the job. In my experience, though, the majority have a lot of opportunities for improvement. They are stuck using just the basics, which don't cut it anymore. They need to raise their game with new approaches, in particular to be mastering dynamic complexity.

Whether it is with our personal productivity, our team-based productivity, or other core aspects of our operational productivity, often we are just "tickling" the problem not truly "tackling" it. That's why this driving discipline says "Tackling" Operational Productivity. As we discussed earlier in this chapter, systemic problems require systemic solutions (refer to Enhancing Strategic Productivity) for which we must be "tackling" the whole problem, not just "tickling" parts of the problem. Productivity problems are some of the most systemic, complex, and insidious, and therefore intractable. Therefore, we must be truly "tackling" them, not just "tickling" them; otherwise we are just wasting our time. When we do, we liberate management bandwidth to invest elsewhere in our Execution Excellence agenda, and everything else gets easier. When we don't, we remain gridlocked, and everything else gets harder.

The most common wheel$pin I see is applying detail complexity solutions to dynamic complexity problems and, as a result, not triaging our time well. Let's revisit our example of agile software development which we touched upon in Chapter 4. The problem with the traditional "waterfall method" of software development is that it is an old, detail complexity solution for a new, dynamic complexity problem. A slow moving aim for a fast moving target. A constantly moving target! The goalposts are always being moved on us, faster and faster. It's a mistake to try harder and harder to apply the "waterfall" method in a whitewater world.

We need the more agile approach, of a fast moving aim for a fast moving target, of "agile software development." Not too structured and not too unstructured, not too tight and not too loose, not overplanned and not underplanned. An "and" proposition right down the middle, leveraging the power of our opposable mind and integrative thinking. Think jet fighter plane.

We need similar, more agile approaches, to tackle other aspects of our operational productivity. Among other things you can do to develop this driving discipline (read more at www.mydrivingseat.com/booklinks booklink #26), the number one thing I recommend as part of a 90-Day Plan, is to single out one operational productivity bottleneck to tackle. Choose one that is causing wheel$pin, maybe:

- The productivity of your meetings
- The productivity of your customer service and customer complaints process
- The productivity of your product development process

Single out just one aspect of your operational productivity, as a subsystem of your whole productivity challenge, and truly tackle it. Try to choose the most bottlenecked aspect that has a choke hold on your productivity.

One of the biggest operational productivity challenges in the cleanup of the BP oil spill in the Gulf of Mexico was the coordination of the more than 5,000 vessels involved. A software solution called PortVision, provided by one of my Vistage members called Airsis, was pressed into service by BP to tackle this operational productivity challenge. PortVision is a web based tool that provides vessel tracking software, allowing users to view their locations, not just as GPS points on a map, but with other historical data and analysis of their movements. Smaller vessels, which wouldn't normally have the transmitters on board, were hurriedly equipped with battery-powered units, so that more of the fleet could be better coordinated for a more agile response. When we don't have enough boom and skimmers to go around, we have no choice but to triage our resources with more agile approaches.

Think about more agile approaches you could take. Don't be put off by ideas that are so elegantly simple, they are almost embarrassingly so, which is why most people don't do them. Get over it! Earlier in this chapter (refer to Accentuating Short-Range Culture), I gave some examples of some of the things I have done through the years. When you are done truly tackling this first aspect, look for the next bottleneck that now has a chokehold on your operational productivity, and truly tackle that. You will be progressively debottlenecking things. Your organizational agility depends upon it!

Holding a Recurring, Rigorous, and Rallying Strategy Process

This is the seventh of our 13 driving disciplines. As we progressively debottleneck our operational productivity and increasingly liberate more of our management bandwidth to invest elsewhere in our Execution Excellence agenda, we need to improve the rigor of our recurring process of strategy, to be rallying our journey-oriented focus as a team.

Holding a Recurring, Rigorous, and Rallying Strategy Process:
• The essence of strategy is conversation; if you don't have much conversation, you probably don't have much strategy. Unless we hold ourselves fully accountable, a strategy process can easily become ill-disciplined, open ended, and laborious.

Common Source of Wheel$pin:
- Infrequent "strategy process," dominated by annual business planning/budgeting/goal setting.

90-Day Plan:
- Conduct a current state assessment and strategic tri-fold review session with your team.

Resources:
- Read more about the related concepts, models, tools, and other resources at: www.mydrivingseat.com/booklinks booklink #27.

How many ill-disciplined, open ended, and laborious strategy processes have you experienced through the years? Whether it is with corporations, business units, or not-for-profits, if your experience is anything like mine, you have experienced plenty that are not rallying, rigorous, or recurring.

They typically happen infrequently and on an ad hoc basis, rather than as a recurring process, discipline, and cycle; they typically address some of the parts of our strategy and execution challenge, but are not rigorous in addressing the whole equation; they typically rally our hopes for a better future, but not our commitment and accountability for what it's really going to take to create it. All in all, we typically aren't holding ourselves fully accountable for our investment in our strategy process and for our commitment to maximize the return on investment (ROI) we are getting from it. As a result, we aren't driving our strategy and execution conversation as much as we should be. As a result, we are risking Wrong Hazelwoods, Eastern Airlines, and constant whitewater scenarios in our future.

The most common wheel$pin I see is an infrequent strategy process, dominated by annual business planning, budgeting, and goal setting. Don't get me wrong, annual business planning, budgeting, and goal setting are important parts of a good strategy and execution process, but they are far from the whole of it, as our Execution Excellence agenda outlines. This one-year-at-a-time, year-to-year, "annual" orientation to strategy can be very limiting, as five one year plans do not a five year plan make.

In fact, more than just limiting, this one-year-at-a-time orientation can be downright dangerous. Think about how our Eastern Airlines story relates. We can be doing a great job fixing the one year bulb (this year's budget/goals) and a miserable job flying the five year plane (our desired trajectory of profitability and growth). We can be doing well from year to year, one year at a time, fixing the annual bulb, while being in an imperceptible descent in flying the five year plane. Just talk to BP or Toyota, GM or Chrysler!

Among other things you can do to develop this driving discipline (read more at www.mydrivingseat.com/booklinks booklink #27), the number one thing I recommend as part of a 90-Day Plan is to conduct a Current State Assessment and Strategic Tri-Fold review session with your team.

As we saw in Chapter 5, the Strategic Tri-Fold tool lives up in the top right corner of our Execution Excellence agenda model. The Strategic Tri-fold helps you distill the elegant simplicity of your strategy onto one piece of paper, as a methodical combination of key components:

- **The Future** (where do we want to be?) as a collage of Mission, Vision, Values, and Value-Proposition;

- **Key Success Measures** (how will we know when we get there?), laying out the trajectory we want to gain traction on;

- **Today** (where are we now?), getting clear about our current state assessment of things;

- **The Journey** (how do we get there?), finding a path, navigating it well, and creating traction on it;

- **The Shifting Landscape** (what will/may change in our environment in the future?) and scanning our environment.

A Current State Assessment, as part of the "Today (where are we now?)" component of the Strategic Tri-Fold above, helps you distill the issues, problems, and opportunities of your current state, as a methodical combination of the following components:

- Strengths, Weaknesses, Opportunities, and Threats (SWOT)

- What's Working, What's Not Working, What's Missing, and What Are We Not Talking About?

- What Should We Start Doing, What Should We Stop Doing, What Should We Continue Doing, and What Should We Do More Of/Less Of or Modify the Way We Do?

- What are our Most Critical/Strategic Issues, Opportunities, and Drivers (evolving into Core Strategies)?

In Chapter 5, we reviewed the elegant simplicity of a wedge shaped journey. The Strategic Tri-fold and Current State Assessment clarify both the thick end and the thin end of the wedge. The Strategic Tri-Fold clarifies the thick end of the wedge of where we want to be. The Current State Assessment clarifies the thin end of the wedge of where we are now. Our challenge is about architecting the breakthrough journey between the two, with the agility required as things change.

While things are ever changing, and we want to stay abreast of that changing landscape, at any moment in time we need the clarity of a snapshot picture to rally our team in architecting our journey. That's why it is crucial that this is a recurring, rigorous, and rallying process. Our organizational agility depends upon it!

Re-Engineering Structures, Processes, and Systems

This is the eighth of our 13 driving disciplines. With the driving disciplines we have covered so far, we are increasingly liberating management bandwidth from whitewater, for deployment onto our core strategies, oriented to our journey from where we are to where we want to be.

For the next go around of our upward spiral of increasing agility, we'd better be handling more of our mid-range and mid-level planning and execution issues with agility on autopilot. That's what our infrastructure of structures, processes, and systems is for, and we need to be continuously improving and re-engineering these for agile, semi-automation. As we discussed in Chapter 3, we need to strike the right balance for agility, not too tight and not too loose, not too structured and not too unstructured, not too hands on and not too hands off.

As we also reviewed in Chapter 5, our objective is to achieve and sustain the agility of that 80/20 balance, of routine/nonroutine, and keep up with the increases in dynamic complexity and detail complexity we face these days, not letting whitewater creep back into our business.

Re-Engineering Structures, Processes, and Systems:

- The efficacy (capability and capacity to produce a desired result) of our infrastructure of structures, processes, and systems is a key—not just relating to our core business processes, but also our infrastructure of other management mechanisms, such as meetings.

Common Source of Wheel$pin:
- Poor meetings efficacy (too few/many) as central cog in decisions/actions gearbox of your business.

90-Day Plan:
- Define your integrated portfolio, system, and cycle of meetings.

Resources:
- Read more about the related concepts, models, tools, and other resources at: www.mydrivingseat.com/booklinks booklink #28.

"Business Process Re-Engineering" was all the rage in the 90s, and while it has value, it isn't necessarily what we are talking about here. Certainly a key part of this discipline is to be doing some appropriate form of value-stream mapping (mapping how we add value and make money) and figure out where we need to be in streamlining processes, realigning structures, and re-engineering systems for our core business processes.

This deserves a word of caution. In my experience, these kinds of initiatives can easily get out of balance, leaning too far toward the bureaucratic end of our "and" proposition spectrum. When that happens, they can become counterproductive, subtracting from agility rather than adding to it. We must find agile approaches right down the middle, such as the example of Agile Software Development we have mentioned. So often, I encounter businesses, organizations, and teams who think they are excellent at execution because they have a lot of strategic stuff around them. Models for this, spreadsheets for that, and flow charts for the other! And yet, they are experiencing wheel$pin, as evidenced via the lack of traction in their financial results and their frustration as a team.

In my experience, it is often because they are stuck in the complexity of thinking that "more is more." For agility, we also need the "and" proposition that "less is more." By that, I mean we need the elegant simplicity of an organizing concept at the center of this complexity, to bring more order to it. An organizing concept I have always found very valuable, in bringing elegantly simple order to the complexity of organizational agility, is an Integrated Business Model. This is a core structure that can influence everyone's thinking and behavior, enterprise wide and enterprise deep. It should comprise many layers, including, but not limited to:

- Offerings and Channels Model
- Organizational Model
- Financial Model
- Value Chain Process Model
- Meetings Matrix and Annual Calendar

Lost in the complexity of all the strategic stuff they have around them, many businesses, organizations, and teams have not made the investment of crystallizing the elegant simplicity of an Integrated Business Model. This is the central cog in their gearbox, to organize all other cogs around (read more at www.mydrivingseat.com/booklinks booklink #28).

In particular, in my experience, the last item in the bullet list above is often the most common source of wheel$pin: inefficient and ineffective meetings, as part of the central cog in the gearbox of our business!

Most CEOs, executives, and managers undervalue the importance of a well-run portfolio of meetings, as the hub of their workflow management system. They tend to fall into two camps, at either end of our "and" proposition spectrum. They either have far too few meetings, because the CEO, executive, or manager has an aversion to meetings and believes people should be allowed to "just get on with their jobs." Or, they have way too many meetings, because their routine/nonroutine mix is out of balance, and everything nonroutine requires a series of meetings. Also, typically, their individual meetings are poorly run and they don't integrate well as a portfolio.

Recall our discussion about meetings in Chapter 5 and our review of Patrick Lencioni's *Death by Meeting*. It's worth restating one of his main points here:

> "For those of us who lead and manage organizations, meetings are pretty much what we do. Whether we like it or not, meetings are the closest thing to an operating room, a playing field, or a stage that we have. How pathetic is it that we have come to accept that the activity most central to the running of our organizations in inherently painful and un-productive. There is simply no substitute for a good meeting—a dynamic, passionate, and focused engagement—when it comes to extracting the collective wisdom of a team."
>
> –Patrick Lencioni, 2004, *Death by Meeting*

How pathetic is it?! In the absence of a sophisticated workflow management software system (and good luck trying to implement one of those!), meetings are all you've got to stay on top of the never ending flow of detail complexity and dynamic complexity. I'm not saying they can't be supplemented with all kinds of new and virtual technologies, but they are still the central cog in the gearbox of our business, for the revved up collaboration, coordination, and communication of the fast-cycle teamwork we need these days. In the face of the ever evolving nature of work and the never ending flow of detail complexity and dynamic complexity, an efficient and effective portfolio of meetings remains crucial.

And yet, in my experience, many CEOs, executives, and managers woefully underinvest their time, energy, and attention, in designing and continually improving their integrated portfolio, system, and cycle of meetings, as the central cog in the gearbox of their agility as an organization. Among other things you can do to develop this driving discipline (read more at www.mydrivingseat.com/booklinks booklink #28), the number one thing I recommend as part of a 90-Day Plan is to define your integrated portfolio, system, and cycle of meetings.

We talked about this earlier in this chapter (refer to Keeping Our Flight Planning Envelope Expanded to the Full Execution Excellence Agenda), and about insisting that your direct reports do this at their level. Here, it's about you doing it at your level, and, if you aren't the CEO, managing upward so that he or she does it at the top level also for the whole business. As we also discussed earlier in this chapter (refer to Reinforcing the Mindset of Operations Management) one of these meetings might be a morning meeting or a daily huddle at some other time of day. In addition, you will also want to map out the different meetings you need to be having with different frequencies and different participation, to cover the map of your execution excellence agenda. Some examples are:

- Operating Board Meeting (Weekly)
- Sales Meeting (Weekly)
- Management Team Meeting (Monthly)
- Master Production Schedule Meeting (Monthly)
- Quality Assurance Review Meeting (Quarterly)
- Traction Plan Review Meeting (Quarterly)
- Strategic Review (Annually)

Meetings are the central cog in the gearbox of our business. Like it or lump it, your organizational agility depends upon it!

Orchestrating a Goal Setting Cascade and Review Process

This is the ninth of our 13 driving disciplines. With the increasing semi-automation of our infrastructure, the next opportunity for increased agility comes from empowering the breadth and depth of our organization to be aligned and attuned with our goals, in an agile way.

Orchestrating a Goal Setting Cascade and Review Process:
- Agile alignment throughout our business depends upon a well orchestrated cascade and review process of goal setting and performance feedback, balancing the over-engineered rigidity of too much and the organic open-endedness of too little.

Common Source of Wheel$pin:
- Top-down and bottom-up disconnect/ misalignment/ variability throughout the organization.

90-Day Plan:
- Have every executive redefine his or her role in the Frame of Execution Excellence.

Resources:
- Read more about the related concepts, models, tools, and other resources at: www.mydrivingseat.com/booklinks booklink #29.

As we have discussed, organizational agility comes from an "and" proposition of not too tight and not too loose, finding a middle road right down the middle. Empowering too loosely creates more chaos and resulting fragility. Empowering too tightly creates more bureaucracy and resulting fragility. Fragility either way around! Building the bus of high-performance teamwork, with agile alignment and attunement, depends upon a well-orchestrated cascade and review process of goal setting and performance feedback, balancing the over-engineered rigidity of too much, too tightly and the organic open-endedness of too little, too loosely.

As we discussed earlier in this chapter (refer to Reinforcing a Mindset of Operations Management), finding this balance is essential to our distributed agility as an organization to expect and manage the unexpected. In their 2007 book, *Managing the Unexpected: Resilient Performance in an Age of Uncertainty*, Karl Weick and Kathleen Sutcliffe identify five principles including, "deference to expertise," which they explain as follows:

Deference to Expertise:

"High Reliability Organizations push decision making down and around. Decisions are made on the front line, and authority migrates to the people with the most expertise, regardless of their rank. The decisions migrate around these organizations in search of a person who has specific knowledge of the event."

–Karl Weick and Kathleen Sutcliffe, 2007, *Managing the Unexpected: Resilient Performance in an Age of Uncertainty*

This distributed agility by deferring authority to front line expertise works when we find the right balance of a goal setting and review process, which is not too loose and not too tight. The most common form of wheel spin I see is too much variability in the goal setting and review process throughout an organization. This results in misalignments and disconnects in our process of agile alignment and attunement, from gray matter to gray matter. As a result, we have high performance individuals coming together as a medium-to-low performance team.

Also, whatever goal setting and review process does exist, it tends to be the predominant approach for creating focus throughout the organization, with the same year-to-year, one-year-at-a-time, "annualized" approach we cautioned against earlier in this chapter (refer to Holding a Recurring, Rigorous, and Rallying Strategy Process). Dangerous!

Among other things you can do to develop this driving discipline (read more at www.mydrivingseat.com/booklinks booklink #29), the number one thing I recommend as part of a 90-Day Plan is to have your direct reports redefine their roles in the frame of Execution Excellence. This causes them to think about how the goal setting part fits in with the bigger whole, and how they will keep their flight planning envelope expanded to that bigger whole of their full Execution Excellence agenda.

As we reviewed in Chapter 5, the Execution Excellence agenda model is fractal in nature. You can apply it to the whole of your business and to any part of your business, any which way you choose to unbundle your business into its component parts. Having your direct reports apply the Execution Excellence frame to their role, and cascading it down below them to their direct reports and so on, is the last piece in our mindful process of integration, alignment and attunement, from gray matter to gray matter. This is how we build the bus of high performance teamwork, broadly and deeply across an organization, with every seat being a driving seat from which we are getting traction.

You could have your direct reports integrate the 13 driving disciplines of **BREAKTHROUGH!**, which we are reviewing in this chapter, into their job descriptions to describe how they will drive each. You could also have each fill in a Quad Report (see www.mydrivingseat.com/booklinks booklink #30), which is a success description and an ongoing planning and reporting tool. This is a subset of the 13 driving disciplines in four quadrants:

- **Quadrant i**: Key Performance Indicators (Our month by month, quarter by quarter journey)

- **Quadrant ii**: Breakthrough Goals (Our annual plan of SMART Goals— our one year mountain on our multiyear journey)

- **Quadrant iii**: Core Strategies (Driving traction on our multiyear journey)

- **Quadrant iv**: Role Description (Mission/Purpose, Vision/What Success Looks Like, Scope/Activities) and Other Traction "ions" of Our Journey (other things to think about, questions to ask, decisions to make, and actions to take)

Visit www.mydrivingseat.com/booklinks booklink #30

This approach puts the essential part of annual goal setting in the frame of the bigger whole of core strategies, serving our multiyear journey; key performance indicators, serving our month by month and quarter by quarter journey; and other things to be keeping in mind with mental agility. As an ongoing planning and reporting tool, this approach can be used as a platform for performance appraisals, coaching, and reporting at team meetings, helping to synchronize integration, alignment and attunement and sustain traction.

Whether someone is responsible for a department, product, or process; a project, facility, or business unit; a key account, strategic alliance, or issue; this approach will help him or her to be *In the Driving Seat* of his or her role, translating strategy and execution into traction with the organizational agility we need these days. We need traction from every seat on the bus, aligned and attuned, from gray matter to gray matter, enterprise wide and enterprise deep. That's how we build our wheelbase and get more contact footprint between the rubber and the road. Orchestrating this is essential. Your organizational agility depends upon it!

Unlocking and Challenging Mental Models

This is the 10th of our 13 driving disciplines. With the increasing management bandwidth deployed on longer range and more strategic issues, we better also be doing the work to be staying mentally agile.

Unlocking and Challenging Mental Models:
• The paradigms, mindsets, assumptions, and beliefs held by you, your team, and your organization are the mental models through which you interpret the world. Old, used-up, and out-of-date mental models imprison our thinking and ability to see new possibilities and pathways.

Common Source of Wheel$pin:
• Blindness to pivotal importance/atrophied mental agility/unconscious resistance for the creativity involved.

90-Day Plan:
• Hold an "Options and Futures" strategy session with your team.

Resources:
• Read more about the related concepts, models, tools, and other resources at: www.mydrivingseat.com/booklinks booklink #31.

In our framework of Execution Excellence, this is my favorite component, up in the top left corner of our model. In my experience, for many CEOs, executives, and managers, this can be a huge, insidious source of wheel$pin and missed opportunity for traction. As we reviewed in Chapter 5, in *The Fifth Discipline*, Peter Senge said, *"You don't have mental models, you are your mental models."* Mental models are part of our belief system and mind's eye, how we look at something. How we see influences how we think, and how we think is in the flow of the traction "ions" of our journey, of linking and accumulating individual thoughts, questions, decisions, and actions. Therefore, our mental models have a much bigger influence on how our journey unfolds that we might appreciate.

Think about our Eastern Airlines story again. How would the crew's thoughts, questions, decisions, and actions have unfolded differently if they had seen the altimeter earlier, showing their loss of altitude, when they had more time to get cognitively spooled back up? Think about our journey to the Wrong Hazelwood again. How would our thoughts, questions, decisions, and actions have unfolded differently if it had occurred to us to verify where Hazelwood was?

Think about residential real estate, subprime mortgages, and credit default swaps. In October 2008, when Alan Greenspan, the previous chairman of the Federal Reserve Board, was in front of Congress testifying, he eventually wound around to saying, *"Those of us who have looked to the self-interest of lending institutions to protect shareholders' equity, myself included, are in a state of shocked disbelief."* My translation: "My belief system was wrong." When asked, "Do you feel that your ideology pushed you to make decisions that you wish you had not made?" he answered, *"Yes, I've found a flaw."* My translation: "My mental model was wrong." He went on to say: *"This modern risk-management paradigm held sway for decades. The whole intellectual edifice, however, collapsed in the summer of last year. This crisis has turned out to be much broader than anything I could have imagined. It has morphed from one gripped by liquidity restraints to one in which fears of insolvency are now paramount."* My translation: "Nobody had been unlocking and challenging the mental model for decades." The intellectual edifice was a house of cards.

That's a roundabout way of saying that his mental model was flawed, which he now understood with 20/20 hindsight, postadaptively. It's a shame no one could have understood that with 20/20 foresight, preadaptively, although it sounds as if some of the players must have turned a blind eye! The numerous books, documentaries (including *Inside Job* by Charles Ferguson) and movies (including the HBO movie, *Too Big to Fail*) make that pretty clear.

Unlocking and challenging mental models is crucial for preadaptive organizational agility. Indeed, my focus is on helping you unlock and challenge your mental model of traditional strategic planning and implementation. I am inviting you to have a different mental model of strategy, execution, and traction, reframed around the journey orientation dimension of our three dimensional model for the whole challenge, the whole problem, and the whole solution of being *In the Driving Seat* of organizational agility. That's a paradigm shift.

"The greatest danger in times of turbulence is not the
turbulence; it is to act with yesterday's logic."
–Peter Drucker

Turbulence is not the problem. There has always been turbulence. As that turbulence comes at us thicker and faster than ever before, the problem is the logic of our mental model and paradigm. Is our logic staying ahead of the pace preadaptively, keeping up with the pace adaptively, or falling behind the pace postadaptively? The paradigms, mindsets, assumptions, and beliefs held by you, your team, and your organization are the mental models through which you interpret the world. Old, used-up, and out-of-date mental models imprison our thinking in yesterday's logic. They imprison an ability to see new possibilities and pathways.

"We live in and work in an analytic prison.
Working hard within this prison produces nothing.
We cannot remodel the prison, we must get out of it.
To do this a transformation is required."
–W. Edwards Deming

The most common form of wheel$pin I see is that organizations are imprisoned and blind to the pivotal importance of this component, they rarely do any work with this driving discipline, and their mental agility has atrophied as a result. They typically also have a subconscious resistance for the creativity involved in getting limbered up again.

As a result, this component continues to be a largely unconscious source of wheel$pin and missed opportunity for traction which, therefore, they will likely learn about postadaptively, with 20/20 hindsight, as we did with our Wrong Hazelwood; as they did with Eastern Airlines; as Alan Greenspan did with residential real estate, subprime mortgages, and credit default swaps! As Toyota did! As BP did! Learning postadaptively from hindsight can be very expensive, painful, and a matter of life and death. It is much less expensive and painful to be learning as much as possible, preadaptively, from foresight.

This becomes increasingly critical these days as there is so much new, affordable, and paradigm shifting technology to keep up with, not least of all via the Web and associated information and communications technology. It seems as if paradigms are shifting every year, if not every quarter, month, week, or day. It's as if someone hit the fast-forward button for the movie we are participating in called "Darwin's Theory of Evolution by Natural Selection as applied to Business," starring you and me, increasingly with 3-D special effects for which we need to be wearing our 3-D glasses. Talking of movies and as one small example, just look at how the production and distribution costs of video have tumbled over recent years. If we aren't beginning to fully leverage video as a communication tool, both externally for branding and marketing purposes, and internally for the purposes of change leadership and change management, training and development, and cultural integration, alignment and attunement, then we are falling behind the power curve.

As a result, this driving discipline is increasingly differentiating, at an accelerating rate, between those who are postadaptively in wheel$pin and those who are preadaptively in traction. Among other things you can do to develop this driving discipline (read more at www.mydrivingseat.com/booklinks booklink #31), the number one thing I recommend as part of a 90-Day Plan, is to hold an "Options and Futures" strategy session with your team.

Preadaptive organizational agility is about never running out of options, so that we are as future proofed as possible. Options are valuable because they create degrees of freedom to navigate problems and opportunities in front of us. When we have more options, we have more influence in choosing our future. When we don't have options, our future chooses us. And typically, when that happens, it won't be pretty!

An "Options and Futures" strategy session with your team is about getting them limbered up with their mental agility to consider multiple scenarios, a portfolio of plans to deal simultaneously with those scenarios, and the Blue Ocean thinking necessary to generate new options, scenarios, and plans. In their 2005 book, *Blue Ocean Strategy: How to Create Uncontested Market Space and Make the Competition Irrelevant*, W.Chan Kim and Renee Mauborgne say:

> "Imagine a market universe composed of two sorts of oceans: red oceans and blue oceans. Red oceans represent all the industries in existence today. This is the known market space. Blue oceans denote all the industries not in existence today. This is the unknown market space.
>
> The dominant focus of strategy work over the past twenty-five years has been on competition-based red ocean strategies. The result has been a fairly good

understanding of how to compete skillfully in red waters, from analyzing the underlying economic structure of an existing industry, to choosing a strategic position of low cost or differentiation or focus, to benchmarking the competition.

Blue ocean strategy challenges companies to break out of the red ocean of bloody competition by creating uncontested market space that makes the competition irrelevant. Instead of dividing up existing—and often shrinking—demand and benchmarking competition, blue ocean strategy is about growing demand and breaking away from the competition. Our aim is to make the formulation and execution of blue ocean strategy as systematic and actionable as competing in the red waters of known market space—poor understanding exists both in theory and in practice as to how to systematically create and capture blue oceans."

–W.Chan Kim and Renee Mauborgne, 2005, *Blue Ocean Strategy: How to Create Uncontested Market Space and Make the Competition Irrelevant*

In an "Options and Futures" strategy session, we want to be driving the Blue Ocean thinking about the who, what, how, where, when, and why of our business:

As-Is	Could-Be
Who do we serve? • • •	**Who else** could we serve? • • •
What do we serve them with? • • •	**What else** could we serve them with? • • •
How do we serve them? • • •	**How else** could we serve them? • • •

As-Is	Could-Be
Where do we serve them? • • •	**Where else** could we serve them? • • •
When do we serve them? • • •	**When else** could we serve them? • • •
Why do they buy? • • •	**Why else** might they buy? • • •

Driving this kind of Blue Ocean thinking generates new input to an "Options and Futures" process of considering a portfolio of scenarios, options, and plans. Read more at www.mydrivingseat.com/booklinks booklink #32. Across our portfolio of different offerings, in different markets, at different phases of the lifecycle, we must be constantly considering the A, B, C, D, E, and F of our options:

- **Option A:** Accelerating
- **Option B:** Business as Usual/Baseline
- **Option C:** Consolidation/Cost-Cutting
- **Option D:** Downsizing/Downshifting
- **Option E:** Exit
- **Option F:** Fold

In my experience, the mental agility to be holding all of these in mind at the same time, and doing the Blue Ocean thinking which goes hand in hand with them, is often lacking. As a result, we are not as preadaptive as we could be, and we are not as future-proofed as we could be.

I have had the delight of working on organizational agility with a family business called EFI Sports Medicine. You might know them better for their core product called Total Gym, which has been at the leading edge of innovation in athletic training, physical therapy, and home fitness, with functional rehabilitation and conditioning equipment, for nearly 40 years, beginning in 1974. Since then, in this increasingly burgeoning, competitive, and fragmented market, EFI has stayed at the leading edge by always considering its options, alternative futures, and portfolio of plans to find an evolutionary path.

In the 1980s, the rehabilitation community became a focused market segment, in which the company developed the credibility of a strong and well-respected brand. In the 1990s, they launched the infomercial for the home user consumer market (with the actor Chuck Norris, at that point an avid user of Total Gym for more than 20 years, as spokesperson). Broadcast in 85 countries, this continues to be one of the industry's longest-running and most successful fitness infomercials, selling more than 4 million units worldwide, and counting. In the 2000s, they launched their GRAVITYSystem program to the health club industry. Now in the 2010s, they are at it again, evolving a next generation and integration of offerings, aligned and attuned with emerging trends, wants, and needs.

BONUS

http://bit.ly/nJJwBC

EFI's secret has been to understand and develop concepts that tap into the natural order of things with elegant simplicity. "Functional exercise" is a technique that recreates the movements we perform every day with and against gravity, using the individual's body weight as resistance, on a glide-board which can be adjusted to any angle, to vary the body-weight resistance level according to the user's level of strength and fitness. The machine engages all major muscle groups and facilitates more than 250 strength, stretching, and mind-body control exercises, for greater physical agility.

This driving discipline of "Unlocking and Challenging Mental Models" is about our mental agility and a mental workout. It's about the "functional exercise" of our minds, understanding and developing concepts that tap into the natural order of things, relating to our organizational agility, with elegant simplicity. It's about strengthening, stretching, and mind-body control, having the inner world/journey and the outer world/ journey in unison, as a continuum.

Our journey-oriented challenge is a continuum of the outer world/journey, of nuts and bolts things like offerings, markets, and lifecycles, and our inner world/journey, of soft and fleshy things like beliefs and blind spots. In that continuum, doing Blue Ocean thinking in our outer world requires Blue Ocean thinking in our inner world. We could easily be swimming in red oceans in our inner world, imprisoned in old, used up, and out of date mental models, beliefs, and blind spots. We are talking about being more methodical, proactive, and intentional in unlocking and challenging mental models for preadaptive agility. Your organizational agility depends upon it!

Guiding Leadership/Communication Skills and Style

This is the 11th of our 13 driving disciplines. For preadaptive organizational agility, our culture as an organization needs increasingly to embody the principles, practices, and driving disciplines we have been exploring progressively. As CEOs, executives, and managers, our leadership and communication skills and style set the tone for evolving our culture in these dimensions and directions. We are role models and lead by example.

Guiding Leadership/Communication Skills and Style:
• Our style and skills of leadership and communication set the tone for our culture, creating resonance (or dissonance) with the teamwork we desire. We are the role models that our team emulates, founded on our emotional intelligence and resilience.

Common Source of Wheel$pin:
• Void/insufficiently ready, willing, and able to be Breakthrough Leaders, doing the heavy lifting required.

90-Day Plan:
• Regular one-to-ones (weekly or monthly?) with your direct reports based upon their Quad Reports.

Resources:
• Read more about the related concepts, models, tools, and other resources at: www.mydrivingseat.com/booklinks booklink #33.

It's about resonance or dissonance with organizational agility. Are you creating resonance with an upward spiral, virtuous cycle, and self-fulfilling prophecy of increasingly preadaptive agility? Or are you creating dissonance with a downward spiral, vicious cycle, self-defeating, and self-fulfilling prophecy of increasingly postadaptive agility, resulting in constant whitewater?

As we reviewed in Chapter 5, it is a closed loop, starting and ending with emotional intelligence, creating resonance or dissonance, which determines whether everything else works as well as it could. In this closed loop manner, the emotional fortitude of the leader influences the emotional fortitude of the organization, creating the upward spiral of resonance or the downward spiral of dissonance.

When it comes to breakthrough leadership, this emotional resonance or dissonance is crucial. Recall the December 2001 *Harvard Business Review* special edition on Breakthrough Leadership, which said: *"Those who would lead these voyages of inner and outer discovery face extraordinary demands on their time, energy and intellectual capacities. The emotional demands are just as daunting."*

Brewing up a **BREAKTHROUGH!** with our organizational agility will certainly test our agility and emotional fortitude as breakthrough leaders. In my experience, this is a common form of wheel$pin. Many CEOs, executives, and managers leave a void of leadership because they are not sufficiently ready, willing, or able to be the breakthrough leaders they need to be, doing the heavy lifting they need to do, intellectually and emotionally.

It is like being a Sherpa for the mountainous journey of brewing up a **BREAKTHROUGH!** Sherpas do the heavy lifting to help teams climb a mountain, providing load carrying support for those mountainous journeys.

> *"Great leaders are educators, entertainers, sages*
> *and Sherpa guides—but not generals."*
> **-Larry Weber, 2001,** *The Provocateur*

"Change has to get into the culture. When that happens it kind of seeps into the bloodstream and you no longer have to be the one guy supporting it all. The problem very often is that people don't allow enough time or they don't get enough of the right kind of behavior producing the right kind of results. So the new way of doing things doesn't take hold. It's always being propped up by the key change leaders."

–John Kotter, 2003, Leader to Leader #27

There is a certain amount of heavy lifting and propping up that has to be done at the front end of a **BREAKTHROUGH!** journey for it to take hold and become more self-propelling. And even then it needs load carrying support along the way at critical junctures.

What I see, time and again, is that no one is stepping in and rolling up their sleeves sufficiently, to do that heavy lifting, provide that load carrying support, and prop things up. Architecting a **BREAKTHROUGH!** is a mountainous journey, whether at the level of the whole business or a part of the business. Instead of truly tackling issues, we tend to be tickling them. Instead of heavy lifting, we get wishful thinking. Instead of undertaking the master's journey, we take the dabbler's journey instead. And we wonder why things aren't really changing. Well architected **BREAKTHROUGH!** journeys don't happen by accident. They happen through design, heavy lifting, and load carrying support. We will review this more in the next chapter.

It's a kind of sweat equity. Rolling up our sleeves as leaders, getting involved with heavy lifting, load carrying support, and breaking into a sweat, when and where the journey demands it of us, intellectually and emotionally. Investing sweat in the equity of a journey, showing our people how, and then, as soon as we can, getting out of their way and seeing them pay back a return on our equity.

Among other things you can do to develop this driving discipline (read more at www.mydrivingseat.com/booklinks booklink #33), the number one thing I recommend as part of a 90-Day Plan, is to make sure you are holding regular one-to-ones with your direct reports based upon their Quad Report success descriptions, which we reviewed earlier in this chapter (refer to Orchestrating a Goal Setting Cascade and Review Process). Make these breakthrough leadership sessions, identifying wheel$pin anywhere in the mix of your direct reports' success description. Discuss how they can engage more as Sherpas, doing heavy lifting, providing load carrying support, and propping things up. Discuss how they can show their people how to truly tackle these wheel$pin issues, not just tickle them, to get into traction with them.

Look in the mirror! As leaders, we are simultaneously the solution and the problem! Our culture of execution excellence and organizational agility starts with us, or not, as the case may be. Maybe we are the solution. Or maybe we are the problem. Are we doing the heavy lifting and providing the load carrying support for an upward spiral of resonance and climbing big mountains with preadaptive organizational agility? Or are we allowing a downward spiral of dissonance and postadaptive organizational agility, falling into big holes in the ground? It starts with you and your organizational agility depends upon it!

Handling Accountability for Long-Range Culture

This is the 12th of our 13 driving disciplines. As we set out to improve our execution excellence and organizational agility, one of the first tests of our leadership and communication skills and style with our team will be the way we handle accountability for long-range thinking and commitment to advance strategic initiatives. We can so easily lose our grip on this aspect of our culture, tolerating excuses for wheel spin.

Handling Accountability for Long-Range Culture:
• Our culture regarding the long-range thinking and commitment to advance strategic initiatives can often be very challenging and prone to excuses rather than results. How we handle this is crucial, to sustain the accountability we need.

Common Source of Wheel$pin:
• Tolerating lack of commitment to "getting an A" with the higher-order executive strengths required.

90-Day Plan:
• Define your core values, including adopting a model of high performance teamwork.

Resources:
• Read more about the related concepts, models, tools, and other resources at: www.mydrivingseat.com/booklinks booklink #34.

This driving discipline is essential to establishing the upward spiral, virtuous cycle, and self-fulfilling prophecy we desire, toward more preadaptive execution excellence and organizational agility. Yet, it is also the component which can allow those efforts to fall backward into a downward spiral.

It goes like this: We decide to invest in a new beginning with a strategy, execution, and traction process. We hold an offsite retreat, orienting and educating our team to execution excellence and organizational agility. We use some of the key tools (including the Traction Plan that we will touch upon in the next driving discipline in this chapter) to capture, divide, and conquer our challenge, helping us get clear about who needs to do what to start brewing up the **BREAKTHROUGH!** we need. At the end of the retreat, there is a new sense of hope and belief that we can prevail and that we are ready, willing, and able to do so as a team. We schedule the first follow-up session to report back to each other and present our progress on the long range, strategic initiatives we each raised our hands to champion. Confident that everyone will be pulling their weight, we are pumped up about pulling ours.

And then everyone walks out the door, and then it begins, slowly at first and then more and more insidiously. Instead of results, we get excuses! When I work with teams, I show them a numbered list of canned excuses, to make it easy for them. If they are going to come back with an excuse, they won't have to waffle about it; they can just pick the number! My point is that we have heard all the excuses before. With each excuse, I suggest a translation and here are some of my favorites:

1. **"I didn't have time."**
   Translation: I've been too busy fixing bulbs to be flying the plane (referring to our Eastern Airlines story).
2. **"I don't understand what I was supposed to do."**
   Translation: I've been waiting to be told and didn't take responsibility to seek clarification.
3. **"We are already doing a lot of things, and I can't think of anything else we aren't already doing."**
   Translation: We have already had all the great ideas we are ever going to have.
4. **"We are already doing our best every day."**
   Translation: Our best can't get any better.
5. **"It's too complicated."**
   Translation: I am a dabbler, obsessive, or hacker, who prefers stupid simple.

…and my personal favorite…

6.   **"My computer crashed, and I lost all my work."**

Translation: The dog ate my homework (and I was cramming last minute and/or I wasn't smart enough to be saving and backing up my work as I went along).

Which numbers are you picking? And your direct reports? It never ceases to amaze me that mature adults, as CEOs, executives, and managers, can come back with excuses like that! Can you believe it? You do believe it because you have heard them all before, too. Many times, no doubt. And our whole future is at stake. A bright future of new possibilities, spiraling upward to better and better things, which is absolutely ours for the taking. And yet it all hangs in the balance because of pathetic excuses like those above.

Earlier in this chapter (refer to Accentuating Short-Range Culture), we talked about falling prey to the downward spiral of "We become what we tolerate, and we encourage what we allow," and it applies here, too, times 10. The most common form of wheel$pin I see is CEOs, executives, and managers tolerating a lack of commitment from their people toward "getting an A" with the higher order strengths required for execution excellence these days, as we have been progressively exploring. Instead, they tolerate B and C players.

All of their excuses are code for the downward spiral into constant whitewater. Whitewater is the mother of all excuses! All of these excuses are saying, "I'm not agile enough to get done what I said I would get done. Whitewater is *In the Driving Seat*, not me, and there is nothing I can do about it, ever."

We tolerate our direct reports and teams dabbling, obsessing, and hacking! As we discussed in Chapter 2, the journey to mastery of anything is a long and rocky path, with no quick and easy payoffs. Being *In the Driving Seat* of organizational agility is complicated, as a CEO, executive, or manager and certainly entails a journey to mastery, which can be long and arduous. We must make it clear to our direct reports and team that we expect them to be undertaking that journey and that we will accept nothing less.

Among other things you can do to develop this driving discipline (read more at www.mydrivingseat.com/booklinks booklink #34), the number one thing I recommend as part of a 90-Day Plan, is to define your core values, including adopting a model of high performance teamwork. When I do this work with teams, there are several aspects to it:

• Defining the headline core values (honesty, customer service, etc.) and a model of high performance teamwork to be adopted (I often use Patrick Lencioni's model from his book, *The Five Dysfunctions of a Team*, which we touched upon in Chapter 5).

• Translating each headline into a one paragraph definition of what we want that core value to mean.

• Translating those one paragraph descriptions into observable operating norms of things we always do and things we never do.

• Notice the language, "always" and "never," to make things unambiguous, in black and white terms.

• Notice also that these have to be "observable" operating norms. If we can't observe (or hear) someone doing or not doing something (or saying or not saying something), then it's very difficult to hold them accountable. We are left having to talk in generalities and opinions, while the first rule of conflict resolution, which is at the heart of accountability, is to stick to the facts and be specific. Observable operating norms help us do that.

• When we have made a first pass at these, we then go around again and extend the framework with three columns: 1.0, 2.0, and 3.0, reflecting our three modes of organizational agility. We ask ourselves, what do we need to do to rev up these core values and operating norms into a 3.0 mode, for the revved up 3.0 world we live in these days?

• Figuring out a process to engage and enroll others in this process is crucial, so it is bottom up and top down.

• Then, as we discussed earlier in this chapter (refer to Accentuating Short-Range Culture), I challenge my Vistage members and clients to institutionalize these core values in 100 places around the business.

If you already have a set of core values, look at how well they are defined, how observable they are, and how revved up they are in a 3.0 mode for a 3.0 world. Your organizational agility depends upon it!

!ntegrating Our Enterprise Execution Capability and Capacity

This is the 13th and last of our driving disciplines. With improving organizational agility coming from each of the other driving disciplines, as the component parts of our execution excellence agenda model, we need to be integrating them well. For preadaptive organizational agility, we must integrate all of the driving disciplines into our overall capability and capacity to execute as an enterprise. This doesn't happen by accident! Hence the "!" mark substituting for the "I" of "Integrating." When we experience the preadaptive execution excellence and organizational agility that comes from this integration, it is extraordinary!

!ntegrating Our Enterprise Execution Capability and Capacity:

• The execution capability and capacity of our enterprise is more than the sum of the above parts—often all of the parts are there but the whole hasn't emerged. Some integration is required to combine the art and science of a unifying architecture of execution. This doesn't happen by accident (hence the "!" in "!ntegrating") and includes recognizing and teaching execution as a system and a discipline, of accumulating knowledge, tools, and techniques, broadly and deeply throughout the organization.

Common Source of Wheel$pin:

• Disintegration and disaggregation/seeing execution as common sense versus uncommon sense to invest in.

90-Day Plan:

• Holding a Traction Planning session with your team, establishing an ongoing discipline and process.

Resources:

• Read more about the related concepts, models, tools, and other resources at: www.mydrivingseat.com/booklinks booklink #35.

The art and science of integrating all the component parts into the whole, of a unifying architecture of execution excellence, may be the most difficult challenge of all. In my experience, many CEOs, executives, and managers massively underinvest their time, energy, and attention in this driving discipline.

Somehow they expect the integration to happen just as a matter of common sense. Wrong! Extraordinary integration doesn't happen by accident; it happens by design, requiring uncommon sense, in which we need to invest our time, energy, and attention.

This is a common source of wheel$pin. In my experience, many of the component parts are there, but the whole hasn't emerged or isn't working well. It remains disaggregated and disintegrated. More integration is required. It's this integration that ties together and establishes the self-fulfilling prophecy, virtuous cycle, and upward spiral of increasingly preadaptive execution excellence and organizational agility. Without this degree of integration, we are constantly at risk of things beginning to unravel again, allowing a self-fulfilling and self-defeating prophecy, vicious cycle, and downward spiral to re-establish itself, and take us back down into constant whitewater.

Among other things you can do to develop this driving discipline (read more at www.mydrivingseat.com/booklinks booklink #35), the number one thing I recommend as part of a 90-Day Plan, is to engage your team in the ongoing and dynamic process and discipline of "Traction Planning." In our mindful process of integration, alignment, and attunement, from gray matter to gray matter, "Traction Planning" lives between the rubber and the road, as the final phase of translating strategy and execution into traction. It's where we make sure that nothing gets lost in translation. It's an unconventional approach for unconventional times. Read more at www.mydrivingseat.com/booklinks booklink #36.

In my experience, teams are often in a state of being overwhelmed with the array of strategic initiatives they are trying to tackle. One of the reasons is that they don't have a container in which to capture everything, which can also act as an agile tool to communicate, synchronize, and track work in progress. Instead, they are immersed in an array of minutes of meetings, spreadsheets, and presentations. I often work with teams who think they are in pretty good shape, with a lot of this strategic stuff around them. Much of it is very good and very relevant, but their track record of profitable growth says they aren't in as much traction as they would like. So they are puzzled about why so much is getting lost in translation. Yet, as soon as we open up a Traction Planning tool and start building it together electronically, a whole bunch of issues emerge that they realize are the sources of wheel$pin in their business.

As we discussed in Chapter 1, this wheel$pin is costing them a fortune, in avoidable costs and opportunity costs. They can increase tra¢tion for cents on the dollar by doing some of the simple things we have been reviewing in this chapter, as part of a 90-Day Plan, all of which cost only cents on the dollar. One of those is Traction Planning itself. It's an unconventional approach for unconventional times. Your organizational agility depends upon it!

Iterative, Concurrent Engineering

So far in this chapter, we have reviewed each of the elements of our *Journey-Judgment* Opportunity Assessment. This translates the 13 moving parts of our Journey-judgment model of Execution Excellence 3.0 into 13 driving disciplines, for reducing wheel$pin, increasing traction, and brewing up a **BREAKTHROUGH!** with our execution excellence and organizational agility. It provides a template with which to judge where we are in our journey, from postadaptive 1.0 through 2.0 to preadaptive 3.0, for each of the 13 driving disciplines, and assessing opportunities for improvement.

The 90-Day Plan gives you tips, techniques, templates, and tools that you can use during the next 90 days to shift up a gear with traction and building momentum. If you hired me as a general manager for your business, these are the kinds of things I would be doing in the first 90 days and then a lot more beyond. It is a nonlinear process and is not meant to be 13 sequential steps. It all depends on the nature of your situation and where we judge you are in your journey. We can use the Journey-Judgment Opportunity Assessment to capture a diagnosis of the 13 driving disciplines of **BREAKTHROUGH!**, marking each in the corresponding column of 1.0, 2.0, or 3.0, reflecting the modalities we are in, as follows:

- **1.0 = Wheel$pin**: You are spinning your wheels with this discipline.
- **2.0 = Mixed**: You have some wheel$pin and some traction.
- **3.0 = Traction**. You are in traction with this discipline.

Maybe go back through this chapter and mark up your gut-check assessment for each of the 13 driving disciplines on the template you downloaded. Are you in a 1.0, 2.0, or 3.0 mode? You can join up the dots to create the shape of your profile down the 13 items. Looking down the shape of this profile will help you see those driving disciplines that are in the red zone, holding you back in a postadaptive mode of organizational agility 1.0. You will see those driving disciplines that are in the orange zone, helping you be in a more adaptive mode of organizational agility 2.0. You will see those driving disciplines that are in the green zone, propelling you forward in a preadaptive mode of organizational agility 3.0.

Relative to the green zone, you will have diagnosed the gaps of orange and red between the mode you are in and the preadaptive mode of organizational agility 3.0 you want to be in. This will determine how you can best focus your treatment plan during the next 90 days, referring to the corresponding items in the 90-Day Plan. If you have downloaded the pdf file of the Journey-Judgment Opportunity Assessment and 90-Day Plan (www.mydrivingseat.com/booklinks booklink #19), you can visit the links for additional resources and tools to help you.

If you are in any doubt, you can also use the **BREAKTHROUGH!** driving disciplines as 13 sequential steps. Recognize, though, that after your first cycle, you will need to start diagnosing what's working, what's not working, and what's missing in a nonlinear way to continue the iterative process of preventing a downward spiral and of establishing an upward spiral. It has to be an iterative and concurrently engineered process of diagnosis and treatment, in nonlinear phases, virtuous cycles, and upward spirals. That's how we break the natural pattern of things tending toward decay, atrophy, and spiraling downward as a vicious cycle, self-defeating and self-fulfilling prophecy, resulting in Wrong Hazelwoods, Eastern Airlines and constant whitewater!

Certainly if we are growing, and even if we aren't, there is no such thing as the status quo these days. We are either spiraling upward or downward. One or the other! You choose, with bottom-line consequences, not least of all for the cash flow journey of our business.

The Bottom Line

Our framework of strengths, understandings, and intelligences is now looking increasingly complete.

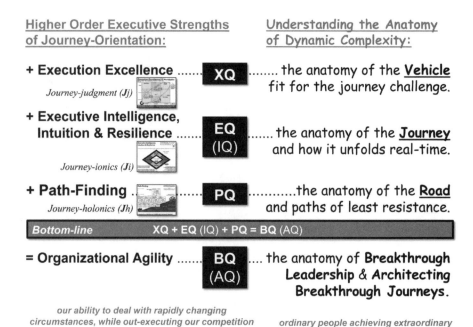

Higher Order Executive Strengths of Journey-Orientation:		Understanding the Anatomy of Dynamic Complexity:
+ Execution Excellence	**XQ**	the anatomy of the **Vehicle** fit for the journey challenge.
Journey-judgment (Jj)		
+ Executive Intelligence, Intuition & Resilience	**EQ (IQ)**	the anatomy of the **Journey** and how it unfolds real-time.
Journey-ionics (Ji)		
+ Path-Finding	**PQ**	the anatomy of the **Road** and paths of least resistance.
Journey-holonics (Jh)		
Bottom-line	XQ + EQ (IQ) + PQ = BQ (AQ)	
= Organizational Agility	**BQ (AQ)**	the anatomy of **Breakthrough Leadership & Architecting Breakthrough Journeys.**

our ability to deal with rapidly changing circumstances, while out-executing our competition and stakeholder expectations (of customers, employees, suppliers and shareholders)

ordinary people achieving extraordinary things, making possible tomorrow, what seems impossible today

We have reviewed each of the three levels, of the higher order strengths of journey orientation, and the corresponding model for each, which helps us understand the anatomy of dynamic complexity involved and the underlying intelligence that is the foundation of that strength.

This brings us to the bottom line, where it all gets put together. The bottom line is about the higher order strength of organizational agility and understanding the associated anatomy of breakthrough leadership and architecting **BREAKTHROUGH!** journeys. It is about the underlying intelligences of business acumen and handling adversity, which are the foundation of this strength.

In chapter 7, we will look at the anatomy of architecting **BREAKTHROUGH!** journeys, the breakthrough leadership involved, and who we need to be as breakthrough leaders. First, in the rest of this chapter, we will look at the bottom-line, higher order strength of organizational agility. As we reviewed in Chapter 2, our definition of organizational agility is:

Organizational Agility:
Our ability to deal with rapidly changing circumstances,
while out-executing our competition and stakeholder expectations
(of customers, employees, suppliers, and shareholders)

To be *In the Driving Seat* of organizational agility, we have to understand the whole challenge, the whole problem, and the whole solution, dissected into its component parts and put back together as an integrated whole.

That's what we have been doing as we have progressed. We started by understanding the whole challenge in its three dimensions, as a mindful process of integration, alignment, and attunement, from gray matter to gray matter. We have progressed to the whole problem of our new framework of strengths, understandings, and intelligences. We have dissected this into three levels, with each level further dissected into the component parts of its associated model, and with our *Journey-judgment* model of Execution Excellence acting as the master, unifying model of the whole problem. We have progressed to the whole solution by looking at the 13 driving disciplines associated with the master unifying model of Execution Excellence, together with the tools that map into it and the other tips, techniques, and templates referenced in the 90-Day Plan and in the online resources. Now we start putting it all back together as an integrated whole.

As we are discovering, it's complicated! But no more complicated than it needs to be. Remember what Einstein told us, that *"Everything should be made as simple as possible, but no simpler."* It is necessarily as complicated as it needs to be. If it were easy, anybody could do it, everybody would already be doing it, nobody would be struggling with it, and somebody would have taken the lead in your organization. In his 2001 book, *Reframing Business: When the Map Changes the Landscape*, Richard Normann puts it this way:

> "Every true renewal process takes place in stages (not necessarily sequential but often better described as modes of thinking and acting) characterized by the generation of new diversity and information, and then stages of reduction of it and focus on certain types of action. A successful organization must learn to live in both these modes.

> Business and other Institutions today have to be very skilled at conceptualizing. Today's free flow of information needs to be transformed into unique

concepts and frameworks which then focalize action. Action orientation and conceptual thinking are two sides of the same coin."

–Richard Normann, 2001, *Reframing Business:*
When the Map Changes the Landscape

This is the bottom line of the whole challenge, the whole problem, and the whole solution, which we have been dissecting into its component parts and putting back together as an integrated whole. We must develop the skills to be ready, willing, and able to live in both of these modes, of thinking and acting, divergence and convergence, conceptualizing and focalizing, all at the same time.

Just like *In the Driving Seat* of our cars, when we get it wrong, we can end up in the Wrong Hazelwood! Just like in the flying seat of a commercial jet, when we get it wrong, we can end up with an Eastern Airlines! Just like in the flying seat of a jet fighter plane, when we get it wrong, we can end up losing the dogfight!

As Richard Normann says, *"Today's free flow of information needs to be transformed into unique concepts and frameworks which then focalize action."* That's what our *In the Driving Seat* concept suite, model set, and tool box is. That's what our framework of strengths, understandings, and intelligences is. A framework of unique concepts, models, and tools that focalize action for today's free flowing reality of dynamic complexity coming at us thicker and faster, with unprecedented uncertainty, volatility, and turbulence.

For organizational agility, our new framework of strengths, understandings, and intelligences, together with the concepts, models, and tools associated with each level, lives in the eye of the storm, where we have been filling a void. This is where my sense of void lives, and we have been filling it.

BONUS

http://bit.ly/n82YV9

In the eye of the storm, our new framework helps us understand the anatomy of dynamic complexity involved and the higher-order executive strengths of journey orientation we need to cope, together with the intelligences that are the underlying foundation of each. For the first time, we have a concept suite, model set, and tool box which are up to the job of being *In the Driving Seat* of things. Despite being in the eye of the storm, we are able to be driving things and not letting things drive us! This doesn't happen by accident; it happens by design.

This model of organizational agility we call *Jhij* as it integrates our other three models of *Journey-holonics* (*Jh*), *Journey-ionics* (*Ji*), and *Journey-judgment* (*Jj*) adding up to:

$$Jhij = Jh + Ji + Jj$$

As a result, we are able to create and sustain traction on a higher (hij'er) road. We are able to architect a journey of successive breakthroughs, unlocking, uplifting, and unfolding our desired trajectory of profitability and growth. We are ready, willing, and able to be *In the Driving Seat* of organizational agility, translating strategy and execution into traction. We are driving our thinking and acting, divergence and convergence, conceptualizing and focalizing, living in both modes, all at the same time, as an "and" proposition.

For organizational agility not to be an ordeal in our business, it must be this "and-deal." It must be the "and-deal" of all of the above, dissected into all of the component parts and put back together as an integrated whole. Without this new framework of understandings, strengths, and intelligences, organizational agility can easily remain an "or-deal" in our business. As a result we can easily be suffering the ordeal of Wrong Hazelwoods, Eastern Airlines, and constant whitewater, and the associated ordeals of losing our best talent, customers, suppliers, and investors.

As we have been reviewing progressively, mastering the challenge of the "and" is complicated. How could it not be?! Mastering anything worthwhile is complicated. Getting an A, as a great CEO, executive, or manager *In the Driving Seat* of organizational agility, is not easy! If it were easy, you would already have done it, a long time ago.

So, in our mindful process of integration, alignment, and attunement, from gray matter to gray matter, our new framework of strengths, understandings, and intelligences has progressed to completeness:

Higher Order Executive Strengths of Journey-Orientation:	Understanding the Anatomy of Dynamic Complexity:

+ Execution Excellence .... **XQ** .... the anatomy of the **Vehicle** fit for the journey challenge.

Journey-judgment (Jj)

+ Executive Intelligence, Intuition & Resilience .... **EQ (IQ)** .... the anatomy of the **Journey** and how it unfolds real-time.

Journey-ionics (Ji)

+ Path-Finding . ... **PQ** ....the anatomy of the **Road** and paths of least resistance.

Journey-holonics (Jh)

Bottom-line	XQ + EQ (IQ) + PQ = BQ (AQ)

= Organizational Agility .... **BQ (AQ)** .... the anatomy of **Breakthrough Leadership & Architecting Breakthrough Journeys.**

(Jhij = Jh + Ji + Jj)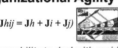

our ability to deal with rapidly changing circumstances, while out-executing our competition and stakeholder expectations (of customers, employees, suppliers and shareholders)

ordinary people achieving extraordinary things, making possible tomorrow, what seems impossible today

We now have a model at each level, embedding the anatomy of dynamic complexity involved at that level, and the intelligences required to master the challenge of the "and," conceptualizing and focalizing, thinking and acting, divergence and convergence. Together they add up to organizational agility and the breakthrough leadership required to be architecting **BREAKTHROUGH!** journeys. That's the subject of our next chapter.

Chapter 6 Summary

It takes will, passion, and insane obsession to develop execution excellence and organizational agility, involving 13 driving disciplines and overcoming common sources of wheel$pin with traction. It is necessarily a nonlinear, iterative process of concurrent engineering, depending upon our judgment of where we are in our journey and how best to link and accumulate the traction "holons" and the traction "ions" of our journey to find a path of least resistance. Here are some more ideas for traction "ions" you can link and accumulate as part of your journey.

Things to Think About

► *Think about* the will, passion, and insane obsession you are investing in execution excellence, or not, as the case may be.

► *Think about* the integration of the component parts of your efforts into the whole capability and capacity of your enterprise to execute.

► *Think about* the path you are finding with your business as a result and the degree to which it is of low resistance or higher resistance.

Questions to Ponder

► *Ask yourself* if you are dabbling, obsessing, or hacking at execution excellence and organizational agility, instead of taking the mastery journey?

► *Ask yourself* what is stopping you from switching to the mastery journey with the requisite will, passion, and insane obsession?

► *Ask yourself* who do you need to bring along on that journey?

Decisions to Make

► *Decide* how best to triage the 13 driving disciplines, depending upon your judgment of where you are in your journey.

► *Decide* how to sequence the 90 Day Plan items.

Actions to Take

► *Execute* on a small number of 90 Day Plan items, driving them through to be traction creating/momentum building.

Who Do We Need To Be As Breakthrough Leaders In The Driving Seat of Organizational Agility?

"Brick walls are there to give us a chance to show how badly we want something."

–**Randy Pausch, 2008, *The Last Lecture***

Well architected **BREAKTHROUGH!** journeys don't happen by accident! Any time we set out to create a breakthrough, we are going to run into barriers, hurdles, and brick walls, which test how much we really want the breakthrough we are setting out to create. To help us persevere, we need to understand the anatomy of Breakthrough Leadership and architecting **BREAKTHROUGH!** journeys.

In his last lecture, Randy Pausch put it so well, saying, *"Brick walls are there to give us a chance to show how badly we want something."* As we have discussed, architecting a breakthrough journey involves compounding our interest in a succession of breakthroughs, by linking and accumulating the traction "ions" and the traction "holons" of our journey.

> *"You are today where your thoughts have brought you.*
> *You will be tomorrow where your thoughts take you."*
>
> **–James Allen**

The thoughts (and questions, decisions, and actions) in the unfolding of how we link and accumulate the traction "ions" and "holons" of our journey have brought us here and will determine where we go from here. The traction "ions" and "holons" of our journey link and accumulate as "breakthrough equity." We often talk about how "brand equity" and "breakthrough equity" are similar in concept. They are largely intangible and invisible but are assets that are there, nevertheless, when you need them.

It's like "Sully" said, after successfully ditching US Airways Flight 1549 in the Hudson and saving all on board: "I've been making small, regular deposits in this bank account of experience, education and training. And on January 15th, the balance was sufficient that I could make a very large withdrawal." He had built up enough breakthrough equity, not just in his flying hours, but also in ongoing education and training, and it was there as an asset when he needed it. As a result, the journey was more able to end with a breakthrough, not a breakdown.

To be building up our breakthrough equity, our challenge is to be going on the journey to mastery, plodding along, learning to love the plateau, and waging war against the quick fix, fast temporary relief, anti-mastery mentality we run into. That's actually what I love most about the anatomy of breakthrough journeys and breakthrough leadership. In my experience, many CEOs, executives, and managers hate the plateau, and they aren't willing to stay the course, go the distance, and see it through. They gradually check out and their desired **BREAKTHROUGH!** journey comes to a grinding halt, imperceptibly at first and then increasingly perceptibly.

Instead, I love the plateau! Why? Because I know that, if I just keep plodding along, with every step that I take, more and more are checking out, and I am in a smaller and smaller minority of those willing to stay the course, go the distance, and see it through. Success becomes more and more inevitable, and I am more and more certain to win.

It helps to understand the anatomy of breakthrough leadership and architecting **BREAKTHROUGH!** journeys, so that we know what the journey holds in store and what to expect, with no surprises. Knowing this, we can be ready, willing, and able. Understanding the anatomy of breakthrough leadership and architecting **BREAKTHROUGH!** journeys is the last component of our framework of understandings, strengths, and intelligences.

To provide breakthrough leadership with your team and architect breakthrough journeys with your business requires a coming together of everything we have progressed through in our framework so far. We have defined breakthrough leadership and architecting breakthrough journeys as follows:

Breakthrough Leadership
(and Architecting Breakthrough Journeys):

ordinary people achieving extraordinary things,
making possible tomorrow what seems impossible today.

It's about ordinary people, like you and me, achieving extraordinary things by putting together everything we have reviewed so far, with the mastery of elegant simplicity. Not getting overwhelmed, lost, and stuck in complexity! Not bouncing off complexity and choosing stupid simplicity instead! Not majoring in detail complexity and minoring in dynamic complexity! It's an "and" proposition of everything we have reviewed.

In my experience, this is the acid test of our leadership. Do we have what it takes to architect a **BREAKTHROUGH!** journey? Can we be the breakthrough leaders we need to be? Can we put it all together? Are we ready, willing, and able? Breakthrough leaders are ready to architect a business vehicle that is fit for the journey challenge, with the organizational agility required. Breakthrough leaders are willing to undertake the arduous journey to mastery, with the patience, persistence, and determination required. Breakthrough leaders are able to put it all together to find a path through, with the mental agility required. If we are ready, willing, and able, that puts us in the minority of CEOs, executives, and managers on the planet!

In my experience, our success in architecting **BREAKTHROUGH!** journeys pivots on three critical anatomical aspects of such journeys:

- Dangerous Detours and Mental Modes to Avoid Them
- Getting Going in the Dark
- The Three Biggest Barriers

Let's look at each in turn.

BONUS

GET 11

http://bit.ly/o7pjml

Dangerous Detours and Mental Modes to Avoid Them

This is the first critical aspect of the anatomy of breakthrough leadership and architecting **BREAKTHROUGH!** journeys. We have been exploring the mindful process of alignment with the longitudinal dimension of journey orientation and attunement with the dynamic complexity of the challenge, from the gray matter to gray matter. From the gray matter of our brain and our mental mode to the gray matter of the asphalt, between the rubber and the road.

As we have seen from some of the stories and examples we have been using throughout, it is so easy to veer off track on a dangerous detour. We need to sustain mental modes to avoid dangerous detours and stay on track. In my experience, the following are the five dangerous detours to which we are most prone and the associated mental modes we must sustain to avoid them.

Dangerous Detours	Mental Modes to Avoid Them
1. Being Half-Brained (Left or Right)	• **A Whole-Brain/Whole-Mind/Whole-Person Challenge** • **The Power of Visual Tools & Metaphors**
2. Simplicity this Side of Complexity	• **Elegant Simplicity on the Far Side of Complexity** • **Detail Complexity and Dynamic Complexity**
3. Giving in to the Pressure of Premature Closure.	• **Divergence & Convergence** • **Holding Problems in Mind**—long enough, fiercely enough, with the requisite will, passion, and insane obsession; a willingness to get going in the dark and let the sun rise on the path. "One of the most common errors— I am tempted to say tragedies—I see in business and other organizations is giving in to the pressure of premature closure. If you have not opened up first, there is very little to close in on to. If choice has not been preceded by enough generation of diversity to create many options, and with generation of real tension with the present, it is a pseudo-exercise, a ritual of little consequence. We will be faced with an organization which has not realized its opportunities." (Richard Normann, 2001, Reframing Business).
4. Living in an Analytic Prison	• **Systems Thinking**—integrating the parts and the whole. • **Navigating a Middle Road**—a paradoxical blend/mastering the challenge of the "and." "We live in and work in an analytic prison. Working hard within this prison produces nothing. We cannot remodel the prison, we must get out of it. To do this a transformation is required. (- W. Edwards Deming)
5. Talking Ourselves Out of Planning	• **Strategy is Conversation**—if we don't have much conversation we probably don't have much strategy. • **Implanting a new Chassis of Business Acumen**—aligned and attuned to longitudinal dimension of the journey and the whole problem/solution of being in the driving seat of organizational agility, translating strategy and execution into traction. Unconventional times call for unconventional approaches.

It never ceases to amaze me how prone many CEOs, executives, and managers are to veering off track on these dangerous detours. To avoid them we must sustain these mental modes in ourselves, in our teams, and in our organizations. Read more at www.mydrivingseat.com/booklinks booklink #37. This is the first of our three critical success factors. Then we run into our second.

Getting Going in the Dark

This is the second critical aspect of the anatomy of breakthrough leadership and architecting **BREAKTHROUGH!** journeys. Suppose we manage to sustain the mental modes necessary to avoid dangerous detours. Then we have to get going in the dark.

Before getting married, my wife and I were on a rough and ready budget trip around Egypt and the Sinai Peninsula. Late one evening, we arrived in utter darkness at a monastery hostel at the foot of Mount Sinai. As we ate supper, our guide asked if anyone would like to see the sunrise the following morning at 6 a.m. from the top of Mount Sinai. The only problem being that we would have to be up at 2 a.m. to make the trek, to get up there in time! Although it was already very late and that meant very little sleep, many people enthusiastically said yes, and we promptly gathered outside the hostel at 2 a.m.

It was utter darkness, as it had been when we arrived late the previous evening. We had no concept of the mountain we were about to climb. We didn't know how much higher it was from our starting point, where it was, or what kind of path we were going to have to trek to get to the top. We couldn't see a thing. We had a few flashlights, which allowed us to see a few steps in front of us, but that was it.

So we all set out. We went around and around, up and down, and around and around some more. It soon got pretty steep with loose rubble and craggy outcrops. The going got harder, and we had to sustain a good pace, or we wouldn't make it in time. The going got harder still. Not surprisingly, after a while, a number of people stopped, thought better of it, decided it wasn't worth it, turned around and went back down the mountain.

But we stayed focused. We stayed focused on the feeling of achievement, of what it would be like to stand at the top of Mount Sinai, with the warmth of the sun rising on our faces, taking wonderful photographs for our photograph album. We kept going, trudging along in the darkness, putting one foot in front of the other, sustaining a sufficient pace. As the pre-dawn light started to come up, we began, ever so slightly at first, to be able to make out the looming profile of the mountain, gradually getting a sense of where it was and how much higher it was.

Little by little, as the light came up gradually and very hazily, we were able to make out the path that would take us the rest of the way up to the peak. Our enthusiasm grew as we could gradually begin to see through the gloom that we were on pace and were going to make it in time. Indeed we did, and it was wonderful. In fact, it was better than we had imagined, taking fabulous photographs with the warmth of the sun rising on our faces. Those photos are now one of our favorite memories of our vacation that we look back on most fondly. So what's the moral of my story?

- "Begin with the start in mind." Sometimes we can't wait for the light, as it will be too late. We have to be willing to get going in the dark, just putting one foot in front of the other. We have to let the sun rise on the path. Sometimes, we are faced with problems, opportunities, or challenges that are so complex and tangled up that we feel as if we are in utter darkness. We aren't sure where the mountain is, how high it is, or where the path is. We don't have the time or luxury to wait for the light. We must be willing to get going in the dark and, in so doing, let the sun rise on the path. The mountain and the path will gradually present themselves to us and we will have the opportunity to make it to the peak on time.

- "Begin with the end in mind." Even though we have no concept of the mountain, we can still focus on the feeling of achievement of what it will be like when we get there and imagine those photographs in our photograph album. Begin with the end in mind, to the degree that you can, making it as vividly visual and visceral as possible, so you can see it and feel it. That is what keeps us going.

- "When the end-in-mind is so shrouded in darkness, get going anyway, trusting that the sun will rise on the path." The demands on us these days for organizational agility mean that we don't always have the luxury to "begin with the end in mind"—when we know we can't stay where we are but don't have a clue what mountain we are trying to climb and what the path looks like. Nevertheless, get going anyway, and figure it out along the way. Putting things in motion will help the mountain and the path present themselves to us.

It never ceases to amaze me how paralyzing many CEOs, executives, and managers find the darkness of not knowing exactly where the mountain and the path they are trying to climb are. Getting going in the dark is crucial to being a breakthrough leader and architecting **BREAKTHROUGH!** journeys. Read more at www.mydrivingseat. com/booklinks booklink #38. This is the second of our three critical success factors. Then we run into our third.

The Three Biggest Barriers

Suppose we manage to get going in the dark. Then we run into the three biggest barriers to architecting a **BREAKTHROUGH!** journey:

1. Agility requires mastery of dynamic complexity, not just detail complexity. Despite everything we have reviewed, I am constantly amazed at the denial many CEOs, executives, and managers are in regarding the increasing dynamic complexity they face. While they experience increasing whitewater, they don't seem ready, willing, or able to experiment with new ways of doing things to master dynamic complexity. They seem reluctant to try elegantly simple techniques and approaches. Maybe because they are so elegantly simple, they are almost embarrassingly so?

2. Agility requires systemic solutions to systemic problems. It still surprises me how often I see CEOs, executives, and managers tickling systemic problems rather than truly tackling them with systemic solutions. Maybe they just feel better tickling a larger number of problems than truly tackling a smaller number and compounding their interest in the heavy lifting, load carrying support, and mastery required?

3. Agility requires us to rev up the frequency of our communication, collaboration, and coordination as a team. As the world continues to rev up, we must rev up with it, to handle the dynamic complexity coming at us thicker and faster. Strangely, in my experience, when things get busier, the stakes get higher, and the crises threaten to wash over us, many CEOs, executives, and managers let their communication, collaboration, and coordination as a team decelerate, not accelerate. They say they "don't have time!" Wrong answer! You must make time. When crisis increases, many CEOs, executives, and managers let their organizational OODA Loop get larger, weaker, and more open loop. Meetings get canceled and become more ad hoc because, "We

don't have time." Wrong answer! When crisis increases, it's time for crisis management to increase. Our organizational OODA Loop needs to get smaller, stronger, and more closed loop, not larger, weaker, and more open loop. We must make time.

Overcoming the three biggest barriers is crucial to being a breakthrough leader and architecting **BREAKTHROUGH!** journeys. Read more at www.mydrivingseat.com/booklinks booklink #39.

If we are ready, willing, and able to sustain the mental modes to avoid dangerous detours, get going in the dark, and overcome the three biggest barriers to architecting **BREAKTHROUGH!** journeys, then there is only one issue left. Ourselves! As the saying goes, "We have met the enemy and we are it!" It's about who we are in the process and who we are willing to be, as breakthrough leaders *In the Driving Seat* of Organizational Agility.

"The journey of a business is also the journey of its leader. The leader is in the driver's seat. My management challenge was to get extraordinary results from a large number of people over long periods of time. It was their response to the challenges we faced together that made success possible."
-Peter Schutz (former CEO of Porsche), 2005,
The Driving Force: Extraordinary
Results with Ordinary People

Getting an A

"Getting an A" as a great CEO, executive, or manager these days is not easy. It means fully filling our role *In the Driving Seat* of organizational agility, translating strategy and execution into traction, with nothing getting lost in translation. In my experience, the majority of CEOs, executives, and managers don't do that well and aren't getting an A. They are getting a B or a C or worse!

As we reviewed in Chapter 3, in their 2007 book, *Leadership Agility*, Bill Joiner and Stephen Josephs agree, saying: *"Less than 10% of managers have mastered the level of agility needed for sustained success in today's turbulent business environment.*

Leadership agility is directly analogous to organizational agility: it's the ability to take wise and effective action amid complex, rapidly changing conditions. Leadership agility isn't just another tool for your toolkit. It's the master competency needed for sustained success in today's turbulent economy."

Who do we need to be as breakthrough leaders *In the Driving Seat* of organizational agility? We need to be ready, willing, and able to do what it takes to get into that special minority of CEOs, executives, and managers who are getting (and keeping) an A. We have been progressively understanding the whole challenge, the whole problem, and the whole solution of doing that, dissecting the component parts and putting them back together as an integrated whole.

As we discussed in Chapter 5, there are many moving parts. And yet, at its core, when we distill it down to its most elegantly simple essence, we are really talking about a culture of agility, execution, and the strengths, understandings, and intelligences required. We are talking about your leadership and communication skills and style, creating a resonance loop of the emotional fortitude, beliefs, behaviors, and results required for agility. Flowing from you, it evolves into the DNA of your organization and its evolution as an agile organism, preadaptively attuned and aligned with its rapidly changing environment. When there is less and less we can count on these days with any certainty, we must be able to count more and more on our organizational agility to cope, no matter what. We become increasingly future proofed. Success becomes increasingly inevitable. We are more and more certain to win.

> *"What lies behind us and what lies before us are small matters compared to what lies within us. And when we bring what is within us out into the world, miracles happen."*
>
> **–Ralph Waldo Emerson**

As Ralph Waldo Emerson reminds us, it starts with you and what is within you. It has to be part of your DNA. When you persevere with the journey to mastery, it becomes an instinctive part of you. I call it Sherpa-Sense. We become of the mountain and the mountain becomes of us.

Strategy
 Higher
  Execution
   Road
    Profitability and Growth
   TrAction
    SENSE

This has been the recurring theme of this book—translating strategy and execution into traction, on a higher road of profitability and growth. Read more at www.mydrivingseat.com/booklinks booklink #40. As we develop our Sherpa-Sense, we become of the mountain, and the mountain becomes of us. Mountainous breakthrough journeys become intuitive, instinctive, and sensory. As we develop the higher-order executive strengths of journey orientation, we become of the equation, and the equation becomes of us:

$$Jhij'er\ road = Jh + Ji + Jj$$

This equation is the elegantly simple distillation of our new framework of strengths, understandings, and intelligences, in our mindful process of integration, alignment, and attunement, from gray matter to gray matter. The higher (hij'er) road emerges as we use our judgment to link and accumulate the traction "holons" and traction "ions" of our journey, avoiding any deficit disorders.

It is a mountainous journey to mastery of our framework of understandings, strengths, and intelligences. Being a Breakthrough Leader is hard, as you will be tested in many different ways. There are so many aspects of breakthrough leadership to bring together. When you master these, in my experience, that will put you in the minority of executives.

Chapter 7 Summary

In our journey to execution excellence and organizational agility, we are going to run into brick walls! That's why breakthrough leadership is also at the heart of things. Architecting breakthrough journeys is not for the faint of heart and involves breaking through common barriers. Breakthrough journeys are mountainous, and breakthrough leaders are Sherpas, doing the heavy lifting to provide the load carrying support to prop up the journey for it to become self-propelling. Sherpas are of the mountain, and the mountain is of them. Here are some more ideas for traction "ions" you can link and accumulate as part of your journey.

Things to Think About

◀▶ *Think about* the mountainous nature of the breakthrough journey you want to architect with your organization and business, career, and life, and the heavy lifting and load carrying support required.

◀▶ *Think about* the mental modes you are prone to lapsing into as an organization, the dangerous detours you end up taking as a result, and your willingness to get going in the dark or not, as the case may be, and what prevents that.

◀▶ *Think about* your role as a Sherpa.

Questions to Ponder

◀▶ *Ask yourself* how can you show up more as a Sherpa, judging where you are in your breakthrough journey and where heavy lifting and load carrying support are needed?

◀▶ *Ask yourself* who else can you develop as Sherpas on your team to spread the load, and how can you ultimately develop everyone as Sherpas?

◀▶ *Ask yourself* how can you promote and protect the mental modes you need to avoid dangerous detours, how you increase your organization's readiness, willingness, and ability to get going in the dark and let the sun rise on the path; how you can break through, go around, under or over the three biggest barriers to unlock, uplift, and unfold a breakthrough journey with your organization?

Decisions to Make

◀▶ *Decide* to be even more of a Sherpa than you already are, for your team, organization, and business and develop your team with the Sherpa-Sense they need.

◀▶ *Decide* to be getting an A as a great CEO, executive, or manager, joining the minority.

◆ *Decide* that you will navigate the challenges of architecting breakthrough journeys, no matter what, and that your perseverance will make success inevitable, no matter what.

Actions to Take

◆ *Continue* executing on the 13 driving disciplines in an iterative and progressive cycle and upward spiral.

◆ *Keep* your team focused on the longitudinal dimension of your journey and reinforce your agility to find a path through, no matter what.

Are You Ready, Willing, And Able?

"Champions do not become champions when they win the event, but in the hours, weeks, months and years they spend preparing for it. The victorious performance itself is merely the demonstration of their championship character."

–T. Alan Armstrong

So, are you? Are you ready, willing, and able, that is? After our journey through this book together, that's all we are left with. Are you ready, willing, and able to be the breakthrough leader you need to be *In the Driving Seat* of organizational agility, translating strategy and execution into traction? Are you ready, willing, and able to go on the journey to mastery? Are you ready, willing, and able to become a Sherpa, being of the mountain and the mountain being of you? Being of the equation of higher-order executive strengths of journey orientation and the equation being of you?

Do you have that "championship character" which T. Alan Armstrong refers to above? Organizational agility is *the* core differentiator in business these days. As we have discussed, we need it on the way into a recession, as we find bottom during a recession, and on the way out of a recession. We need it as we start to grow again organically, as we innovate more rapid growth, and as we sustain our desired growth trajectory. No matter what phase of business we are in, we need to have confidence in our organizational agility. We must be ever ready, ever willing, and ever able. How ready, willing, and able are you?

Are you ready, willing, and able to invest "the hours, weeks, months and years they [champions] spend preparing"? It's not easy. If it were easy, you would have mastered it a long time ago. If you are serious about "getting an A" as an executive, then you must go on the journey to mastery, mastering the detail complexity and dynamic complexity of the challenge. We must not bounce off this complexity in any way, shape, or form, adopting stupid simplicity which ignores complexity. Rather, we must persevere through complexity, achieving the mastery of elegant simplicity on the other side. It's not going to get any easier, only more difficult through time, so the sooner we start the better.

Are You Ready?

In my experience, many executives are not ready. They are prone to veering off track on some dangerous detours. Are you ready to sustain the mental modes to avoid those dangerous detours?

Are You Willing?

In my experience, many executives are not willing. They are not willing to get going in the dark.

Are You Able?

In my experience, many executives are not able. They are not able to overcome the three biggest barriers.

Are you ready, willing and able? I hope so, as we need more people like you. Read more at www.mydrivingseat.com/booklinks booklink #41.

> *"The world is moved along not only by*
> *the mighty shoves of its heroes,*
> *but also by the aggregate on the tiny pushes*
> *of each honest worker."*
>
> **–Helen Keller**

As Helen Keller reminds us, the world gets moved by linking and accumulating the tiny pushes (the traction "ions") and the mighty shoves (the traction "holons") of our journey, by both our honest workers and our heroes. In my experience, the more you are ready, willing, and able to do the honest work of everything we have been reviewing in this book, the more ready, willing, and able you will be to become one of the heroes of your world, whatever that is.

My wife's hometown is a quaint little place in the southern border region of Scotland called Moffat, which is where we got married. It's picturesque, with a backdrop of rolling green hills, a high street full of pubs, shops, and cafes, and old stone buildings and houses. At the bottom part of town, there is a town park with a duck pond and a boating lake. There, in pride of place at the top of the park and near the main entrance, is a memorial to Air Chief Marshal Sir Hugh Dowding (April 24, 1882–February 15, 1970), who was born in Moffat and spent his early childhood there. He became an officer in the Royal Air Force and was the commander of the RAF Fighter Command during the Battle of Britain.

In his 2009 book, *With Wings Like Eagles: A History of the Battle of Britain*, Michael Korda says, *"Few moments in British history are so firmly fixed in people's minds as the summer of 1940, when, after the fall of France, fewer than 2,000 young fighter pilots seemed to be all that stood between Hitler and the victory that was almost within his grasp."* As he goes on to explain, we were massively outgunned by a much larger, more powerful, and warlike enemy. Korda goes on to say:

> "Victory against the Luftwaffe in 1940 came about neither by luck nor by last-minute improvisation. In photographs of the period, the fighter pilots tend to look like young, carefree, happy warriors, if there is such a thing, but the reason they won the Battle of Britain was above all that Fighter Command was prepared for it.

The architect of this victory was Air Chief Marshal Sir Hugh Dowding, who took over as Air Officer Commanding-in-Chief of RAF Fighter Command on its formation in 1936.

Above all, in 1936 Dowding was perhaps the one man of consequence in the United Kingdom—perhaps the world—who did *not* believe that the bomber would "always get through."

–Michael Korda, 2009, *With Wings Like Eagles:*
A History of the Battle of Britain

We won because of Dowding's perseverance as a breakthrough leader in architecting our journey to greater organizational agility as a fighting force. Not least of all, he had to break through the prevailing mental model of the time that "the bomber will always get through."

That was the orthodox doctrine of air power at the time. The majority of politicians and Air Ministry staff believed that there was no effective defense against air attack by bombers, and the only form of defense was offense—having a bomber force big enough to deter an enemy and a willingness to use it, with the associated collateral damage. That's attrition warfare and an early precursor to the cold war of nuclear escalation. Because no one had the stomach for the collateral damage which would ensue, the prime minister at the time, Stanley Baldwin, was arguing against increasing military expenditure. No investment in offense. No investment in defense. That only left appeasement. Fortunately, Sir Hugh Dowding was of a different mindset. As reported in Wikipedia:

"He conceived and oversaw the development of the 'Dowding System'. This comprised an integrated air defence system which included (i) radar (whose potential Dowding was among the first to appreciate), (ii) human observers (including the Royal Observer Corps), who filled crucial gaps in what radar was capable of detecting at the time (the early radar systems, for example, did not provide good information on the altitude of incoming German aircraft), (iii) raid plotting, and (iv) radio control of aircraft.

The whole network was tied together, in many cases, by dedicated phone links buried sufficiently deep to provide protection against bombing. The network had its apex (and Dowding his own headquarters) at RAF Bentley Priory, a converted country house on the outskirts of London, which became Fighter Command's Operations Room. Dowding also introduced modern aircraft into service during the pre-war period, including the eight-gun Spitfire and Hurricane.

Beyond the critical importance of the overall system of integrated air defense, which he had developed for Fighter Command, his major contribution was to marshal resources behind the scenes (including replacement aircraft and air crew) and to maintain a significant fighter reserve, while leaving his subordinate commanders' hands largely free to run the battle in detail. At no point did Dowding commit more than half his force to the battle zone in Southern England.

Because of his brilliant detailed preparation of Britain's air defenses for the German assault, and his prudent management of his resources during the battle, Dowding is today generally given the credit for Britain's victory in the Battle of Britain."

–Source: Wikipedia

"You go to war with the army you've got" is a saying we unfortunately hear a lot these days. Sir Hugh Dowding knew he had to go to war with the RAF Fighter Command force he had, maximizing its strengths, mitigating its weaknesses, and leveraging its agility. His ashes rest below the Battle of Britain Memorial Window in Westminster Abbey in London. There is also a statue on the Strand, for which the inscription reads:

"Air Chief Marshal Lord Dowding was commander-in-chief of Fighter Command, Royal Air Force, from its formation in 1936 until November 1940. He was thus responsible for the preparation for and the conduct of the Battle of Britain. With remarkable foresight, he ensured the equipment of his command with monoplane fighters, the Hurricane and the Spitfire. He was among the first to appreciate the vital importance of R.D.F. (radar) and an effective command and control system for his squadrons. They were ready when war came. In the preliminary stages of that war, he thoroughly trained his minimal forces and conserved them against strong political pressure to disperse and misuse them. His wise and prudent judgment and leadership helped to ensure victory against overwhelming odds and thus prevented the loss of the Battle of Britain and probably the whole war. To him, the people of Britain and of the Free World owe largely the way of life and the liberties they enjoy today."

–Inscription from the Lord Dowding statue,
St. Clement Dane's, the Strand, London

Think about what Sir Hugh Dowding did in the context of Execution Excellence, organizational agility, and the unifying architecture, framework, and system we have been reviewing in this book. He was fully filling his role *In the Driving Seat*. Not too structured and not too unstructured. Not too tight and not too loose. Preadaptive not postadaptive. Human as hero not human as hazard. Traction not wheel$pin. He understood organizational agility and the integration, alignment, and attunement of all the component parts. He knew we couldn't win at attrition warfare, so he conceived a precursor to the modern approach of maneuver warfare—outthink and outmaneuver your adversary, from gray matter to gray matter.

From the gray matter of the central brain of the system, in the Fighter Command Operations Room, being fed real time information for its organizational OODA Loop of Observe, Orient, Decide and Act. To the gray matter, where the rubber meets the road, with Spitfires and Hurricanes in dogfights in the airspace all over Southern Britain, with young pilots operating their individual OODA Loops. With the integration, alignment, and attunement of everything in between. A true three-dimensional challenge. Any shortfall in Sir Hugh Dowding fully filling his role *In the Driving Seat* of the Battle of Britain would have become very evident very quickly, very fully, and very finally, with few second chances.

As Michael Korda says: *"With a clairvoyance exceeding that of his fellow air marshalls, let alone the government, Dowding had a good picture in his mind of the battle to come, and what it would take to win. Fighter Command Headquarters, he had already determined, would not just control the fighter squadrons; it would have to control the entire battle… in what we would now call "real time."* He continues saying that Hermann Goring, the founder and commander in chief of the Luftwaffe, was *"about to launch a new kind of war; and it was a war for which the British were better prepared than he (or anyone else) supposed. Over the past decade they had devoted an astonishing amount of thought, innovation, and preparation to it."*

Sir Hugh Dowding was ready, willing, and able. Are you? Do you have a clairvoyant picture in your mind of the battle to come with your business and your industry? Do you have a good understanding of what it will take to win? Are you devoting an astonishing amount of thought, innovation, and preparation to the real time agility you need, preemptively and preadaptively, just like Sir Hugh Dowding did? Are you putting all of the component parts in place, addressing the whole challenge, the whole problem, and the whole solution, not just some of the parts? Are you ready, willing, and able to fully fill your role *In the Driving Seat* avoiding any shortfalls? Here's what Winston Churchill famously said of the Battle of Britain:

> *"The gratitude of every home in our Island, in our Empire, and indeed throughout the world, except in the abodes of the guilty, goes out to the British airmen who, undaunted by odds, unwearied in their constant challenge and mortal danger, are turning the tide of the World War by their prowess and by their devotion. Never in the field of human conflict was so much owed by so many to so few. All our hearts go out to the fighter pilots, whose brilliant actions we see with our own eyes day after day."*
> **–Winston Churchill, August 20, 1940**

That's breakthrough leadership, against the odds. The many owing so much to the few. Which group will you belong to? The many of the majority who aren't ready, willing, and able? Or the few of the minority who are? In this book, I have tried to educate, inform, and inspire you to join the minority. Join the few. Your organizational agility depends upon it!

BONUS

http://bit.ly/owWRkA

Chapter 8 Summary

In my experience, the majority of managers, executives, and CEOs aren't ready, willing, and able to undertake the journey to mastery we have been reviewing in this book. For whatever reason, they aren't ready, they aren't willing, or they aren't able. Many never will be! Don't let that be you. Join the minority by being ready, willing, and able to undertake the journey to mastery, ready to sustain the mental modes required to avoid dangerous detours, willing to get going in the dark, and able to break through the three biggest barriers along the way. There is no time like the present to begin. Here are some more ideas for traction "ions" you can link and accumulate as part of your journey.

Things to Think About

◆ *Think about* the thin end of the wedge traction "ions" of your journey to get you started, getting going in the dark.

◆ *Think about* the traction "holons" you will need to bring into focus in the longitudinal path of your journey thereafter.

◆ *Think about* the bigger barriers you will need to break through and the traction "ions" and traction "holons" you will need to link and accumulate to do so.

Questions to Ponder

◆ *Ask yourself* how you will progressively enroll and engage enough Sherpas on your team?

◆ *Ask yourself* what heavy lifting and load carrying support will be most needed in the first phase of the journey?

◆ *Ask yourself* what kind of execution excellence and organizational agility challenges you will run into and how you will evolve through them?

Decisions to Make

◆ *Decide* to be a breakthrough leader, who is ready, willing, and able *In the Driving Seat* of organizational agility, translating strategy and execution into traction.

◆ *Decide* to do what it takes to be fully filling that seat and getting an A as a great CEO, executive, or manager.

Actions to Take

◆ *Never, ever, ever give up!*

Index

W

waterfall method   136, 247

wedge   204, 209-11, 238-9, 251

Weick, Karl   102-3, 120, 163, 225, 256

wheel   26-7, 77-8, 92, 117, 181-2, 186-7, 197, 200-1, 230-5, 246-7, 252, 258, 260-1, 265-6, 272-4

whitewater   58, 63, 145, 149, 167, 169, 176-7, 234, 241, 251, 270

Wichita   21, 94-5

wisdom   90, 120, 122, 220

work   16-18, 21, 25-6, 39, 44, 86-8, 114-16, 130-1, 146-9, 173-5, 190-2, 194-6, 207, 245, 269-70

world/journey, inner   113-17, 124, 146-7, 196, 235, 265

Wrong Hazelwoods   109, 120, 125, 128, 157, 169, 177, 194, 198, 201, 204, 222, 241, 259-60, 278-9